THE FIRST AGA KHAN

The Institute of Ismaili Studies
Ismaili Texts and Translations Series, 24

Editorial Board: Farhad Daftary (general editor), Wilferd Madelung (consulting editor), Carmela Baffioni, Nader El-Bizri, Heinz Halm, Abbas Hamdani, Hermann Landolt, Mehdi Mohaghegh, Roy Mottahedeh, Azim Nanji, Ismail K. Poonawala, Ayman F. Sayyid, Paul E. Walker

Previously published titles:

1. Ibn al-Haytham. *The Advent of the Fatimids: A Contemporary Shiʿi Witness*. An edition and English translation of Ibn al-Haytham's *Kitāb al-Munāẓarāt*, by Wilferd Madelung and Paul E. Walker (2000).
2. Muḥammad b. ʿAbd al-Karīm al-Shahrastānī. *Struggling with the Philosopher: A Refutation of Avicenna's Metaphysics*. A new Arabic edition and English translation of al-Shahrastānī's *Kitāb al-Muṣāraʿa*, by Wilferd Madelung and Toby Mayer (2001).
3. Jaʿfar b. Manṣūr al-Yaman. *The Master and the Disciple: An Early Islamic Spiritual Dialogue*. Arabic edition and English translation of Jaʿfar b. Manṣūr al-Yaman's *Kitāb al-ʿĀlim wa'l-ghulām*, by James W. Morris (2001).
4. Idrīs ʿImād al-Dīn. *The Fatimids and their Successors in Yaman: The History of an Islamic Community*. Arabic edition and English summary of Idrīs ʿImād al-Dīn's *ʿUyūn al-akhbār*, vol. 7, by Ayman Fu'ad Sayyid, in collaboration with Paul E. Walker and Maurice A. Pomerantz (2002).
5. Naṣīr al-Dīn Ṭūsī. *Paradise of Submission: A Medieval Treatise on Ismaili Thought*. A new Persian edition and English translation of Naṣīr al-Dīn Ṭūsī's *Rawḍa-yi taslīm*, by S. J. Badakhchani with an introduction by Hermann Landolt and a philosophical commentary by Christian Jambet (2005).
6. al-Qāḍī al-Nuʿmān. *Founding the Fatimid State: The Rise of an Early Islamic Empire*. An annotated English translation of al-Qāḍī al-Nuʿmān's *Iftitāḥ al-daʿwa*, by Hamid Haji (2006).
7. Idrīs ʿImād al-Dīn. *ʿUyūn al-akhbār wa-funūn al-āthār*. Arabic critical edition in 7 volumes by Ahmad Chleilat, Mahmoud Fakhoury, Yousef S. Fattoum, Muhammad Kamal, Ma'moun al-Sagherji and Ayman Fu'ad Sayyid (2007–2014).

8. Aḥmad b. Ibrāhīm al-Naysābūrī, *Degrees of Excellence: A Fatimid Treatise on Leadership in Islam.* A New Arabic Edition and English Translation of al-Naysābūrī's *Ithbāt al-imāma,* by Arzina Lalani (2009).
9. Ḥamīd al-Dīn Aḥmad b. ʿAbd Allāh al-Kirmānī. *Master of the Age: An Islamic Treatise on the Necessity of the Imamate.* A critical edition of the Arabic text and English translation of Ḥamīd al-Dīn Aḥmad b. ʿAbd Allāh al-Kirmānī's *al-Maṣābīḥ fī ithbāt al-imāma,* by Paul E. Walker (2007).
10. *Orations of the Fatimid Caliphs: Festival Sermons of the Ismaili Imams.* An edition of the Arabic texts and English translation of Fatimid *khuṭbas*, by Paul E. Walker (2009).
11. Taqī al-Dīn Aḥmad b. ʿAlī al-Maqrīzī. *Towards a Shiʿi Mediterranean Empire: Fatimid Egypt and the Founding of Cairo.* The reign of the Imam-caliph al-Muʿizz, from al-Maqrīzī's *Ittiʿāẓ al-ḥunafāʾ bi-akhbār al-aʾimma al-Fāṭimiyyīn al-khulafāʾ*, translated by Shainool Jiwa (2009).
12. Taqī al-Dīn Aḥmad b. ʿAlī al-Maqrīzī. *Ittiʿāẓ al-ḥunafāʾ bi-akhbār al-aʾimma al-Fāṭimiyyīn al-khulafāʾ.* Arabic critical edition in 4 volumes, with an introduction and notes by Ayman F. Sayyid (2010).
13. Naṣīr al-Dīn Ṭūsī. *Shiʿi Interpretations of Islam: Three Treatises on Theology and Eschatology.* A Persian edition and English translation of Naṣīr al-Dīn Ṭūsī's *Tawallā wa tabarrā*, *Maṭlūb al-muʾminīn* and *Āghāz wa anjām*, by S. J. Badakhchani (2010).
14. al-Muʾayyad al-Shīrāzī. *Mount of Knowledge, Sword of Eloquence: Collected Poems of an Ismaili Muslim Scholar in Fatimid Egypt.* A translation from the original Arabic of al-Muʾayyad al-Shīrāzī's *Dīwān*, translated by Mohamed Adra (2011).
15. Aḥmad b. Ibrāhīm al-Naysābūrī. *A Code of Conduct: A Treatise on the Etiquette of the Fatimid Ismaili Mission.* A critical Arabic edition and English translation of Aḥmad b. Ibrāhīm al-Naysābūrī's *Risāla al-mūjaza al-kāfiya fī ādāb al-duʿāt*, by Verena Klemm and Paul E. Walker with Susanne Karam (2011).
16. Manṣūr al-ʿAzīzī al-Jawdharī. *Inside the Immaculate Portal: A History from Early Fatimid Archives.* A new edition and English translation of Manṣūr al-ʿAzīzī al-Jawdharī's biography of al-Ustādh Jawdhar, the *Sīrat al-Ustādh Jawdhar*, edited and translated by Hamid Haji (2012).

17. Nāṣir-i Khusraw. *Between Reason and Revelation: Twin Wisdoms Reconciled.* An annotated English translation of Nāṣir-i Khusraw's *Kitāb-i Jāmiʿ al-ḥikmatayn*, translated by Eric Ormsby (2012).
18. al-Qāḍī al-Nuʿmān. *The Early History of Ismaili Jurisprudence: Law and Society under the Fatimids.* An Arabic edition and English translation of al-Qāḍī al-Nuʿmān's *Kitāb minhāj al-farāʾid*, edited and translated by Agostino Cilardo (2012).
19. Ḥātim b. Ibrāhīm al-Ḥāmidī. *The Precious Gift of the Hearts and Good Cheer for Those in Distress. On the Organisation and History of the Yamanī Fatimid Daʿwa.* A critical edition of the Arabic text and summary English translation of Ḥātim b. Ibrāhīm al-Ḥāmidī's *Tuḥfat al-qulūb wa furjat al-makrūb*, by Abbas Hamdani (2012).
20. Abū Ṭāhir Ismāʿīl al-Manṣūr bi'llāh. *The Shiʿi Imamate: A Fatimid Interpretation.* An Arabic edition and English translation of al-Manṣūr's *Tathbīt al-imāma* attributed to Abū Ṭāhir Ismāʿīl al-Manṣūr bi'llāh, edited and translated by Sami Makarem (2013).
21. Idrīs ʿImād al-Dīn. *The Founder of Cairo: The Fatimid Imam-Caliph al-Muʿizz and his Era.* An English translation of the section on al-Muʿizz from Idrīs ʿImād al-Dīn's *ʿUyūn al-akhbār*, edited and translated by Shainool Jiwa (2013).
22. Ibn al-Walīd. *Avicenna's Allegory on the Soul: An Ismaili Interpretation.* An Arabic edition and English translation of Ibn al-Walīd's *al-Risāla al-mufīda*, edited by Wilferd Madelung and translated and introduced by Toby Mayer (2015).
23. Ḥasan-i Maḥmūd-i Kātib. *Spiritual Resurrection in Shiʿi Islam: An Early Ismaili Treatise on the Doctrine of* Qiyāmat. A new Persian edition and English translation of the *Haft bāb* by Ḥasan-i Maḥmūd-i Kātib, edited and translated by S. J. Badakhchani (2017).

Aga Khan I, official portrait photograph taken in Bombay after 1848.

The First Aga Khan

Memoirs of the 46th Ismaili Imam

A Persian edition and English translation of the
ʿIbrat-afzā of Muḥammad Ḥasan al-Ḥusaynī,
also known as Ḥasan ʿAlī Shāh

by
Daniel Beben
and
Daryoush Mohammad Poor

I.B.Tauris *Publishers*
LONDON • NEW YORK
in association with
The Institute of Ismaili Studies
LONDON

Published in 2018 by
I.B.Tauris & Co. Ltd
London • New York
www.ibtauris.com

in association with The Institute of Ismaili Studies
210 Euston Road, London, NW1 2DA
www.iis.ac.uk

ISBN: 978 1 78831 505 0
eISBN: 978 1 78672 551 6
ePDF: 978 1 78673 551 5

A full CIP record for this book is available from the British Library
A full CIP record is available from the Library of Congress

Library of Congress Catalog Card Number: available

Typeset in Minion Tra for The Institute of Ismaili Studies

Printed and bound in Great Britain by T.J. International, Padstow, Cornwall

FSC www.fsc.org MIX Paper from responsible sources FSC® C013056

The Institute of Ismaili Studies

The Institute of Ismaili Studies was established in 1977 with the object of promoting scholarship and learning on Islam, in the historical as well as contemporary contexts, and a better understanding of its relationship with other societies and faiths.

The Institute's programmes encourage a perspective which is not confined to the theological and religious heritage of Islam, but seeks to explore the relationship of religious ideas to broader dimensions of society and culture. The programmes thus encourage an interdisciplinary approach to the materials of Islamic history and thought. Particular attention is also given to issues of modernity that arise as Muslims seek to relate their heritage to the contemporary situation.

Within the Islamic tradition, the Institute's programmes promote research on those areas which have, to date, received relatively little attention from scholars. These include the intellectual and literary expressions of Shiʿism in general, and Ismailism in particular.

In the context of Islamic societies, the Institute's programmes are informed by the full range and diversity of cultures in which Islam is practised today, from the Middle East, South and Central Asia and Africa to the industrialised societies of the West, thus taking into consideration the variety of contexts which shape the ideals, beliefs and practices of the faith.

These objectives are realised through concrete programmes and activities organised and implemented by various departments of the Institute. The Institute also collaborates periodically, on a programme-specific basis, with other institutions of learning in the United Kingdom and abroad.

The Institute's academic publications fall into a number of inter-related categories:

1. Occasional papers or essays addressing broad themes of the relationship between religion and society, with special reference to Islam.
2. Monographs exploring specific aspects of Islamic faith and culture, or the contributions of individual Muslim thinkers or writers.
3. Editions or translations of significant primary or secondary texts.
4. Translations of poetic or literary texts which illustrate the rich heritage of spiritual, devotional and symbolic expressions in Muslim history.
5. Works on Ismaili history and thought, and the relationship of the Ismailis to other traditions, communities and schools of thought in Islam.
6. Proceedings of conferences and seminars sponsored by the Institute.
7. Bibliographical works and catalogues which document manuscripts, printed texts and other source materials.

This book falls into category three listed above.

In facilitating these and other publications, the Institute's sole aim is to encourage original research and analysis of relevant issues. While every effort is made to ensure that the publications are of a high academic standard, there is naturally bound to be a diversity of views, ideas and interpretations. As such, the opinions expressed in these publications must be understood as belonging to their authors alone.

In commemoration of the Diamond Jubilee of
His Highness the Aga Khan

Contents

List of Maps xv

List of Illustrations xvii

Acknowledgements xix

Foreword by Farhad Daftary xxi

Introduction 1
Daniel Beben

English Translation of the *'Ibrat-afzā* 75
Daniel Beben and Daryoush Mohammad Poor

Bibliography 135

Index 145

Persian Index

Persian Edition of the *'Ibrat-afzā*
Daniel Beben and Daryoush Mohammad Poor

List of Maps

1. Persia (Iran) showing sites associated with the Nizārī Ismailis 71

2. South-eastern Persia showing the routes taken by Aga Khan I in 1840–1841 72

3. Afghanistan and 19th-century India showing sites associated with Aga Khan I 73

List of Illustrations

Frontispiece Aga Khan I, official portrait photograph taken in Bombay after 1848 (The Institute of Ismaili Studies, Ismaili Special Collections Unit)

1. Handle of Aga Khan I's dagger with his likeness (President and Fellows of Harvard College) xxii
2. Fatḥ ʿAlī Shāh Qājār, 1815, by Mihr ʿAlī (Brooklyn Museum, 2005.56) 30
3. Muḥammad Shāh Qājār and Ḥājjī Mīrzā Āqāsī, 1840s (MMA, 2014.739) 35
4. General view of the citadel of Bam in the 1980s (Courtesy of Farhad Daftary) 40
5. Maḥallāt, a section of the wall encircling Aga Khan I's residential compound (Courtesy of Farhad Daftary) 41
6. Aga Khan I in India (Courtesy of Farhad Daftary) 44
7. General Sir Charles Napier, by Henry William Pickersgill (Bridgeman Images, MOU133220) 52
8. Aga Khan I and Aga Khan II (Courtesy of Farhad Daftary) 60
9. Mausoleum of Aga Khan I in Hasanabad, Bombay (Courtesy of Hussain Jasani) 61
10. Title Page of the lithographic edition of *ʿIbrat-afzā*, 1278/1862 64

Acknowledgements

I have benefited from the support and generosity of a number of colleagues throughout the course of this project. At the Institute of Ismaili Studies, I would like to thank first and foremost Farhad Daftary for encouraging me to undertake this project, for contributing the foreword and for sharing his knowledge and insight throughout; Daryoush Mohammad Poor for his partnership on the edition of the Persian text and the English translation; Isabel Miller for her careful editorial work; Karim Javan for his careful proof-reading of the Persian text; Russell Harris for his work on the maps; Hussain Jasani for his assistance procuring images for the volume; Wafi Momin, Walid Ghali, Nour Nourmamadshoev and Naureen Ali for their assistance with manuscripts and library materials; and Shainool Jiwa, Julia Kolb and Tara Woolnough for their assistance at various stages during this project.

This project developed from an MA thesis completed during my graduate studies at Indiana University in 2010. I would like to thank Paul Losensky, Ron Sela, Scott Levi and Michael Dodson for their guidance on the earlier iteration of the project, and Paul additionally for his later help with some of the thornier verse sections of the text. In addition, I would like to thank Alexander Morrison and Rozina Ladhani for their feedback on the introduction; Shahrad Shahvand for his help procuring digital images of the Tehran manuscript; and Bindu Draksharam for her assistance procuring materials from the Salar Jung Museum. Last but not least, I would like to thank my family, and especially Zohra and Sinan, for their love and support throughout.

This project was supported by research funding from the Institute of Ismaili Studies and Nazarbayev University. I am grateful to both institutions for their support.

Daniel Beben
Nazarbayev University, June 2018

Foreword

The *'Ibrat-afzā* is the partial biography of Ḥasan 'Alī Shāh Aga Khan I (1219–1298/1804–1881). Also known as Muḥammad Ḥasan al-Ḥusaynī, he was the forty-sixth Imam of the Nizārī Ismailis. This Persian text was written as an autobiography, although it was committed to writing in 1266/1850 in Bombay, not by the Imam himself but by a Persian luminary. The *'Ibrat-afzā* is here edited and translated for the first time into English. It was lithographed in Bombay in 1278/1862, and reprinted subsequently with numerous errors three times in Tehran. A Gujarati translation of the work appeared in India in 1865, soon after its original publication.

Ḥasan 'Alī Shāh succeeded to the Imamate of the Nizārī Ismaili Shi'i Muslims on the death of his father Shāh Khalīlullāh in 1232/1817, when he was only thirteen years old. Shāh Khalīlullāh himself had succeeded his father Abu'l-Ḥasan 'Alī to the Imamate in 1206/1792. By that time, close ties had developed between the Ismaili Imams' family and the Ni'matullāhī Sufi order. While Imam Abu'l-Ḥasan 'Alī governed the province of Kirmān almost independently during the Zand period, from around 1170/1756, the Ni'matullāhī Sufi order was revived in Persia by Ma'ṣūm 'Alī Shāh (d. 1211/1796), who had been dispatched there by the order's master, Riḍā 'Alī Shāh, then residing in the Deccan. Soon after his arrival in Persia in 1184/1770, Ma'ṣūm 'Alī Shāh acquired a growing number of devoted disciples, including Nūr 'Alī Shāh (d. 1212/1797), who eventually settled in Māhān, Kirmān, to be near the shrine of the order's eponymous founder Shāh Ni'matullāh Valī (731–834/1330–1431). Imam Abu'l-Ḥasan 'Alī supported Nūr 'Alī Shāh and other prominent Ni'matullāhī Sufis, such as Mushtāq 'Alī Shāh, who was murdered in Kirmān in 1206/1792.

Shāh Khalīlullāh transferred the seat of the Imamate from Kirmān to Kahak, a village near Qumm and Maḥallāt where the Ismaili Imams possessed extensive properties. He married Bībī Sarkāra, a daughter of Muḥammad Ṣādiq Maḥallātī, who bore the next Imam, the author of the *'Ibrat-afzā*, in 1219/1804 in Kahak. Muḥammad Ṣādiq Maḥallātī, a

Nizārī Ismaili sayyid who carried the Sufi name Ṣidq ʿAlī Shāh, was also a poet and a Niʿmatullāhī Sufi initiated by Muẓaffar ʿAlī Shāh (d. 1215/1800), a physician and one of the leading members of the order in Kirmān. Ṣidq ʿAlī Shāh, the maternal grandfather of Aga Khan I, died in 1230/1815 and was buried in Qumm. Ṣidq ʿAlī Shāh's son, better known by his Sufi name of ʿIzzat ʿAlī Shāh, was another prominent Niʿmatullāhī dervish. This maternal uncle of Aga Khan I was initiated by Majdhūb ʿAlī Shāh (d. 1238/1823), the thirty-eighth master (*quṭb*) of the order. Subsequently, ʿIzzat ʿAlī Shāh developed close relations with Zayn al-ʿĀbidīn Shirvānī (d. 1253/1837), who carried the Sufi name of Mast ʿAlī Shāh and became the chief successor to Majdhūb ʿAlī Shāh as the *quṭb* of the Niʿmatullāhīs, who were now split into several branches. ʿIzzat ʿAlī Shāh spent the greater part of his life in Maḥallāt, where his nephew, Aga Khan I, was then also residing.

Shāh Khalīlullāh, who was not actively interested in Sufism, moved his residence to Yazd, between Iṣfahān and Kirmān, in 1230/1815. There, in 1232/1817, the Ismaili Imam became a victim of certain intrigues of the local Twelver Shiʿi clerics and lost his life in the course of a dispute between some of his followers and the local shopkeepers. The contemporary Qājār monarch, Fatḥ ʿAlī Shāh (1212–1250/1797–1834), who had good relations with the murdered Imam, punished the culprits after a fashion. This was in response to Bībī Sarkāra's pleading for justice at the Qājār court in Tehran. In addition, Fatḥ ʿAlī Shāh added to the youthful Imam's land holdings in the Maḥallāt area and gave one of his daughters, Sarv-i Jahān Khānum, in marriage to the Imam. At the same time, the Qājār monarch appointed the Imam to the governorship of Qumm and bestowed upon him the honorific title (*laqab*) of Āghā Khān (simplified later in Europe to Aga Khan), meaning lord and master. Henceforth, this title remained hereditary among Aga Khan I's successors to the Imamate.

1. Handle of Aga Khan I's dagger with his likeness.

The events of Aga Khan I's early decades and his conflict with the Qājār establishment in the reign of Fatḥ ʿAlī Shāh's grandson Muḥammad Shāh (1250–1264/1834–1848), who succeeded to the throne of Persia as the third Qājār monarch, and the Imam's departure from Persia in 1257/1841 and his eventual settlement in India are all fully covered in the *ʿIbrat-afzā*. As first noted by W. Ivanow (*A Guide to Ismaili Literature*, London, 1933, p. 114), this work was actually committed to writing by Mīrzā Aḥmad Viqār-i Shīrāzī (1232–1298/1817–1881), who spent a year in India in 1266/1850 and enjoyed the Ismaili Imam's hospitality in Bombay. A poet himself, Viqār was the eldest son of the Persian poet, calligrapher and Sufi, Mīrzā Viṣāl-i Shīrāzī (1197–1262/1783–1846). The *ʿIbrat-afzā* is filled with extensive details, including those related to confrontations in various localities between the government armies and the Imam's forces, often commanded by his brother Sardār Abu'l-Ḥasan Khān (d. 1297/1880). The detailed nature of the *ʿIbrat-afzā,* written several years after the events, may indicate that the Imam must have kept some sort of a diary, which at least partly had survived the pillaging of his books and other valuable possessions in Sindh.

The text of the *ʿIbrat-afzā* as a primary source is particularly significant in terms of three distinct contexts: the Nizārī Ismaili Imamate, power politics at the contemporary Qājār court with its strong Sufi underpinnings, and the evolving relations between Aga Khan I and the British in India.

As a result of a succession dispute, the Ismaili Imamate of the Fatimid times was split in 487/1094 into two rival branches, the Mustaʿlian and the Nizārī. While the Mustaʿlian Ismailis recognised al-Mustaʿlī (d. 495/1101) and the later Fatimids as their Imams, the Nizārī Ismailis, led initially by Ḥasan-i Ṣabbāḥ (d. 518/1124), traced their Imamate through the progeny of al-Mustaʿlī's older brother Nizār b. al-Mustanṣir (d. 488/1095), who had been deprived of his succession rights to the Fatimid caliphate by the all-powerful vizier, al-Afḍal. The Nizārī Ismailis founded a state of their own with its capital centred at the fortress of Alamūt in northern Persia. From around the middle of the 6th/12th century, this state was ruled by the Nizārī Imams themselves. Following the destruction of their state in 654/1256 by the Mongols, the Nizārī Ismaili Imams, descendants of the last ruler of Alamūt, Rukn al-Dīn Khurshāh, remained in hiding for several generations while their followers disguised themselves under Sunni, Sufi and other guises to escape rampant persecution. From the middle of the 9th/15th century, the Imams emerged in the village of Anjudān, near Qumm, and initiated a revival in the *daʿwa* and literary activities of their community. By the time the Safavids established their rule over Persia in 907/1501, the Nizārī Imams had achieved great success in Persia, Central Asia and India, where their followers were commonly known as the Khojas. The fortieth Nizārī Imam, Shāh Nizār (d. 1134/1722) transferred his seat from Anjudān to the nearby village of Kahak, and, subsequently, his successors established their residence in Kirmān. Meanwhile, the Imams and their followers had been observing precautionary dissimulation (*taqiyya*) as Twelver Shiʿis, the official religion of Persia under the Safavids, while maintaining close ties with the Niʿmatullāhī Sufi order in Kirmān.

After his grandfather Abu'l-Ḥasan ʿAlī, also known as Sayyid Kahakī, Aga Khan I was the first Nizārī Ismaili Imam to acquire political prominence as governor of Kirmān and son-in-law of Fatḥ ʿAlī Shāh, the Qājār monarch of Persia. From the time of his accession to the Imamate in 1232/1817 until the death of Fatḥ ʿAlī Shāh in 1250/1834, he enjoyed honour and respect at the Qājār court in Tehran.

As far as we know, Aga Khan I was also the first Ismaili Imam to have composed an autobiography. The eventful career of this Imam coincided with the final decades of the Nizārī Ismaili Imamate in Persia. The Aga Khan's departure from Persia in 1257/1841, which proved permanent, actually marked the transference of the seat of the Nizārī Ismaili Imamate after more than seven centuries from Persia to India. The *ʿIbrat-afzā* sheds invaluable light on the events leading to this watershed in Ismaili history.

Furthermore, the *ʿIbrat-afzā* depicts in vivid terms the circumstances, financial and otherwise, under which Aga Khan I succeeded to the Imamate, providing an excellent basis for comparison with later circumstances under this Imam and his successors. It was indeed after the arrival of Aga Khan I in India, marking the first visit of a Nizārī Imam there, that the Imamate came to possess a sound financial basis also permitting the development of institutional and organisational structures for the evolving global Ismaili community. All this effectively marked the initiation of the modern era in Nizārī Ismaili history. In no small measure these achievements had resulted from the direct contact between the Ismaili Imam and his Khoja *murīd*s or disciples, accounting perhaps for the largest group of contemporary Nizārī Ismailis, although in earlier times the Khojas in small numbers had embarked on the perilous journey to Persia for seeing (*dīdār*) their Imam. The *'Ibrat-afzā* bears witness to the fact that delegations from various Nizārī communities, in Central Asia and elsewhere, had continued to visit the Imam in Persia and India, revealing that the Nizārī Ismailis had maintained their contacts with their Imams even under the most difficult circumstances. Indeed, this *imām–murīd* bond characterised the very essence of the Nizārī Ismaili ethos and identity, attributes that have continued to define the distinctive religious identity of this Shiʿi community with an unbroken line of hereditary living and present Imams.

Soon after his succession to the throne in 1250/1834, Muḥammad Shāh Qājār, in consultation with his learned chief minister Qāʾim-maqām-i Farāhānī (d. 1251/1835), appointed Aga Khan I to the governorship of Kirmān. The Imam speedily restored law and order to the province by checking the ongoing Afghan and Balūchī raids, without receiving any payment from the Qājār treasury. The Ismaili Imam received invaluable help from the local ʿAṭāʾullāhī and Khūrāsānī tribesmen who were his followers. By 1252/1837, however, he was abruptly dismissed. Thereafter ensued several years of confrontations and sporadic military conflicts between the Imam and the Qājār establishment, all recounted in great detail in the *'Ibrat-afzā*, reflecting the Imam's own version of the events. However, the Imam's motivations behind the same events were subsequently depicted differently in a number of Qājār chronicles, such as Riḍā Qulī Khān Hidāyat's *Rawḍat al-ṣafā-yi Nāṣirī*, Lisān al-Mulk Sipihr's *Nāsikh al-tawārīkh: taʾrīkh-i Qājāriyya* and Muḥammad Ḥasan Khān Iʿtimād al-Salṭana's *Taʾrīkh-i muntaẓam-i Nāṣirī*.

Modern scholarship has not been able to identify with absolute certainty and objectivity the root causes and the intentions driving these confrontations, which also coincided with the opening phase of the Anglo-Russian rivalries in the region. Aga Khan I's dismissal from the governorship of Kirmān was probably instigated also by complex rivalries for the leadership of the Niʿmatullāhī Sufi order in Persia. As noted, Aga Khan I himself and his maternal family had close links with this order, which witnessed incessant internal rivalries after the death of Majdhūb ʿAlī Shāh, the thirty-eighth master of the order, in 1238/1823. The majority of the Niʿmatullāhī Sufis had, in fact, recognised Zayn al-ʿĀbidīn Shirvānī as Majdhūb's successor. According to the Niʿmatullāhī sources, the Aga Khan himself had been initiated in his youth into this order by Zayn al-ʿĀbidīn Shirvānī, better known by his *ṭarīqa* name of Mast ʿAlī Shāh. It should be noted, however, that this initiation is not substantiated by the Nizārī Ismaili sources. Be that as it may, the Aga Khan did lend his support to the claims of Mast ʿAlī Shāh. Even earlier, in the reign of Fatḥ ʿAlī Shāh Qājār, the Aga Khan had given refuge near Maḥallāt to Mast ʿAlī Shāh, who had then escaped persecution at the hands of the Twelver Shiʿi *ʿulamāʾ* of Fars; and, on the occasion of Muḥammad Shāh's coronation, Mast ʿAlī Shāh, who had been enjoying the Aga Khan's hospitality at Maḥallāt for some time, had accompanied the Ismaili Imam to Tehran.

Muḥammad Shāh himself had strong Sufi inclinations; he had been initiated into the Niʿmatullāhī order, before his accession, probably by Mast ʿAlī Shāh, who later joined the entourage of the Qājār monarch. Before long, however, Mast ʿAlī Shāh was obliged to confront a powerful rival in the person of Ḥājjī Mīrzā Āqāsī, Qāʾim-maqām's successor as chief minister, who as a Niʿmatullāhī Sufi himself aspired to the leadership of the order. Muḥammad Shāh soon came under the influence of Ḥājjī Mīrzā Āqāsī, who exercised complete control over the affairs of the Persian state until the end of that Qājār monarch's reign. In fact, Muḥammad Shāh acknowledged his chief minister also as the master of the Niʿmatullāhī order, and dismissed Mast ʿAlī Shāh from the court. It was under such circumstances that the Aga Khan, who had continued to support Mast ʿAlī Shāh, now aroused the enmity of the all-powerful Ḥājjī Mīrzā Āqāsī, who caused the Ismaili Imam's dismissal from his governorship and then continued to intrigue against him at court.

Be that as it may, to the annoyance of the chief minister, Aga Khan I did not relinquish his support of Mast ʿAlī Shāh, and after the latter's death in 1253/1837 recognised his son Raḥmat ʿAlī Shāh (d. 1278/1861) as the new master of that Niʿmatullāhī branch. The nature of Aga Khan I's conflict with the Qājār establishment, then under the control of a Sufi chief minister with his own aspirations for leading the order, requires further investigation. However, there is no evidence, as alleged by some modern scholars, substantiating that Aga Khan I was encouraged by the British to confront the Qājārs so that Persia would be prevented from achieving any victory in its contemporary military operations in Afghanistan against Herat, then in the British zone of influence. At any rate, close relations were established between Aga Khan I and the British only after the departure of the Imam from Persia. On leaving Persia, Aga Khan I was accompanied by an extensive retinue of several hundred individuals, comprised of family, attendants, soldiers and others. Later, he built numerous houses for these people, in addition to elaborate living compounds and palaces in Bombay, Poona and Bangalore for his family.

Once inside Afghanistan in 1257/1841, Aga Khan I advanced to Qandahār, the major city of western Afghanistan, which had been occupied by an Anglo-Indian army in 1254/1839. Henceforth, a close association developed between the Aga Khan and the British Raj. Aspects of this association are recorded in the *ʿIbrat-afzā* and elsewhere, including in a variety of British sources and archival materials. Early on, while the Aga Khan was staying in Qandahār, Henry Rawlinson, the local British political agent, granted him a daily stipend of one hundred rupees. Subsequently, the Aga Khan headed for Sindh, and rendered valuable help to the British in their conquest of the region. For these services, the Aga Khan was granted an annual pension of £2000 by General Sir Charles Napier (1782–1853), the British conqueror of Sindh who had maintained friendly relations with the Imam from the time of his arrival in Sindh in 1842. Subsequently, Aga Khan I continued to assist the British with his cavalry and in other ways. During these early years of his exile, Aga Khan I provided assistance to the British in the hope that they would arrange for his safe return to Persia, which remained the Imam's overriding objective throughout the 1840s.

In 1261/1845, Aga Khan I arrived in Gujarāt and visited his Khoja followers in several towns there. These represented the first contacts of an Ismaili Imam with the communities of his followers in India, then the jewel of the British empire. Subsequently, in 1262/1846, the Imam arrived in Bombay; and, shortly afterwards, the Persian government, then still controlled by Ḥājjī Mīrzā Āqāsī, demanded the Aga Khan's extradition from British India, citing the Anglo-Persian treaty of 1229/1814. However, the British refused to comply and only transferred the Imam's residence to Calcutta in 1263/1847, farther removed from Persia. The Imam was now clearly benefiting from British protection while still aiming to return to his ancestral homeland. In 1263/1847, Justin Sheil, the British minister in Tehran, forwarded yet another unsuccessful appeal to the Persian government for the Aga Khan's return to Persia.

On the death of Muḥammad Shāh Qājār in 1264/1848, the Aga Khan returned to Bombay and the British now made new efforts to obtain permission for his return to Persia, while the Aga Khan himself wrote a letter to the same effect to the new chief minister (Amīr Kabīr) under

Muḥammad Shāh's son and successor, Nāṣir al-Dīn Shāh. All these efforts proved futile, however, and the Imam finally resigned himself to settlement in India. It was under such circumstances that two years later, in 1266/1850, he received Viqār as a guest and decided to commit the *'Ibrat-afzā* to writing.

With the Imam's permanent settlement in Bombay, there began the modern phase in the history of the Nizārī Ismailis. The Imam now had more immediate reasons for retaining his close relations with the British, as substantiated by subsequent events. Most obviously, the Imam needed the support of the British Raj in establishing the seat of his Imamate in Bombay and overseeing the affairs of a substantial community of his Khoja followers in South Asia and East Africa, who were then loyal subjects of the British empire. Indeed, the Khojas had for several centuries comprised the most important faction of the Nizārī Ismaili community. As the spiritual head of a Muslim community, Aga Khan I valued the protection of the British establishment in India, which strengthened his position and helped him to exercise his authority. In this context, he received invaluable help from the British judiciary system in India when his leadership and the very identity of the Ismaili community of his followers were called into question by certain dissident members of the Khoja community who were confused about their religious identity. The so-called Aga Khan Case of 1866, brought before the Bombay High Court, put an end to all such challenges as the Aga Khan was formally recognised as the spiritual leader of the Ismailis with full control over all the community properties. At the same time, the distinctive religious identity of the Khojas was articulated as 'Shia Imami Ismailis' and not as Sunnis as claimed by the dissidents. Muḥammad Ḥasan al-Ḥusaynī, Aga Khan I, died after an eventful Imamate of sixty-four years in 1298/1881. He was buried in a domed mausoleum in the Mazagaon district of Bombay. The Ismaili identity of the Khojas was further defined and delineated by Aga Khan I's successors to the Nizārī Ismaili Imamate. In sum, Aga Khan I's Imamate coincided with a crucial period in the history of the Nizārī Ismailis, a period that can be appreciated much better in the light of the Imam's own testimony as faithfully recounted in the *'Ibrat-afzā*.

Farhad Daftary

Introduction

Daniel Beben

This book offers a new edition of the Persian text and the first English translation of the *'Ibrat-afzā*, the memoirs of Ḥasan 'Alī Shāh also known as Muḥammad Ḥasan al-Ḥusaynī (1219–1298/1804–1881), the forty-sixth Imam of the Nizārī Ismailis and the first Ismaili Imam to bear the title of Āqā Khān (hereafter Aga Khan).[1] The *'Ibrat-afzā* was composed in the year 1266/1850, following the Imam's exile from Persia and his permanent settlement in the city of Bombay in British India.[2] The text, whose title may be translated as 'A Book of Exhortation, or Example', has served as an important source for a handful of studies on the career of the Aga Khan and modern Ismaili history. However, on account of the rarity of copies of the text, it has so far remained poorly known among the broader community of scholars, not to mention among the general public.

The figure of the Aga Khan is generally known today for his military clashes with the Qājār government of Persia and as the Imam subsequently responsible for the shift of the seat of the Ismaili Imamate from Persia, where it had been based since the end of the 5th/11th century, to India. However, knowledge of the circumstances surrounding this revolt and the subsequent transfer of the Imamate remains imperfect. Moreover, there is an even greater gap in our understanding of the background to these events and the historical context of the Aga Khan's Imamate and those of his immediate forebears. For centuries Europeans, at least, believed that the Ismailis, whom they mistakenly designated as 'the Assassins', had been entirely vanquished in the course of the Mongol invasions. Although the existence of the Ismailis as a living community

1 The title is also more commonly, but less accurately, transliterated from the Persian as Āghā Khān. I have utilised the anglicised spelling 'Aga Khan' in this book. All further references in the text to the Aga Khan, unless otherwise noted, are to Aga Khan I.

2 The text is also occasionally cited under the title *Tārīkh-i 'ibrat-afzā*.

first came to the notice of Europeans in the early 19th century, it was not until the early 20th century that any serious attempt at scholarly study of the post-Mongol period of their history began. While this opaque period in the history of the Ismailis has now become the focus of work by a small but growing number of scholars, it nonetheless still remains largely ignored by scholarship in the broader field of Ismaili studies. To date only a small number of studies have been produced on Ismaili history in the period from the 7th/13th to the 19th century. This may be compared with the far more voluminous body of writings that surrounds the Fatimid era or the modern Ismaili community. To this we may add the vast body of popular and journalistic writings focused on the lives and careers of the two most recent Imams, Aga Khans III and IV, which abounds with tales of their reputed wealth, their involvement in international politics and diplomacy, and their extensive philanthropical activities.

Yet the story of the transition of the Ismaili Imams from the relative obscurity that characterised their history in the post-Mongol period, to the global profile they attained from the mid-19th century onwards, is one that has still not been fully told. Doubtless, a key figure in this transition is Aga Khan I himself, whose life saw the transformation of the institution of the Imamate which initiated the modern era of Ismaili history. His memoirs, the *ʿIbrat-afzā*, present a critical first-hand account of this transformation, and hence deserve to be much better known, both by scholars and by a broader readership. However, the Aga Khan did not initiate this transformation *ex nihilo*, nor was he alone responsible for the transition of the Imamate from obscurity to prominence. Rather, the dramatic developments witnessed under his leadership were based upon a more gradual transformation in the Imamate that had been under way for several centuries, and especially since the early 18th century.

The chronology of the Aga Khan's career, and particularly the circumstances surrounding his revolt and subsequent move to India, have been covered in detail elsewhere, most notably in studies by Hamid Algar and Farhad Daftary, which will be discussed further below. Moreover, the most complete primary source available for these events, namely the memoirs of the Aga Khan himself, is now in our hands. Therefore, this introduction will not include a detailed reconstruction of these events, for which the interested reader may refer to one of the aforementioned studies. Instead, for the convenience of the general reader a more abbreviated survey of this chronology will be set out, along with some contextual discussion that will assist in understanding the events detailed in the *ʿIbrat-afzā* in their broader context. However, the objectives in this introduction extend beyond providing simply a survey of events to providing an interpretative framework for understanding the significance of the Aga Khan's career, which it is hoped will offer a necessary corrective to some of the gaps and misunderstandings found in the current scholarship on this topic. In particular, an interpretation is presented that may allow for a more holistic view of the Aga Khan's career and its various facets, including his roles as an Ismaili Imam and as a political actor, which have largely been treated separately or seen in tension with one another in previous scholarship.

In the first part of this introduction the history of scholarship on the figure of Aga Khan I is outlined and an interpretative framework presented for assessing his career that addresses some of the gaps and misconceptions in this body of work. The second part consists of a brief historical survey of Ismailism from the Mongol conquests to the Imamate of Aga Khan I, which demonstrates how many of the critical developments that occurred during his career had their precedence in changes within the Ismaili Imamate in preceding centuries. The third and largest part of the introduction focuses on the life and career of Aga Khan I himself, while the fourth and final part discusses the *ʿIbrat-afzā* along with its authorship and textual history.

Part I: Aga Khan I in Western Scholarship

The Aga Khan and the 'Assassins' Legacy

The Aga Khan became known to European observers at a time when Western perceptions of the Ismailis were still deeply mired in the myths and legends that had come down to them from medieval chroniclers and travellers.[3] This tradition of legends had emerged from the medieval European experience with the Ismaili community in the Near East

3 For a general overview of the historiography of Ismaili studies, see Farhad Daftary, *Ismaili Literature: A Bibliography of Sources and Studies* (London, 2004), pp. 84–103; his *The Ismāʿīlīs: Their History and Doctrines* (2nd ed., Cambridge, 2007), pp. 1–33; and his 'Ismaʿilism i: Ismaʿili Studies', *EIr.*

during the Crusades, at a time when the community, with its headquarters at the fortress of Alamūt in northern Persia, was engaged in a military struggle, first against the Saljūqs, and later against the Latin Crusader kingdoms as well.[4] The stories reported from this period consequently morphed into a general set of fables regarding the 'Old Man of the Mountain', the legendary Ismaili lord who allegedly used a combination of drugs and mystical powers to control and unleash bands of fanatical, self-sacrificing assassins upon his enemies.[5] These fables crossed over from popular mythology to scholarship in a work by Joseph von Hammer-Purgstall, who drew upon a mixture of medieval European accounts and newly available primary sources from hostile Sunni Muslim authors to paint a dark and terrifying portrait of his subject matter, published in 1818.[6] It was then published in an English translation in 1835.[7] The same year as von Hammer-Purgstall's initial publication, there appeared a ground-breaking article by the French orientalist Silvestre de Sacy, based on an earlier lecture given to the Institut Royal de France in 1809, in which he resolved for the first time the etymology of the term 'assassin'. De Sacy's article connected the term with the Arabic epithet *ḥashīshīn*, or 'hashish-takers', which was the derogatory term used by some of the opponents of the Ismaili community in the medieval period to refer to them, and subsequently

4 For an overview of this period, see Daniel Beben, 'Remembering Saladin: The Politics of Heresy and the Legacy of the Crusades in Persian Historiography', *Journal of the Royal Asiatic Society*, 28 (2018), pp. 231–253; Farhad Daftary, 'The Isma'ilis and the Crusaders: History and Myth', in Zsolt Hunyadi and József Laszlovszky, ed., *The Crusades and the Military Orders: Expanding the Frontiers of Medieval Latin Christianity* (Budapest, 2001), pp. 21–42; Bogdan Smarandache, 'The Franks and the Nizārī Ismāʿīlīs in the Early Crusade Period', *Al-Masāq*, 24 (2012), pp. 221–239.

5 On the history and development of these legends, see Farhad Daftary, *The Assassin Legends: Myths of the Isma'ilis* (London, 1994); Meriem Pagès, *From Martyr to Murderer: Representations of the Assassins in Twelfth- and Thirteenth-Century Europe* (Syracuse, 2014).

6 Joseph von Hammer-Purgstall, *Die Geschichte der Assassinen aus morgenländischen Quellen* (Stuttgart and Tübingen, 1818).

7 Joseph von Hammer-Purgstall, *The History of the Assassins*, tr. Oswald Charles Woods (London, 1835). See also a review article on this work by Farhad Daftary, 'The "Order of the Assassins": J. von Hammer and the Orientalist Misrepresentations of the Nizari Ismailis', *Iranian Studies*, 39 (2006), pp. 71–82.

rendered into European discourse by the 13th-century Venetian traveller Marco Polo and others where it became a term for those who engaged in the targeted killing of political opponents.[8]

Before the 19th century, European transmitters of the 'assassins' legends believed that the subject of these tales had long since disappeared, having been extirpated in the course of the Mongol conquests in the Middle East in the 7th/13th century. It was only in the early 19th century, with the intensifying involvement of European colonial powers in India and the Middle East, that Western observers started to become dimly aware of the continued existence of the Ismailis in these territories, albeit in a form that bore little resemblance to the dreaded assassins of medieval chronicles and legends. Among the earliest such notices is that of Jean Baptiste Rousseau, the French consul-general in Aleppo, who reported on the existence of Ismailis living in Syria and Persia, and noted as well the presence of their Imam, Khalīlullāh ʿAlī, residing in the town of Kahak in Persia.[9] A decade later, the British traveller James Fraser also recorded some important notices on Imam Khalīlullāh and his following in both Persia and India.[10] These early European notices on Imam Khalīlullāh demonstrated a clear fascination with his reputed status as a descendant of the 'Old Man of the Mountain', which was extended also to Khalīlullāh's successor, the Aga Khan.[11]

---

8 Antoine Isaac Silvestre de Sacy, 'Mémoire sur la dynastie des Assassins, et sur l'étymologie de leur nom', *Mémoires de l'Institut Royal de France*, 4 (1818), pp. 1–84; English trans. in Daftary, *The Assassin Legends*, pp. 129–188.

9 J. B. Rousseau, 'Mémoire sur les Ismaélis et les Nosaïris de Syrie', *Annales des Voyages*, 14 (1811), pp. 271–303.

10 James Baillie Fraser, *Narrative of a Journey into Khorasan in the Years 1821 and 1822* (London, 1825), pp. 376–377.

11 See also John Macdonald Kinneir, *A Geographical Memoir of the Persian Empire* (London, 1813), pp. 157–158; Robert Ker Porter, *Travels in Georgia, Persia, Armenia, Ancient Babylonia, etc., during the years 1817, 1818, 1819, and 1820* (London, 1821–1822), vol. 1, pp. 286–289. It should be noted here that, technically speaking, the Nizārī Imams are not descendants of the mythologised 'Old Man of the Mountain'. The historical figure to whom this appellation probably should be applied was Rāshid al-Dīn Sinān, the chief *dāʿī* of the Syrian Nizārī Ismailis in the 6th/12th century. Sinān was not an Imam, but a *dāʿī* or 'missionary', who served under the Imams. However, these distinctions were not known to European scholars at the time; the notion of 'descent' found in these Western accounts may be more correctly understood here in a broader

As will be outlined further below, the first documented contacts between the Aga Khan and the British occurred in 1841, following the failure of the Aga Khan's revolt against the government of Persia and his flight into neighbouring Afghanistan, where the British were in the midst of their first ill-fated occupation of the country. The Imam whom the British first encountered at this time was in their eyes a latter-day descendant of the feared 'Old Man of the Mountain', who continued to be much maligned in contemporary Western historiography. It would seem that this reputation and legacy was foremost in the minds of virtually every European who interacted with the Aga Khan during this period, as one sees constant references to this narrative in nearly all the Western accounts of the mid-19th century that mention him.

One of the first Westerners to meet the Aga Khan after his arrival in Afghanistan was the Anglican clergyman Isaac Allen, who was serving as a chaplain with the British forces in Qandahār. Allen records of the Aga Khan in his travelogue that 'he is of the royal family of Persia, and an exile on account of some attempt to raise rebellion in that country. He is said to be the head of the Assassins, the lineal representative of the Old Man of the Mountains, and to derive a considerable income from the offerings of his sect'.[12] Similar material was also repeatedly recorded by the British General Charles Napier, who frequently referred to the 'assassins' legend in his notices on his interactions with the Aga Khan.[13] For example, in a campaign dispatch from February 1843, he writes:

> I have sent the Persian prince, Agha Khan, the assassin king of the mountain, and divinity according to his sect, to Jurruck on the right bank of the Indus: his influence is great, and he will with his own followers secure our communication with Kurrachee. He is lineal chief of the assassins of the Crusades, who still exist as a sect and are spread over all the interior of Asia: they have great influence though no longer dreaded as in days of yore.[14]

---

sense, referring to a political and spiritual continuity between the Ismailis of the Crusading era and the modern Nizārī Ismailis.

12 Isaac Nicholson Allen, *Diary of a March through Sinde and Affghanistan with the Troops* (London, 1843), p. 198.

13 I discuss the relationship between the Aga Khan and Napier later in the Introduction.

14 William F. P. Napier, *The Life and Opinions of General Sir Charles James Napier* (London, 1857), vol. 2, p. 342.

While these early encounters displayed a sincere admiration for the Aga Khan and his followers, they were not accompanied by any substantial revision of the 'assassins' narrative to which they referred. By contrast, part of the admiration evinced for the Aga Khan in this period appears to have rested precisely on the degree to which he and his community were perceived to have distanced themselves from their seemingly dreadful past. However, this situation changed in the second half of the 19th century, following the Imam's permanent settlement in Bombay. Historiographical surveys of Ismaili studies have suggested that it was not until the early 20th century, when newly discovered source material on the subject became available, that scholars such as Wladimir Ivanow (1886–1970) were first able to present a substantially revised account of Ismaili history that discarded the 'assassins' fables. However, this overlooks the fact that in the second half of the 19th century a number of British authors had already begun to formulate a substantially revised narrative of Ismaili history, albeit one based not on scholarly evidence, but rather on political considerations, reflecting their increasingly warm relationship with the Aga Khan and the Ismailis, as well as considerations stemming from their deepening colonial involvement in the internal political affairs of the Islamic world.

The most critical source in this regard is a tract prepared by Edward Irving Howard, a British lawyer who represented the Aga Khan in the 1866 lawsuit known as the 'Aga Khan Case', in which a number of the Ismailis of India, known as Khojas, challenged his authority to represent them as the Ismaili Imam. The case and its ramifications will be discussed later in this introduction. Here it suffices to note that the Aga Khan Case entailed not only an appeal to British colonial law, but also more broadly to a historical argument concerning his ancestry and the historical relationship between the Ismaili Imamate and the Khoja communities of South Asia. Consequently, while Howard's brief in the case has hitherto been treated primarily in the rather narrow context of its role as a legal document, it also constitutes a critical revisionist work of historiography. In presenting his case, Howard directly addressed the issue of the 'assassins' legacy attached to the Aga Khan, and did so not by denying any connection between his client and the dreaded sectarians, but rather by offering a sweeping reappraisal of the medieval history of the Ismailis, describing them as a persecuted and free-thinking sect, akin to the early Christian community, who pursued violence purely in self-defence.[15] Anticipating many of the arguments made by a later generation of historians, Howard was highly critical of von Hammer-Purgstall's work, especially his naive reliance upon Sunni sources that were so transparently biased against their subject.

This new approach was also in strong evidence in the writings of Sir Henry Bartle Frere, a British colonial administrator who held several key posts in the mid-19th century which put him in a position where he worked closely with the Aga Khan, including a posting as chief commissioner of Sindh province and as governor of Bombay. In 1876, Frere published an extended two-part article in *Macmillan's Magazine* titled 'The Khojas: The Disciples of the Old Man of the Mountain', which was intended to introduce the Aga Khan and the Ismaili community of India to a general British audience.[16] Like Howard's tract, Frere's article presented nothing less than a radically new version of Ismaili history, one that challenged many of the fundamental aspects of the 'assassins' narrative of contemporary Western historiography. He depicted the military actions of the Nizārī Ismailis against the Saljūq Turks as a defensive struggle against a persecuting regime and offered a general reappraisal of the history of Ismaili–European relations during the Crusades. He noted that while many authors, such as von Hammer, had focused on the hostility between the Ismailis and the Crusaders, it was also the case that at several junctures during this period, the Ismailis and the Crusaders had found themselves in alliance as partners in a common cause against the Saljūq Turks, and later against Saladin. He reminded the reader of the pacts formed by various Crusader leaders, such as the Grand Master of the Templars and Baldwin II, King of the Latin Kingdom of Jerusalem, with the Ismailis, which were given as a precedent for the alliance between the British and the Aga Khan in his own day. Frere's article concluded with a stirring summation of the flourishing friendship between the British and the Ismaili community and a reflection on the benefits brought to this community by British rule:

> It is noteworthy that the Wahabis and Sunni fanatics who have earned such an evil name for their co-religionists in India have

15 E. I. Howard, *The Shia School of Islam and its Branches, especially that of the Imamee-Ismailies* (Bombay, 1866).

16 H. Bartle E. Frere, 'The Khojas: The Disciples of the Old Man of the Mountain', *Macmillan's Magazine*, 34 (1876), pp. 342–350, 430–438.

> hitherto found no imitators among the Indian Shia sects. In the eyes of the Aga and his followers, the British Government of India can hardly appear in any other light than as the one really tolerant power they know, securing to them liberty to follow their own views in religion, and equality before the law, such as they would seek in vain in most parts of Islam.[17]

A number of British travellers as well as other colonial officials also recorded important notices and observations on the Aga Khan and his reputation in the Islamic world.[18] A rather detailed account of the Aga Khan's revolt was included in the work of the British historian Robert Watson, while the British orientalist Sir Percy Sykes, who travelled widely through Persia in the last two decades of the 19th century, also recorded a number of notices on the history of the Aga Khan's career in Persia and its legacy.[19] Beginning in the 1870s, a number of British travellers in Central Asia and the Badakhshān region began recording observations on the influence of the Aga Khan among the Ismailis of the region as well.[20]

Modern Scholarship on Aga Khan I

Under the Imamate of the Aga Khan's grandson, Sultan Muhammad Shah, Aga Khan III, the Ismailis became even better known in the

17 Frere, 'The Khojas', pp. 437–438.

18 For example, see 'Biographies (with Portraits) of Their Highnesses, the Present and the Two Preceding "Aga Sahibs" of Bombay, the Chiefs of the Khojas and Other Ismailians, the Disciples of "The Old Man of the Mountain", the So-Called "Assassins" of the Crusades', *Imperial and Asiatic Quarterly Review*, New Series, 8 (1894), pp. 150–163.

19 Sir Percy Molesworth Sykes, *Ten Thousand Miles in Persia or Eight Years in Irán* (London, 1902), pp. 69–70, 78, 105–106, 217, 409; Robert G. Watson, *A History of Persia from the Beginning of the Nineteenth Century to the Year 1858* (London, 1866), pp. 331–335.

20 Among the earliest of such accounts, see Douglas Forsyth, *Report of a Mission to Yarkund in 1873* (Calcutta, 1875), p. 56; T. E. Gordon, *The Roof of the World; being the narrative of a journey over the high plateau of Tibet to the Russian frontier and the Oxus sources on Pamir* (Edinburgh, 1876), p. 134. Many more notices on the Ismailis of Central Asia were recorded by Russian and British observers in the following decades, under the Imamates of Aga Khans II and III. For surveys of this literature, see Frank Bliss, *Social and Economic Change in the Pamirs, Tajikistan* (London, 2005), pp. 82–89; Munir Pirumshoev, *Pamir v russkoĭ istoriografii vtoroĭ poloviny XIX–nachala XX vv.* (Dushanbe, 2012).

Western world. A number of journalistic and popular histories of the Ismailis were produced in the early 20th century, focusing chiefly upon the life and career of Aga Khan III and the contemporary Ismaili community, but which also contained some background history on Aga Khan I and the earlier Imams.[21] Yet as the figure of Aga Khan I transitioned from a subject of contemporary British policy into the realm of history, a significant historiographical gap began to emerge, which in some ways still characterises the field of Ismaili studies. The period from the 1920s to the 1960s witnessed some momentous developments in the study of Ismailism, pioneered by scholars such as Wladimir Ivanow, Marshall Hodgson and Aleksandr Semenov. These groundbreaking studies, however, were primarily concerned with the medieval history of the Ismailis, while the later phases were left largely untouched.[22] While the Aga Khan's arrival and subsequent career in India were examined in some early academic studies of the Ismaili tradition in the subcontinent, the Iranian phase and background of his career were treated only summarily.[23] The study of the Iranian phase of the Aga Khan's career was initially left to Iranian scholars, most notably Farīdūn Ādamīyat, who, in the context of his masterful study of the renowned chief minister Mīrzā Taqī Khān Amīr Kabīr (first published in 1944), provided one of the earliest studies of the Aga Khan's career in Persia and his revolt against the Qājār government.[24] In addition, in 1946 a new edition of the

---

21 For example, see Naoroji M. Dumasia, *A Brief History of the Aga Khan* (Bombay, 1903), pp. 66–95; his *The Aga Khan and His Ancestors: A Biographical and Historical Sketch* (Bombay, 1939), pp. 25–58; A. S. Picklay, *History of the Ismailis* (Bombay, 1940), pp. 69–82.

22 One notable exception is a study by Ivanow on the tombs of the Nizārī Ismaili Imams in Persia, which also included some brief notes on oral traditions preserved by the communities living in the vicinity of the tombs; see Wladimir Ivanow, 'Tombs of Some Persian Ismaili Imams', *Journal of the Bombay Branch of the Royal Asiatic Society*, New Series, 14 (1938), pp. 49–62.

23 In particular, see John N. Hollister, *The Shiʿa of India* (London, 1953), pp. 364–370; Syed Mujtaba Ali, *The Origin of the Khojāhs and Their Religious Life Today* (Bonn, 1936).

24 Farīdūn Ādamīyat, *Amīr Kabīr va Īrān* (7th ed., Tehran, 1362 Sh./1983), pp. 255–261. The Aga Khan's career in Kirmān was also the subject of a number of studies by Muḥammad Ibrāhīm Bāstānī Pārīzī, who also edited some of the key primary sources concerning the history of the Ismailis in Kirmān; among them, see his *Farmānfarmā-yi ʿālam* (Tehran, 1364 Sh./1985), pp. 305–323, 337–353.

ʿIbrat-afzā was published (the first since its initial lithograph edition in 1861) by Ḥusayn Kūhī Kirmānī, which included a journalistic-style introduction to the Aga Khan and the Ismailis.[25]

An important breakthrough in Western scholarship on the career of the Aga Khan came with the Master's thesis by Zawahir Noorally (Moir), submitted in 1964 to the School of Oriental and African Studies, which examined the engagement between the Aga Khan and the British.[26] Although it did not deal directly with the *ʿIbrat-afzā* or the other Persian sources on the Aga Khan's career, it remains the only study to date to draw on the British archival records, including the unpublished diaries of some of the British officials who dealt directly with the Aga Khan. As such, Noorally's thesis, which remains unpublished, contains a wealth of information on the Aga Khan's activities that is not contained in his own memoirs or in the other published sources. Following Noorally's thesis, in 1969 a ground-breaking article was published in *Studia Islamica* by Hamid Algar, which was the first study to examine the full range of Persian sources on the life and activities of the Aga Khan, including the *ʿIbrat-afzā*.[27] Algar's study in many respects remains the leading source on the subject of the Aga Khan's revolt. A few years after this, another article was published in the same journal by Nasrollah Pourjavady and Peter Wilson, which examined the historical relationship between the Ismailis and the Niʿmatullāhī Sufi order, containing some information that also bears on the history of the Aga Khan's revolt and its causes.[28] Finally, in 1990, Farhad

25 Muḥammad Ḥasan al-Ḥusaynī Āqā Khān Maḥallātī, *ʿIbrat-afzā*, ed. Ḥusayn Kūhī Kirmānī (Tehran, 1325 Sh./1946). The manuscripts and editions of the *ʿIbrat-afzā* will be discussed in Part IV of this Introduction.

26 Zawahir Noorally, 'The First Agha Khan and the British, 1838–1868: A Study in British Indian Diplomacy and Legal History' (MA thesis, School of Oriental and African Studies, University of London, 1964).

27 Hamid Algar, 'The Revolt of Āghā Khān Maḥallātī and the Transference of the Ismāʿīlī Imāmate to India', *Studia Islamica*, 29 (1969), pp. 55–81. Algar has also published a number of shorter entries on the Aga Khan; among them, see 'Maḥallātī, Āg͟hā K͟hān', *EI2*; 'Āqā Khan', *EIr*. See also the brief remarks in his *Religion and State in Iran, 1785–1906: The Role of the Ulama of the Qajar Period* (Berkeley, 1969), pp. 55–56. For his study Algar was unfortunately dependent upon the edition of the *ʿIbrat-afzā* published in Tehran in 1946.

28 Nasrollah Pourjavady and Peter Lamborn Wilson, 'Ismāʿīlīs and Niʿmatullāhīs', *Studia Islamica*, 41 (1975), pp. 113–135.

Daftary published the first edition of his survey of Ismaili history and doctrines, which included some further source material on the Aga Khan and his career and, more critically, placed it within the broader historical context of Ismaili history to an extent that had not happened previously.[29]

More recently, James Gustafson has considered the Aga Khan's time as governor of Kirmān in his study of the history of Kirmān in the Qājār era.[30] Aside from this, however, the history of the Aga Khan's activities in Persia has received little additional attention in recent decades. Following the general turn in academia in the 1980s towards postcolonial studies, research over the past three decades has largely focused on the phase of the Aga Khan's life following his settlement in India and his relationship there with the British. In particular, much attention has been given to the Imam's efforts to deploy the British and their authority in extending and consolidating his authority among the Khoja communities of South Asia. While the large majority of Khojas had traditionally recognised the Aga Khan and his ancestors as their spiritual leaders, the authority exercised by the Imams among their followers in India down to the 19th century was largely indirect in nature. Beginning in the early 19th century, a small minority of Khojas expressed their opposition to the Aga Khan's efforts to centralise the Imamate's authority in India, efforts which increased in scope following his settlement in India. As noted above, this led to the well-known court case of 1866 in which a small group of Khoja dissenters declined to render the customary tithes to the Imam. The resolution of this case in favour of the Aga Khan is the focus now of a growing number of studies.[31]

---

29 Farhad Daftary, *The Ismāʿīlīs: Their History and Doctrines* (Cambridge, 1990), pp. 504–517; (2nd ed., Cambridge, 2007), pp. 463–477 (please note: all further references to this work are to the second edition).

30 James M. Gustafson, *Kirman and the Qajar Empire: Local Dimensions of Modernity in Iran, 1794–1914* (New York, 2016).

31 The most thorough treatment of this topic so far is found in the studies by Soumen Mukherjee, *Ismailism and Islam in Modern South Asia: Community and Identity in the Age of Religious Internationals* (Cambridge, MA, 2017); and Teena Purohit, *The Aga Khan Case: Religion and Identity in Colonial India* (Cambridge, 2012). Among other key studies on this topic, see Iqbal Akhtar, *The Khōjā of Tanzania: Discontinuities of a Postcolonial Religious Identity* (Leiden, 2016); Ali S. Asani, 'The Khojahs of Indo-Pakistan: The Quest for an Islamic

Interpreting the Career of the Aga Khan: A New Approach

Both popular and academic writings on the Aga Khans have long struggled to reconcile the worldly and spiritual roles performed by these Imams, often viewing these two roles as, at best, unrelated, and at worst as contradictory. This perspective emerges from a long-standing suspicion in the Western world, rooted in the Protestant critique of the Catholic Church, of involvement by spiritual entities in worldly affairs.[32] However, as will be explained further below, this notion finds far less historical resonance in the Islamic world, where there is a long-standing precedence for the involvement by spiritual leaders in political and social affairs. In particular, in the regions where the Aga Khan's career was based, including Persia, Afghanistan and India, there exists a time-honoured tradition for individuals endowed with sayyid status, that is, descent from the Prophet Muḥammad, to act as political agents and as mediators of conflicts.[33] For the Nizārī Ismaili Imams, this

Identity', *Journal of the Institute of Muslim Minority Affairs*, 8 (1987), pp. 31–41; his 'From Satpanthi to Ismaili Muslim: The Articulation of Ismaili Khoja Identity in South Asia', in F. Daftary, ed., *A Modern History of the Ismailis: Continuity and Change in a Muslim Community* (London, 2011), pp. 95–128; Michel Boivin, 'Contestation et identité chez les Khojas Indo-Pakistanais (1866–1986)', *Lettre d'information – La transmission du savoir dans le monde musulman périphérique*, 17 (1997), pp. 4–23; his *La rénovation du Shīʿisme Ismaélien en Inde et au Pakistan* (London, 2003); Raj Kumar Hans, 'The Legitimation of the Agha Khan's Authority over the Khojas of Western India under Colonial Dispensation in the Nineteenth Century', *Islamic Culture*, 71 (1997), pp. 19–35; James C. Masselos, 'The Khojas of Bombay: The Defining of Formal Membership Criteria During the Nineteenth Century', in Imtiaz Ahmad, ed., *Caste and Social Stratification among Muslims in India* (New Delhi, 1978), pp. 97–116; Zawahir Moir, 'Historical and Religious Debates amongst Indian Ismailis 1840–1920', in Mariola Offredi, ed., *The Banyan Tree: Essays on Early Literature in New Indo-Aryan Languages* (Venezia, 2000), pp. 131–153; Amrita Shodhan, 'Legal Formulation of the Question of Community: Defining the Khoja Collective', *Indian Social Science Review*, 1 (1999), pp. 137–151; and her *A Question of Community: Religious Groups and Colonial Law* (Calcutta, 2001), pp. 82–116.

32 For an early example of this tendency, see Robert L. Baker, 'The Aga Khan: Moslem Pontiff', *Current History*, 42 (1935), pp. 591–597.

33 For an overview of this phenomenon, see Kazuo Morimoto, ed., *Sayyids and Sharifs in Muslim Societies: The Living Links to the Prophet* (Abingdon, 2012).

position has been employed, since at least the 10th/16th century, to legitimise their involvement in political and social affairs that extend far beyond the scope of their immediate Ismaili following. In other words, it is precisely because of their spiritual standing, and their genealogical claim of descent from the Prophet Muḥammad, that the Ismaili Imams have wielded socio-political authority in the Islamic world down to the present, and not despite it.[34]

In the case of Aga Khan I, one trend in scholarship, beginning with the studies by Noorally and Algar, has been to turn attention away from his role as the Ismaili Imam, emphasising instead his political and economic roles. The most extreme example of this trend is presented in a recent work by Teena Purohit. While Purohit's study offers some valuable insights into the impact of the colonial state on notions of religious identity among the Khojas, her analysis of the historical background of the Aga Khan and his relationship with the Ismailis of South Asia demonstrates a number of omissions and severe oversimplifications. This includes, among others, the argument that the Aga Khan was merely a 'Persian nobleman' and not 'the official Imam of the Isma'ilis' (leaving unanswered the question of what exactly determines the 'official' status of an Ismaili Imam), as well as the extraordinary claim that the Nizārī Imamate was dormant until it was 'reconstituted' by the Aga Khan's father, Imam Khalīlullāh.[35] In Purohit's view, the Aga Khan's claims to the historical institution of the Nizārī Imamate appear to be based on nothing more than a desire to extract money from credulous Indians, who were somehow duped into believing that this Persian newcomer held a historical claim to their tithes. These claims, it should be noted, stand in direct contradiction to the sources cited by Purohit herself in their support, which include the studies by Algar and Daftary, both of which in fact present substantial evidence confirming the historical legitimacy of the Aga Khan's genealogical claim to the Nizārī Imamate, as well as the history of the Imamate's relationship with communities in South Asia.

---

34 For a discussion of these issues in the context of the modern Ismaili Imamate, see Daryoush Mohammad Poor, *Authority without Territory: The Aga Khan Development Network and the Ismaili Imamate* (New York, 2014).

35 Purohit, *The Aga Khan Case*, pp. 22–23. Purohit's book inexplicably omits any reference to the *'Ibrat-afzā*, which is an essential source for any scholarly discussion of the Aga Khan's career.

A far more equitable approach in this vein is taken by Nile Green in his recent study of Muslim communities in colonial-era Bombay.[36] While Green does not dismiss the legitimacy of the Aga Khan's claim to the legacy of the Ismaili Imamate, he rightfully argues that the emphasis on genealogical continuity found in much of the literature in Ismaili studies obscures the far-reaching changes in practices and doctrines that marked the Imamate of the Aga Khan. Green argues against the essentialist approach to Ismailism that is found in much of the Ismaili studies literature, maintaining that 'While Ismāʿīlism is conventionally regarded as a stable religious formation passed down through an ancient pedigree of familial imams … the prominence and characteristics of the Āghā Khāns' "family firm" were very much a product of the religious economy of nineteenth-century Bombay'.[37] Green characterises the function of the Aga Khan's Imamate in the religious environment of colonial-era Bombay as 'Neo-Ismāʿīlism', implying a fundamental paradigm shift from the practices of a seemingly unreformed Imamate which, 'by 1800 … had long slipped into provincial obscurity'. However, whereas Green sees the Aga Khan's Imamate as constituting a radical departure from his predecessors', these developments may be better understood as marking the fruition of a much more gradual shift in the Ismaili Imamate that had taken place in previous centuries, in some respects going back to the time of the Mongol conquests, and more substantially since the Safavid era.

Here a new framework is outlined which may provide a better analytical lens through which to understand the nature of the Aga Khan's career in the 19th century. The approach here builds upon a body of scholarship in the study of Sufism and holy persons in the Islamic tradition, which may provide a useful framework for a more holistic understanding of the Aga Khan's career, including his roles as the Ismaili Imam and as a prominent and active political and economic figure in Persia and British India. Many of the earlier authors examining the place of holy persons in the Islamic world, dating back to the 19th century, focused their studies on the early Sufi tradition, and particularly the ascetic trends evidenced in it, and tended to draw parallels

---

36 Nile Green, *Bombay Islam: The Religious Economy of the Western Indian Ocean, 1840–1915* (Cambridge, 2011).

37 Green, *Bombay Islam*, p. 156.

between the Sufi saints and the Christian monastic traditions.[38] Within this framework, the increasing involvement of Sufi saints in worldly and political affairs in later centuries was taken as evidence of decline and vulgarisation.[39] Since the late 1960s, however, increasing focus has been placed in Western scholarship on the social and political roles performed by Muslim holy figures in both historical and contemporary contexts. One of the earliest studies of this type was Ernest Gellner's *Saints of the Atlas*, which examined the role of Sufi saints in the highlands of Morocco and the social and meditational role performed by these figures among the fissiparous Berber tribes of North Africa.[40] Gellner argued that, in the absence of any strong state authority or court system, such holy men and representatives of sacred lineages, whose genealogical claims traced back to early Muslim saints placed them in a neutral position outside the traditional tribal structure, were widely recognised as mediators of disputes and as sources of legal and social authority. The anthropological approach soon began to be adopted by historians of religion as well, notably in the work of Peter Brown on the social and political roles of Christian saints in the late Roman period.[41]

Building on these studies, in recent years a large number of works have emerged that have highlighted similar historical functions performed by Sufi and charismatic holy figures in the Muslim world. Some of the most extensive applications of this socio-political approach have been taken in the study of Sufism in the Indian subcontinent, such as Richard Eaton's study of the political and social roles of Sufis in the region of Bijapur in the medieval period,[42] and in subsequent studies

38 For an overview of the historiography of Sufism, see Nile Green, 'Making Sense of "Sufism" in the Indian Subcontinent: A Survey of Trends', *Religion Compass*, 2 (2008), pp. 1044–1061; his *Sufism: A Global History* (Malden, 2012), pp. 1–10.

39 See, for example, A. J. Arberry, *Sufism: An Account of the Mystics of Islam* (London, 1950).

40 Ernest Gellner, *Saints of the Atlas* (London, 1969).

41 Peter Brown, 'The Rise and Function of the Holy Man in Late Antiquity', *Journal of Roman Studies*, 61 (1971), pp. 80–101; his *The Cult of the Saints: Its Rise and Function in Latin Christianity* (Chicago, 1981).

42 Richard M. Eaton, *Sufis of Bijapur, 1300–1700: Social Roles of Sufis in Medieval India* (Princeton, 1978).

by scholars such as Simon Digby,[43] Nile Green[44] and Sarah Ansari.[45] Several scholars have similarly highlighted the political and social roles of Sufi shaykhs and lineages in Central Asia. Jo-Ann Gross, for instance, has explored the economic and political functions of the 9th/15th-century Naqshbandī shaykh Khwāja Aḥrār,[46] while Devin DeWeese has highlighted the role of sacred lineages in the Syr Darya region where Sufi shaykhs and holy men positioned themselves as intermediaries with the Russian colonial government in the 19th century.[47] Similar arguments have been advanced for the role and functions of the Ismaili *pīrs* in the Badakhshān region of Central Asia.[48]

---

43 Simon Digby, 'The Sufi Shaykh and the Sultan: A Conflict of Claims to Authority in Medieval India', *Iran: Journal of the British Institute of Persian Studies*, 28 (1990), pp. 71–81; his 'The Sufi Shaikh as a Source of Authority in Medieval India', in Richard M. Eaton, ed., *India's Islamic Traditions, 711–1750* (Delhi, 2003), pp. 234–262.

44 Nile Green, *Indian Sufism since the Seventeenth Century: Saints, Books and Empires in the Muslim Deccan* (London, 2006); his 'Blessed Men and Tribal Politics: Notes on Political Culture in the Indo-Afghan World', *Journal of the Economic and Social History of the Orient*, 49 (2006), pp. 344–360; his 'The *Faqir* and the Subalterns: Mapping the Holy Man in Colonial South Asia', *Journal of Asian History*, 41 (2007), pp. 57–84; and his *Islam and the Army in Colonial India: Sepoy Religion in the Service of Empire* (Cambridge, 2009).

45 Sarah F. D. Ansari, *Sufi Saints and State Power: The Pirs of Sind, 1843–1947* (Cambridge, 1992).

46 Jo-Ann Gross, 'The Economic Status of a Timurid Sufi Shaykh: A Matter of Conflict or Perception?', *Iranian Studies*, 21 (1988), pp. 84–104; her 'Multiple Roles and Perceptions of a Sufi Shaykh: Symbolic Statements of Political and Religious Authority', in Marc Gaborieau et al., ed., *Naqshbandis: Cheminements et situation actuelle d'un ordre mystique musulman* (Istanbul, 1990), pp. 109–121.

47 Devin DeWeese, 'The Politics of Sacred Lineages in 19th-Century Central Asia: Descent Groups Linked to Khwaja Ahmad Yasavi in Shrine Documents and Genealogical Charters', *International Journal of Middle East Studies*, 31 (1999), pp. 507–530.

48 Daniel Beben, 'Religious Identity in the Pamirs: The Institutionalization of the Ismāʿīlī *Daʿwa* in Shughnān', in Dagikhudo Dagiev and Carole Faucher, ed., *Revisiting Pamiri Identity in Central Asia and Beyond* (London, forthcoming); Abdulmamad Iloliev, '*Pirship* in Badakhshan: The Role and Significance of the Institute of the Religious Masters (*Pirs*) in Nineteenth and Twentieth Century Wakhan and Shughnan', *Journal of Shiʿa Islamic Studies*, 6 (2013), pp. 155–176; Ėl'bon Khodzhibekov, *Ismailitskie dukhovnye nastavniki (piry) i ikh rol' v obshchestvenno-politicheskoĭ kul'turnoĭ zhizni Shugnana*

The following pages will demonstrate how a similar framework may allow for a better understanding of the career of the Aga Khan and its significance in the broader Muslim world. Beginning in the wake of the Mongol conquests, the Ismaili Imamate underwent a number of critical changes in response to developments in the wider religious environment in which it operated. One of the major developments that can be traced throughout this period is the increasing adoption on the part of Ismaili authors of Sufi motifs and later, in the Safavid era, of discourses emphasising the sayyid lineage of the Imams. While these adaptations have traditionally been described under the framework of *taqiyya*, or merely precautionary efforts to 'blend in' with neighbouring religious communities, it can be argued that these developments should be seen as much more deeply rooted and meaningful for the Imamate than previous studies have allowed.[49] Thus these changes and adaptations reflect not merely an effort at survival and disguise, but also, and more significantly, an effort to project a sense of legitimacy within the social and spiritual realm in a manner that appealed to a wider circle of Muslim constituencies beyond the Imams' Ismaili followers. Above all, the Ismaili Imams can be seen undertaking the political and mediational roles performed by sayyids and holy men in many Muslim societies, a practice which reached fruition in the career of the Aga Khan.

Part II: The Historical Context

Ismailism in Post-Mongol Persia

The destruction of the Nizārī Ismaili headquarters at Alamūt and the murder of Imam Rukn al-Dīn Khūrshāh by the Mongols in 655/1257 initiated two centuries of the utmost concealment for the Nizārī Imamate. For most of this period the history of the Imamate is obscure and little is

---

(vtoraia polovina XIX–30-e gody XX vv.) (Dushanbe, 2015); Otambek Mastibekov, *Leadership and Authority in Central Asia: An Ismaili Community in Tajikistan* (London, 2014).

49 I have discussed this issue at length elsewhere; see Daniel Beben, 'Re-imagining *Taqiyya*: Strategies of Secrecy among the Ismāʿīlīs of Central Asia', in A. Akasoy et al., ed., *Religious Secrecy as Contact: Secrets as Promoters of Religious Dynamics* (Leiden, forthcoming).

known of it beyond the barest outlines.[50] While the decentralised political climate of late 9th/15th-century Persia permitted a brief public re-emergence of the Imamate, in the period known in modern Ismaili historiography as the 'Anjudān revival', the Safavid conquest of Persia in the early 10th/16th century once again forced the Imams into a perilous position. For a time it was believed by scholars that the Safavids, as a Shiʿi dynasty, would have been naturally more favourably disposed towards the Ismailis. This was suggested by Wladimir Ivanow, who proposed that 'the advent of the Safavids, with their adoption of Shiʿism as the religion of the state, together with the generally inflamed Shiʿite sentiment of the population, brought another period of relief in the history of Persian Ismaʿilism'.[51] However, the Safavid era had been poorly studied at the time of Ivanow's writing, and subsequent research into the religious policies of the Safavid state have not borne out his presumptions. On the contrary, it is clear now that the form of Shiʿism expressed by the Safavids was an exclusionary one, and hence the claims of the Nizārī Imams as living successors to Imam ʿAlī presented an ideological challenge to Safavid prerogatives to rule on behalf of the authority of the hidden Twelfth Imam.[52] At least one of the Nizārī Imams from the Safavid period, Murād Mīrzā (d. 981/1574), was executed on the charge of spreading heresy, while others were forced into hiding or dissimulation.[53]

Nonetheless, the state of Ismaili communities in the Safavid era was not altogether bleak. Nizārī communities outside Persia, particularly in

---

50 The most thorough overview of Nizārī history in the centuries immediately following the Mongol conquests is given in Shafique N. Virani, *The Ismailis in the Middle Ages: A History of Survival, a Search for Salvation* (Oxford, 2007). See also Daftary, *The Ismāʿīlīs*, pp. 403–422; Nadia Eboo Jamal, *Surviving the Mongols: Nizārī Quhistānī and the Continuity of Ismaili Tradition in Persia* (London, 2002).

51 Wladimir Ivanow, *Brief Survey of the Evolution of Ismailism* (Leiden, 1952), p. 18.

52 On Safavid persecution of the Ismaili Imams, see Said Amir Arjomand, *The Shadow of God and the Hidden Imam: Religion, Political Order and Societal Change in Shiʿite Iran from the Beginning to 1890* (Chicago, 1984), pp. 112–116; Farhad Daftary, 'Shāh Ṭāhir and the Nizārī Ismaili Disguises', in Todd Lawson, ed., *Reason and Inspiration in Islam: Theology, Philosophy and Mysticism in Muslim Thought: Essays in Honour of Hermann Landolt* (London, 2005), pp. 395–406.

53 On Murād Mīrzā, see Qāḍī Aḥmad al-Qummī, *Khulāṣat al-tavārīkh*, ed. Iḥsān Ishrāqī (Tehran, 1383 Sh./2004), vol. 1, pp. 582–584.

South Asia, underwent remarkable growth in this period, a development that would prove to be a critical factor in the fate of the Imamate in the post-Safavid era. Within Persia, the position of the Imamate underwent several critical developments in the Safavid era that likewise had lasting implications. Ever since the establishment of the Nizārī Ismaili Imamate in Persia, which occurred following the schism within the Ismaili community and the murder of Imam Nizār in Egypt in 488/1095, the Nizārī Imams in Persia had operated within a predominantly Sunni environment. In the wake of the Mongol conquests in the 7th/13th century, this environment became increasingly marked by the presence of the Sufi orders that flourished in this period, and the Imams elaborated their claims to religious authority within the context of the *pīr–murīd* discourse that characterised the Sufi traditions.[54] The Safavid conquest brought further major changes to the religious environment in Persia. In its early years, the Safavid state adopted a fervently messianic doctrine that endowed its rulers with miraculous powers and near-divine status.[55] In this context, the Nizārī Imams, with their own claims to divinely appointed succession to Imam ʿAlī, posed a clear threat to the Safavid regime, and were therefore persecuted and treated as rivals.

Over the course of the 10th/16th century, however, the Safavid state adopted a more normative interpretation of Twelver Shiʿism, relying upon Arab Shiʿi scholars recruited mainly from Lebanon to elaborate a state-sponsored Shiʿi legal and political framework for the regime.[56] In subsequent decades, the majority of the population of Persia converted to Twelver Shiʿism. As a consequence, for the first time in history the Ismaili Imamate found itself situated within a majority-Shiʿi environment. While this context did not afford the Imams any claims to authority on the basis of their Imamate, it did allow them to pursue such claims on the basis of their sayyid status, a position that came to be

54 On the Nizārī relationship with the Sufi orders in the post-Mongol era, see Farhad Daftary, 'Ismaili–Sufi Relations in Post-Alamut Persia', in Daftary, *Ismailis in Medieval Muslim Societies* (London, 2005), pp. 183–203.

55 Kathryn Babayan, 'The Safavid Synthesis: From Qizilbash Islam to Imamite Shiʿism', *Iranian Studies*, 27 (1994), pp. 135–161; see also her *Mystics, Monarchs and Messiahs: Cultural Landscapes of Early Modern Iran* (Cambridge, MA, 2002).

56 On this development, see Rula Jurdi Abisaab, *Converting Persia: Religion and Power in the Safavid Empire* (London, 2004).

broadly revered in Safavid Persia. Consequently, the Nizārī Imams throughout the late 10th/16th and 11th/17th centuries were able to establish themselves as local notables and landholders in the Anjudān region, where they concealed their claim to Imamate, adopting a disguise as Twelver Shiʿis, but earned esteem as sayyids. One piece of evidence for this is an edict dated 1036/1627 from Shāh ʿAbbās, addressed to the Nizārī Imam Khalīlullāh Anjudānī (known also as Dhu'l-Fiqār ʿAlī, d. 1043/1634), and to the inhabitants of Anjudān, exempting them from taxes on account of their proximity to the holy city of Qumm and because of their status as sayyids.[57] However, while the Nizārī Imams were able to retain a degree of local standing during the late Safavid period, their ability to operate openly as Ismailis remained very constricted, and there is no evidence that the Imams after Murād Mīrzā made any open expression of their claim to Imamate. However, this situation changed significantly after the fall of the Safavids in the 18th century.

The 18th-Century Transformation in Ismailism

Beginning in the early 18th century, a confluence of political and economic developments led to a drastic shift in the status of the Nizārī Imamate, enabling it to emerge as a political and social force in Persia after centuries of relative obscurity.[58] The most significant of these was the decline and collapse of the Safavid state. In the early 18th century the Safavid realm became subject to repeated incursions by Afghan tribal forces from the east which finally captured the Safavid capital of Iṣfahān in 1134/1722.[59] In the years following the fall of Iṣfahān, the Safavid commander Nādir Qulī-Beg came into a position of great power through a series of successful campaigns against the Afghans, eventually becoming the de facto ruler of Persia. Finally, in 1147/1736 Nādir decided to abandon the pretence of loyalty to the Safavids and had himself

57 Daftary, *The Ismāʿīlīs*, pp. 437–438.

58 On these developments, see further Daniel Beben, 'The Fatimid Legacy and the Foundation of the Modern Nizārī Ismaili Imamate', in Farhad Daftary and Shainool Jiwa, ed., *The Fatimid Caliphate: Diversity of Traditions* (London, 2018), pp. 192–216.

59 On the decline and collapse of the Safavid empire, see Rudolph P. Matthee, *Persia in Crisis: Safavid Decline and the Fall of Isfahan* (London, 2012).

crowned shah of Persia.[60] Following this, the newly crowned Nādir Shāh undertook a series of sweeping reforms in an effort to consolidate his power. Among these was the introduction of a far-reaching change to the religious policy of the state, in which official patronage of Twelver Shiʿism was abandoned in an effort to reduce tensions with his Sunni subjects and the neighbouring Sunni states. In its place, Nādir Shāh espoused a new system in which Shiʿism, under the label of the Jaʿfarī *madhhab*, would be recognised as the fifth school of jurisprudence of Islam, alongside the four widely recognised Sunni schools.[61] While Nādir Shāh's religious reforms met with only limited success and acceptance among his Sunni neighbours, his displacement of the religious institutions established in the Safavid era had far-reaching consequences for the Ismaili Imamate.

Nādir Shāh developed a close relationship with Imam Ḥasan ʿAlī (known also as Sayyid Ḥasan Beg) and employed the Imam as a commander in his army, in whose ranks there also served a number of Nizārīs.[62] It would appear, moreover, that this appointment was made by

---

60 On Nādir Shāh, see Peter Avery, 'Nādir Shāh and the Afsharid Legacy', in Peter Avery et al., ed., *The Cambridge History of Iran*, Volume 7: *From Nadir Shah to the Islamic Republic* (Cambridge, 1991), pp. 3–62; Michael Axworthy, *The Sword of Persia: Nader Shah, from Tribal Warrior to Conquering Tyrant* (London, 2006).

61 On Nādir Shāh's religious policies, see Hamid Algar, 'Shiʿism and Iran in the Eighteenth Century', in T. Naff and R. Owens, ed., *Studies in Eighteenth Century Islamic History* (Carbondale, 1977), pp. 288–302; Hamid Algar, 'Religious Forces in Eighteenth and Nineteenth-Century Iran', in *The Cambridge History of Iran*, vol. 7, pp. 705–731; Ernest Tucker, 'Nadir Shah and the Jaʿfari *Madhhab* Reconsidered', *Iranian Studies*, 27 (1994), pp. 163–179.

62 The relationship between Imam Sayyid Ḥasan Beg and Nādir Shāh is reported in a number of sources. The earliest account of it is provided by Nādir Shāh's chronicler, Muḥammad Kāẓim Marvī, who reports that the Imam served in the royal camp of Nādir Shāh but was later accused of treason and blinded; see Muḥammad Kāẓim Marvī, *ʿĀlamārā-yi Nādirī*, ed. Muḥammad Amīn Riyāḥī (Tehran, 1364 Sh./1985), vol. 3, p. 1182. Somewhat later, an early 19th-century Ismaili text from Central Asia titled the *Silk-i guhar-rīz* reports that the author's grandfather, a Nizārī *pīr* named Khwāja Muḥammad Ṣāliḥ, visited Imam Sayyid Ḥasan Beg in Mashhad and spent six months there in his service. It notes that the Imam served as an officer in Nādir Shāh's army and participated in his capture of Iṣfahān, and later accompanied Nādir to Mashhad, where Khwāja Muḥammad Ṣāliḥ came to meet him. He also notes that many of the Imam's followers likewise served in Nādir Shāh's army. See *Silk-i guhar-rīz*,

Nādir Shāh in the full knowledge of Ḥasan 'Alī's status as the Nizārī Imam. According to some accounts of this relationship, Imam Ḥasan 'Alī also accompanied Nādir Shāh on his invasion of India, after which he was rewarded with the governorship of the region surrounding his ancestral village of Maḥallāt. After some time, however, the Imam's enemies at court intrigued against him, accusing him of heresy, which led Nādir Shāh to blind him. However, Nādir Shāh later pardoned Ḥasan 'Alī and reinstated him in his former position. Despite its hesitant beginnings, the relationship between the Nizārī Imams and the Afshārid dynasty outlived Nādir Shāh and was strengthened significantly under his successors.

Nādir Shāh's cultivation of a relationship with the Nizārī Imamate reflected the broader political and religious agenda he pursued in the course of his short-lived empire. Lacking the genealogical or religious claims to legitimacy afforded to the Safavids, Nādir Shāh instead pursued a series of alternative policies of legitimation in order to establish his authority in post-Safavid Persia.[63] Given his own efforts to combat the influence of the Ithnāʿasharī Shiʿi *'ulamā'* and to displace them from the privileged position they had held under the Safavids, it is likely that Nādir Shāh would have seen a convenient ally in the Nizārī Imamate. Consequently, following the collapse of the Safavid state it would appear that the Nizārī Imams were no longer pressured to conceal their claim to the Imamate. As the sources of this period illustrate, the Ismaili identity of the Imams was clearly known to observers

---

ed. Qudratbek Elchibekov (unpublished typescript in the archives of the IIS), pp. 108–110. Another source from the late 19th century, the *Āthār-i Muḥammadī* (IIS MS 919, pp. 15–16), reports that Nādir Shāh gave the governorship of the town of Kiyāb, located near Maḥallāt, to Imam Sayyid Ḥasan Beg. It likewise reports that the Imam participated in Nādir Shāh's capture of Iṣfahān and was even given the governorship of the city, although this latter detail is almost certainly an embellishment. This account also mentions Nādir Shāh's blinding of the Imam, but adds that Nādir later pardoned him and appointed him as *beglarbegī* (governor) of Kirmān. The early 20th-century Nizārī chronicler Fidā'ī Khurāsānī also relates that the Imam and his followers served in Nādir Shāh's campaign in India, accompanying him to Kabul and as far as Peshawar; see Muḥammad b. Zayn al-ʿĀbidīn Fidā'ī Khurāsānī, *Hidāyat al-mu'minīn al-ṭālibīn*, ed. A. A. Semenov (reprinted, Tehran, 1362 Sh./1983), pp. 142–143.

63 On this, see Ernest Tucker, *Nadir Shah's Quest for Legitimacy in Post-Safavid Iran* (Gainesville, FL, 2006).

during the reign of Nādir Shāh and in later times. However, as will be seen, the Imams also continued to assert broader claims to social and spiritual authority among non-Ismaili constituencies on the basis of their sayyid status.

The Nizārī Ismaili Imamate and Kirmān

Another major development that accompanied the public emergence of the Nizārī Ismaili Imamate under Nādir Shāh was the moving of the seat of the Imamate away from the Qumm region, where it had been based since at least the 9th/15th century, to the region of Kirmān in south-eastern Persia. The main sources chronicling this development are the writings of the late 19th-century historian Aḥmad ʿAlī Khān Vazīrī, among whose works are the *Tārīkh-i Kirmān*, a history of Kirmān from pre-Islamic times to the early Qājār period completed in 1874, and a historical geography of Kirmān titled *Jughrāfiyā-yi Kirmān*.[64] While Kirmān had not historically been an important centre of Ismailism,[65] the Imamate had maintained a following there since at least the late 11th/17th century. During the Imamate of Sayyid Ḥasan ʿAlī's grandfather, Shāh Nizār ʿAlī (Nizār II), a group of nomadic Khurāsānī tribesmen known as ʿAṭāʾullāhīs (after the *takhalluṣ* of Shāh Nizār, ʿAṭāʾullāh), who were followers of the Imam, were resettled in Kirmān, in the region of Sīrjān.[66] One interesting characteristic of this group was that they were explicitly identified by Vazīrī as not being Ismailis, but rather the personal followers of the Imam, drawn to his charismatic authority as a

64 On Vazīrī and his works, see Heribert Busse, 'Kermān im 19. Jahrhundert nach der Geographie des Wazīrī', *Der Islam*, 50 (1973), pp. 284–312; James M. Gustafson, 'Geographical Literature in Nineteenth-Century Iran: Regional Identities and the Construction of Space', *Journal of the Economic and Social History of the Orient*, 59 (2016), pp. 807–811.

65 Kirmān appears to have been the scene of some limited Ismaili activity in the Fatimid and early Nizārī eras, and it was the home of the renowned Ismaili philosopher Ḥamīd al-Dīn Kirmānī (d. after 411/1020), whose career was largely based in Iraq. However, there is no evidence for Ismaili activity in the region in the period following the Mongol conquests and prior to Imam Nizār II (d. 1134/1722).

66 Several of these communities reportedly still resided in the Kirmān region as late as the 1960s; see Peter Willey, *Eagle's Nest: Ismaili Castles in Iran and Syria* (London, 2005), pp. 205–206.

sayyid and a descendant of Imam Jaʿfar al-Ṣādiq. According to Vazīrī, 'this group maintained complete faith and sincerity in the sayyids of the line of Ismāʿīl, son of Ḥaḍrat-i Imām, to speak correctly, Jaʿfar Ṣādiq … from that time forward the Khurāsānī and ʿAṭā'ullāhī communities have been believers and followers of this *silsila*, but like the Ḥaydarābādīs, they are neither Sevener Shiʿas nor Ismāʿīlīs.'[67] The presence of the ʿAṭā'ullāhīs offers one of the earliest signs of the gradual growth and extension of the political and social authority of the Imams in the 18th century, which saw the development of new constituencies for the Imamate outside the context of strictly Ismaili communities.

The strengthening of the position of the Nizārī Imamate in 18th-century Persia was enabled also by another development in this period, namely the increase in the economic fortunes of the Indian Ismaili communities. Notwithstanding various polemical claims to the contrary, the strength of the Nizārī Imams' following in India is well attested in the sources at least since the late medieval period.[68] In the late 11th/17th and 18th

---

67 Aḥmad ʿAlī Khān Vazīrī, *Jughrāfiyā-yi Kirmān*, ed. Muḥammad Ibrāhīm Bāstānī Pārīzī (Tehran, 1376 Sh./1997), p. 265. The reference to the Ḥaydarābādīs in this account probably refers to the town of Ḥaydarābād (Hyderabad) in the Sindh province of present-day Pakistan, where the Nizārī Imams had for centuries maintained a community of followers.

68 The position of the Nizārī Imamate in the history of the Khojas is well attested in both Ismaili and non-Ismaili sources going back several centuries before the time of Aga Khan I. The 10th/16th-century Nizārī author Khayrkhwāh-i Harātī relates an anecdote about one of his contemporaries, a Nizārī *dāʿī* operating in India, who had ten times the number of followers of one of his competitors in Khurāsān; see Khayrkhwāh-i Harātī, *Taṣnīfāt*, ed. Wladimir Ivanow (Tehran, 1961), p. 61. A century later, an early 11th/17th-century Safavid history, the *Khulāṣat al-tavārīkh* of Qāḍī Aḥmad al-Qummī, mentions that the Ismaili Imam of this period, Murād Mīrzā, had many followers in India who regularly dispatched tithes to him; see al-Qummī, *Khulāṣat al-tavārīkh*, vol. 1, p. 582. This same observation is repeated by the 18th-century chronicler of Nādir Shāh, Muḥammad Kāẓim Marvī, who reports that Imam Sayyid Ḥasan Beg received a significant number of pilgrims, as well as notable amounts of tithes from his followers in India, who were centred in the city of Aḥmadabād in the Gujarat region of present-day India; see Marvī, *ʿĀlamārā-yi Nādirī*, vol. 3, p. 1182. A notice from a British official stationed in Gujarat from 1818 also says that 'the Khojas consider themselves of Persian origin, and frequently make a pilgrimage to a spot eight days' march to the N.W. of Isphahan, where they worship a living peer, or saint, to whom they pay an annual tax on their property'; see James Macmurdo, 'An account of the province of Cutch, and of the countries

centuries the Indian Nizārī Ismailis, known as Khojas, began increasingly to migrate from inland regions towards the coastal areas of Sindh and Gujarat, and then into Bombay and across the Indian Ocean to East Africa in the early 19th century.[69] One of the major factors leading to this development was the shifting of patterns of trade away from the overland trade routes of Asia in favour increasingly of a sea-based pattern of trading dominated by the European naval powers. While this development more broadly had negative consequences for many of the economies of the region, contributing in part to the decline and collapse of the Safavid state, which was dependent upon revenues from the overland trade, conversely it also benefited the Ismailis of India, many of whom belonged to merchant communities in a position to profit from the increased volume in the Indian Ocean trade.[70]

The concern for the relationship with the Indian Ismailis and their wealth was a major impetus behind the shift of the seat of the Imamate to Kirmān under Imam Ḥasan ʿAlī. According to Vazīrī, who introduces the Imam as 'from the lineage of Nizār who was, by several degrees removed, among the ancestors of Ismāʿīl b. Imām Jaʿfar al-Ṣādiq', as a result of the disorders in Persia following the fall of the Safavids the Nizārīs in India faced increasing difficulty in travelling to visit and pay tribute to the Imams in central Persia.[71] Many of their

---

lying between Guzerat and the river Indus', *Transactions of the Literary Society of Bombay*, 2 (1820), pp. 245–246. Internal evidence from the *ginān*s relates to even earlier periods; on this, see Azim Nanji, *The Nizārī Ismāʿīlī Tradition in the Indo-Pakistan Subcontinent* (Delmar, NY, 1978).

69 Akhtar, *The Khōjā of Tanzania*, pp. 33–35. On the role of the Ismailis in the economy of Bombay and the Indian Ocean arena in the 19th century, see also Green, *Bombay Islam*, pp. 155–178.

70 Claude Markovits, *The Global World of Indian Merchants, 1750–1947* (Cambridge, 2000). While the overland trade through Persia appears to have declined in the 17th and 18th centuries, at the same time trade between Russia and India through Central Asia saw an increase in this period, on which see Scott C. Levi, 'India, Russia and the Eighteenth-Century Transformation of the Central Asian Caravan Trade', *Journal of the Economic and Social History of the Orient*, 42 (1999), pp. 519–548; and his *The Indian Diaspora in Central Asia and Its Trade, 1550–1900* (Leiden, 2002). This increased volume of trade between India and Central Asia facilitated the closer integration between the Ismaili communities of these two regions in the 18th and 19th centuries as well.

71 Aḥmad ʿAlī Khān Vazīrī, *Tārīkh-i Kirmān*, ed. Muḥammad Ibrāhīm Bāstānī Pārīzī (6th ed., Tehran, 1393 Sh./2014), pp. 698–699.

caravans were plundered by the Bakhtiyārī tribes and the flow of tithes to the Imamate was stifled. As a result, towards the end of the reign of Nādir Shāh the decision was made by Sayyid Ḥasan ʿAlī to move the seat of the Imamate to the town of Shahr-i Bābak in Kirmān in order to position himself closer both to the overland routes from India as well as the southern port of Bandar ʿAbbās, which was also used by many Indian pilgrims in this period. The flow of tithes from India resumed and increased, and the Imam soon became a major landowner in the Kirmān region. Vazīrī further relates that following the death of Nādir Shāh, Sayyid Ḥasan ʿAlī developed a close relationship with Nādir Shāh's grandson, Shāhrukh Khān, the governor of Kirmān, and that the Imam gave one of his daughters in marriage to Shāhrukh Khān's son, Luṭf ʿAlī Khān.

The sources relate few details regarding Imam Sayyid Ḥasan ʿAlī's successor, Qāsim ʿAlī, whose Imamate evidently was quite brief. Much more information is available on the next imam, Sayyid Abu'l-Ḥasan ʿAlī.[72] During Sayyid Abu'l-Ḥasan's Imamate, control of Kirmān passed from the Afshārids to the Zands. The Imam continued to enjoy a close relationship with the Zand governor of the province, Mīrzā Ḥusayn Khān, and later succeeded him as the governor of Kirmān.[73] The Imam successfully repelled a major Afghan invasion of Kirmān in this period, earning him copious accolades from the Zands. In addition, he patronised the construction of a public square adjacent to the Friday mosque as well as a number of prominent buildings in the city of Kirmān. Following the death of the Zand ruler, Karīm Khān, in 1193/1779, Imam Abu'l-Ḥasan ʿAlī continued to receive the support of his successors and governed the province as a virtually autonomous ruler. However, he crucially switched his support to Āghā Muḥammad Khān Qājār during the latter's conflict with the Zands, and with the support of his ʿAṭā'ullāhī followers he repelled an attempt by the Zand ruler Luṭf ʿAlī Khān to

---

72 On this Imam, see also Sayyid ʿAlī Āl-i Dāvūd, ʿAbu'l-Ḥasan Khān Bīglarbigī Maḥallātī', in *Dā'irat al-Maʿārif-i Buzurg-i Islāmī*, vol. 5, ed. Kāẓim Musavī Bujnurdī (Tehran, 1382 Sh./1993), pp. 339–341; English trans. in *Encyclopaedia Islamica*, vol. 2, pp. 29–32; Heribert Busse, 'Abu'l-Ḥasan Khan Maḥallātī', *EIr*; Daftary, *The Ismāʿīlīs*, pp. 459–462.

73 Vazīrī, *Tārīkh-i Kirmān*, pp. 699–705. On Zand rule in Kirmān, see also James M. Gustafson, 'Kerman viii: Afsharid and Zand Period', *EIr*; John R. Perry, *Karim Khan Zand: A History of Iran, 1747–1779* (Chicago, 1979), pp. 134–136.

capture the city of Kirmān in the winter of 1205–1206/1790–1791.[74] This switch of allegiance laid the foundations for a very close and beneficial relationship between the Nizārī Imamate and the Qājārs for the next half-century.

Part III: The Life and Career of the Aga Khan

Imams Khalīlullāh and Aga Khan I

Following the Qājār capture of Kirmān, Imam Abu'l-Ḥasan 'Alī retired to his ancestral home in Kahak, a decision that was probably due to the violent upheavals that continued to take place across Kirmān following the imposition of Qājār authority there. The Imam died a year later, in 1206/1792, and was succeeded by his son Shāh Khalīlullāh, who was appointed mayor of Kahak by Āghā Muḥammad Khān. The French diplomat, Rousseau, in his notice on Khalīlullāh observed that this Imam, although opposed by the local Twelver Shiʿi clergy in the Kahak region, was favoured by the Shāh on account of the revenues brought into the country by his Indian followers.[75] It was in Kahak that Ḥasan 'Alī Shāh, the future Aga Khan I, was born in 1219/1804. In 1815 Shāh Khalīlullāh moved his residence to the city of Yazd in central Persia, in order to once again situate the Imamate more conveniently for pilgrims from India. In 1817, two years after the shift of the seat of the Imamate to Yazd, Imam Shāh Khalīlullāh's residence was attacked by an angry mob instigated by a member of the local Shiʿi *'ulamā'* named Mullā Ḥusayn Yazdī, and the Imam and a number of his Indian followers were murdered.[76]

---

74 On these events, see Ḥājj Mīrzā Ḥasan Ḥusaynī Fasā'ī, *Fārs-nāma-yi Nāṣirī*, English trans. as *History of Persia under Qājār Rule*, tr. Heribert Busse (New York, 1972), pp. 37–38; Riḍā Qulī Khān Hidāyat, *Rawḍat al-ṣafā-yi Nāṣirī* (Tehran, 1339 Sh./1960), vol. 9, pp. 250–252; Muḥammad Fatḥullāh b. Muḥammad Taqī Sārū'ī, *Tārīkh-i Muḥammadī (Aḥsan al-tavārīkh)*, ed. Ghulām Riḍā Ṭabāṭabā'ī Majd (Tehran, 1371 Sh./1992), p. 256.

75 Rousseau, 'Mémoire sur les Ismaélis', pp. 279–280.

76 On the murder of Imam Khalīlullāh, see Hidāyat, *Rawḍat al-ṣafā-yi Nāṣirī*, vol. 9, pp. 551–553; Muḥammad Ḥasan Khān Iʿtimād al-Salṭana, *Mir'āt al-buldān*, ed. 'Abd al-Ḥusayn Navā'ī (Tehran, 1368 Sh./1989), vol. 1, p. 868; Muḥammad Taqī Lisān al-Mulk Sipihr, *Nāsikh al-tavārīkh: Tārīkh-i Qājāriyya*,

This incident clearly illustrates the continuing precarious nature of the Nizārī Imamate's position in Persian society in this period. Yet at the same time, it also reveals the remarkable degree of affinity between the Imamate and the political elite of Persia that had developed over the previous century. While the Imam's murderers were never caught, the Qājār ruler of the period, Fatḥ 'Alī Shāh, ordered Mullā Yazdī to be severely punished for having instigated the disturbances. As further compensation, the Shāh appointed Shāh Khalīlullāh's son and successor to the Imamate, Ḥasan 'Alī Shāh, governor of Qumm and granted him one of his own daughters, Sarv-i Jahān, in marriage.[77] In addition, at this time Fatḥ 'Alī Shāh also bestowed on him the honorific title of Aga Khan, which has since become a hereditary title for the Nizārī Ismaili Imams.[78]

Little more is known about this period of the Aga Khan's life until the death of Fatḥ 'Alī Shāh in 1834 and the accession of his grandson Muḥammad Shāh to the Qājār throne.[79] The Aga Khan, now thirty years old, endeared himself to the new ruler and soon after was appointed governor of Kirmān, the same position that his grandfather had held under the Zands. The Aga Khan's appointment as governor of Kirmān entailed considerable responsibility, as the province had fallen into

---

ed. Jamshīd Kiyān-far (Tehran, 1390 Sh./2011), vol. 1, pp. 290–291. See also the account of the British traveller James Fraser, *Narrative of a Journey into Khorasan*, pp. 376–377.

77 Aḥmad Mīrzā 'Aḍud al-Dawla, *Tārīkh-i 'Aḍudī*, ed. Kāẓim 'Ābidīnī Muṭlaq (Qumm, 1388 Sh./2009), pp. 29–30, 140.

78 The title Āqā Khān (anglicised as Aga Khan) consists of two elements, both loan-words into Persian of Turkic-Mongol origin. The first, 'Āqā', is a Turkic word meaning 'elder brother', more generally also used as a term of respect for older men, which in Qājār-era Iran held the broader connotation of 'chief' or a respected elder. This term is also found sometimes under the variant spelling of 'Āghā'. The second element of the title, 'Khān', is an ancient Turkic-Mongol title referring to a ruler, and from the period of the Mongol conquests onwards was almost exclusively claimed only by patrilineal descendants of Chingīz Khān. While this more restrictive definition was retained in Central Asia and elsewhere down to the 19th century, in Iran by this period the term had come to hold a broader significance, being used generally and as a title of respect, as applied in the case of the Aga Khan, and not implying Chingīzid descent.

79 Unless otherwise noted, the source for most of the following discussion on the life and career of the Aga Khan is the *'Ibrat-afzā*, to which the reader may refer in the main body of the present work.

2. Fatḥ ʿAlī Shāh Qājār, 1815, by Mihr ʿAlī.

disorder and was plagued by a series of tribal uprisings.[80] The Aga Khan agreed to accept this assignment without any remuneration. However, less than two years into his governorship in Kirmān and following, by his own account, a widely successful campaign to restore law and order to the province, the Aga Khan was dismissed from his post and replaced by Nuṣrat al-Dawla, a brother of Muḥammad Shāh Qājār. Rather than accepting his dismissal, however, the Aga Khan decided to garrison himself and his soldiers in the fortress of Bam and called on his brothers, Abu'l-Ḥasan Khān and Muḥammad Bāqir Khān, to join him there with their own troops.[81]

80 On the period of the Aga Khan's governorship of Kirmān, see also James M. Gustafson, 'Kerman ix: Qajar Period', *EIr*; Gustafson, *Kirman and the Qajar Empire*, pp. 41–44; Vazīrī, *Tārīkh-i Kirmān*, pp. 771–773, 782–789.

81 On these events, see also Sykes, *Ten Thousand Miles in Persia*, pp. 69–70, 217.

It is here that the Aga Khan's narrative and that of the Qājār chronicles begin to diverge in their account of his motivations. The Qājār chroniclers of these events suggest that before this event the Aga Khan had begun to nurture the idea of a revolt against the Qājār crown, with his refusal to accept his dismissal being taken as evidence of his intentions.[82] The Aga Khan's narrative traces the origins of his dismissal to the conniving of the monarch's chief minister, Ḥājjī Mīrzā Āqāsī (1783–1848), who targeted the Aga Khan on account of his close relationship with his, Ḥājjī Mīrzā's, rival, the spiritual leader (*quṭb*) of the Niʿmatullāhī Sufi order, Zayn al-ʿĀbidīn Shirvānī. Given that the relationship between the Ismailis and the Niʿmatullāhī order played a key role in the events of this period, here there will be a digression in order to provide some background on this relationship and its significance for the career of the Aga Khan, before returning to a discussion of the events leading up to his campaigns against the Qājārs.

The Nizārīs and the Niʿmatullāhiyya

The relationship between the Niʿmatullāhiyya and the Ismailis was first brought to light in Hamid Algar's 1969 article on the Aga Khan's revolt, and was subsequently the subject of a more extensive study in a 1975 article by Pourjavady and Wilson.[83] While claims have been made for a relationship between the two traditions extending back to the time of Shāh Niʿmatullāh Valī himself, in fact there is no direct evidence testifying to such a relationship before the revival of the Niʿmatullāhiyya in Persia in the late 18th century, as will be explained further below.[84]

---

82 The Qājār sources for these events are discussed further below.

83 Algar, 'The Revolt of Āghā Khān Maḥallātī', pp. 72–74; Pourjavady and Wilson, 'Ismāʿīlīs and Niʿmatullāhīs', pp. 113–135. See also ʿAlī Aṣghar Maẓharī, 'Rābiṭa-yi Ismāʿīliyān bā sūfiyān-i ṭarīqat-i Niʿmatullāhī', *Ṣūfī*, 27 (1374 Sh./1995), pp. 6–18, which adds little to previous studies.

84 The arguments for much earlier relationships between the two traditions rest in part upon such flimsy 'evidence' as the fact that a number of Nizārī Imams had 'Sufic-sounding names'; it also rests, however, upon a misconstrual of evidence from Central Asia, where the Nizārīs of the Badakhshān region maintain a number of literary traditions associated with Shāh Niʿmatullāh Valī. A closer examination of these traditions, however, shows that they present no evidence of any institutional engagement between the Ismailis and the Niʿmatullāhī order; rather, they reflect an Ismaili

The Niʿmatullāhiyya trace their foundation to the Sufi master Shāh Niʿmatullāh Valī (d. 834/1431).[85] Shāh Niʿmatullāh's early career as a Sufi master was based primarily in Central Asia, although he was later expelled from there by Amīr Tīmūr and so he settled in the Kirmān region of south-eastern Persia, where his shrine complex is preserved in the city of Māhān. Later, Niʿmatullāh's son Khalīlullāh established another branch of the order in India, under the patronage of the Bahmanid dynasty of the Deccan.[86] While Shāh Niʿmatullāh and the Sufi tradition he established were Sunni in orientation, following the Safavid conquest of Persia the Niʿmatullāhiyya adopted a Shiʿi alignment in order to preserve the patronage of the Safavids.[87] Yet while the Niʿmatullāhiyya initially enjoyed good relations with the Safavids, by the end of the 10th/16th century this relationship had soured and the majority of the Niʿmatullāhī leadership likewise migrated to India under threat of persecution.

While the Niʿmatullāhiyya almost entirely abandoned its institutional presence in Persia from the end of the 10th/16th century onwards, it was energetically reintroduced to Persia in the late 18th century by the order's master, Riḍā ʿAlī Shāh Dakkanī, whose disciple Maʿṣūm ʿAlī

---

engagement with the popular legacy of Shāh Niʿmatullāh as a Sufi saint and poet in Central Asia. I plan to dedicate a separate study to this topic in the future; for now, see the preliminary discussion in Daniel Beben, 'The Legendary Biographies of Nāṣir-i Khusraw: Memory and Textualization in Early Modern Persian Ismāʿīlism' (PhD dissertation, Indiana University, 2015), pp. 195–197.

85 On Shāh Niʿmatullāh and the Niʿmatullāhī tradition, see Hamid Algar and J. Burton-Page, 'Niʿmat-allāhiyya', *EI2*; Terry Graham, 'Shāh Niʿmatullāh Walī: Founder of the Niʿmatullāhī Order', in Leonard Lewisohn, ed., *The Legacy of Mediaeval Persian Sufism* (London, 1992), pp. 173–190; Nasrollah Pourjavady and Peter Lamborn Wilson, *Kings of Love: The Poetry and History of the Niʿmatullāhī Sufi Order* (Tehran, 1978).

86 On the descendants of Shāh Niʿmatullāh and their Sufi activities in the Deccan, see Jean Aubin, 'De Kûhbanân à Bidar: La Famille Nimatullahī', *Studia Islamica*, 20 (1991), pp. 233–261; Nasrollah Pourjavady and Peter Lamborn Wilson, 'The Descendants of Shāh Niʿmatullāh Walī', *Islamic Culture*, 48 (1974), pp. 49–57.

87 On the Niʿmatullāhiyya in the Safavid era, see Terry Graham, 'The Niʿmatu'llāhī Order Under Safavid Suppression and in Indian Exile', in Leonard Lewisohn and David Morgan, ed., *The Heritage of Sufism*, Volume 3: *Late Classical Persianate Sufism (1501–1750)* (Oxford, 2000), pp. 165–200.

Shāh travelled to Persia from the Deccan in 1184/1770 and began promulgating the order there.[88] The late 18th-century revival of the Niʿmatullāhiyya was particularly vibrant in the region of Kirmān, where the order was able to build upon a popular following connected to the shrine of Shāh Niʿmatullāh Valī in Māhān. In 1199/1785 two of Maʿṣūm ʿAlī Shāh's disciples, Nūr ʿAlī Shāh and Mushtāq ʿAlī Shāh, arrived in Kirmān to revive the order and proselytise for it.[89] Imam Abu'l-Ḥasan ʿAlī, grandfather of the Aga Khan and governor of Kirmān at this time, welcomed these Sufis and offered them protection from persecution by local members of the Twelver *ʿulamā*.[90] In 1206/1792 Mushtāq ʿAlī Shāh was murdered by a mob incited by a local cleric who declared the popular Sufi to be a heretic. Upon his death later that same year, Imam Abu'l-Ḥasan ʿAlī was buried in Mushtāq ʿAlī Shāh's mausoleum in the city of Kirmān, known as the Mushtāqiyya, which remains a popular pilgrimage site today.[91]

The Niʿmatullāhī revival drew sharp opposition from members of the Twelver *ʿulamā*, who considered the Niʿmatullāhī claim to *vilāyat*, or spiritual authority, to usurp the prerogative of their hidden Twelfth Imam.[92] Several high-ranking individuals in the Niʿmatullāhiyya,

---

88 On the Niʿmatullāhī revival in late 18th-century Persia, see Leonard Lewisohn, 'An Introduction to the History of Modern Persian Sufism, Part I: The Niʿmatullāhī Order: Persecution, Revival and Schism', *Bulletin of the School of Oriental and African Studies*, 61 (1998), pp. 437–464; William Royce, 'Mīr Maʿṣūm ʿAlī Shāh and the Niʿmat Allāhī Revival 1776–77 to 1796–97: A Study of Sufism and its Opponents in Late Eighteenth Century Iran' (PhD dissertation, Princeton University, 1979); Fabrizio Speziale, 'A propos du renouveau *Niʿmatullāhī*: Le centre de Hyderabad au course de la première modernité', *Studia Iranica*, 42 (2013), pp. 91–118.

89 On the revival of the Niʿmatullāhiyya in Kirmān, see Lewisohn, 'Introduction to the History of Modern Persian Sufism, Part I', p. 444; Pourjavady and Wilson, *Kings of Love*, pp. 118–125; Royce, 'Mīr Maʿṣūm ʿAlī Shāh and the Niʿmat Allāhī Revival', pp. 152–162.

90 Daftary, *The Ismāʿīlīs*, pp. 461–462.

91 Ivanow, 'Tombs of Some Persian Ismaili Imams', p. 60.

92 On the theological underpinnings of this debate, see Nasrollah Pourjavady, 'Opposition to Sufism in Twelver Shiism', in Frederick de Jong and Bernd Radtke, ed., *Islamic Mysticism Contested: Thirteen Centuries of Controversies and Polemics* (Leiden, 1999), pp. 614–623; Oliver Scharbodt, 'The *Quṭb* as Special Representative of the Hidden Imam: The Conflation of Shiʿi and Sufi *Vilāyat* in the Niʿmatullāhī Order', in Denis Hermann and Sabrina Mervin,

including Ma'ṣūm 'Alī Shāh himself, were murdered at the instigation of the Twelver *'ulamā'* in this period. This experience of persecution was undoubtedly a major factor in bringing the Ni'matullāhiyya and the Nizārīs into a close alliance. While the most vehement expression of this persecution had subsided by the early 19th century, nonetheless the Ni'matullāhīs continued to experience maltreatment by the *'ulamā'* throughout the 19th century and beyond.

Yet while the Ni'matullāhī revival was met with fierce opposition by members of the Twelver clergy in Persia, by contrast, they received a warm reception from Āghā Muḥammad Khān Qājār, who at that time was consolidating his rule over Persia and sought to enlist Ma'ṣūm 'Alī Shāh and his followers as allies in his rivalry with the Zands.[93] Āghā Muḥammad Khān's successor, Fatḥ 'Alī Shāh, adopted a more guarded position towards the Ni'matullāhīs and feared the consequences of their growing influence at court; nonetheless, during his reign many high-ranking courtiers and members of the Qājār elite became followers of the Ni'matullāhiyya. This relationship between the Ni'matullāhiyya and the Qājār court reached its apogee upon the ascension of Muḥammad Shāh to the Qājār throne in 1834. The following year, Muḥammad Shāh appointed his former tutor, a Ni'matullāhī Sufi named Ḥājjī Mīrzā Āqāsī, as his chief minister.[94] From his position as chief minister, Āqāsī engaged in bitter contests for political influence with other Ni'matullāhī figures. The most notable of these was with Zayn al-'Ābidīn Shirvānī (d. 1838, also known as Mast 'Alī Shāh), who upon the death of Majdhūb 'Alī Shāh in 1823 succeeded him as the master (*quṭb*; lit. 'pole') of the Ni'matullāhiyya.[95] Shirvānī, who

---

ed., *Shi'i Trends and Dynamics in Modern Times (XVIIIth–XXth Centuries)* (Beirut, 2010), pp. 33–49.

93 On the relationship between the Ni'matullāhiyya and the state in 19th- and 20th-century Persia, see Matthijs van den Bos, *Mystic Regimes: Sufism and the State in Iran, from the late Qajar Era to the Islamic Republic* (Leiden, 2002).

94 On Āqāsī, see Abbas Amanat, 'Āqāsī, Ḥājjī Mīrzā Abbās Īravānī', *EIr*; Majīd Ashrafī, *Ḥājj Mīrzā Āqāsī: Ṣadr-i a'ẓam-i Muḥammad Shāh Qājār* (Tehran, 1386 Sh./2008).

95 On Shirvānī, see Lewisohn, 'Introduction to the History of Modern Persian Sufism, Part I', pp. 446–448; Muḥammad Ma'ṣūm Shīrāzī, *Ṭarā'iq al-ḥaqā'iq*, ed. Muḥammad Ja'far Maḥjūb (Tehran, 1345 Sh./1966), vol. 3, pp. 280–292.

3. Muḥammad Shāh Qājār and Ḥājjī Mīrzā Āqāsī, 1840s.

throughout his Sufi career had received repeated death threats from members of the *ʿulamāʾ*, had a long friendship with the Aga Khan, who at one point granted him refuge in the village of Dawlatābād near Maḥallāt from his persecutors.[96]

96 Shirvānī travelled widely in the early years of his career and composed a series of books in which he writes affectionately of the Aga Khan and the Ismailis; see Zayn al-ʿĀbidīn Shirvānī, *Riyāḍ al-siyāḥa*, vol. 1, ed. Aṣghar Ḥāmid Rabbānī (Tehran, 1339 Sh./1960), pp. 672–690; Zayn al-ʿĀbidīn Shirvānī, *Būstān al-siyāḥa*, ed. Āghā Mīrzā Ḥabibullāh (Tehran, 1315/1897), p. 530; his *Ḥadāʾiq al-sīyāḥa*, ed. Sulṭān Ḥusayn Tābanda, Riḍā ʿAlī Shāh (Tehran, 1348 Sh./1969), pp. 521–525.

A number of modern authors writing on the relationship between the Nizārī Imams and the Niʿmatullāhiyya have advanced the problematic claim that the association between the former and the latter was one of 'discipleship', in which not only a number of ordinary Ismailis, but even several of the Imams themselves are claimed to have been initiated into the order. According to Hamid Algar, this relationship entailed the Nizārī Imams 'implictly renouncing their title to the Imamate'.[97] While there is not space here to consider fully the theological implications of this assertion, it suffices to mention that such claims of discipleship are found solely within the Niʿmatullāhī sources, and more particularly, in the context of hagiographical works intended to praise the spiritual prowess and influence of the Niʿmatullāhī shaykhs involved in this relationship. Current scholarship on this question has largely relied upon an uncritical reading of these sources in assessing this relationship. Unfortunately, contemporary Nizārī sources on this matter, which may shed additional light on the motivations of the Imams for pursuing this relationship and their perceptions of its significance, are far more sparse. The earliest of such sources available, namely the *ʿIbrat-afzā* itself, in fact appears to squarely discredit this claim of 'discipleship', as will be explained shortly.

The label of 'discipleship' imposed upon this relationship implies a zero-sum equation, in which one party's claims to spiritual authority must necessarily come at the expense of, or on supersession of, another's. While the history of Sufi orders in the Islamic world certainly has no lack of examples of such rivalries and spiritual one-upmanship, it affords countless examples of genuine fealty and mutual affection between spiritual claimants as well. Moreover, the Aga Khan's own work presents multiple examples of offers of fealty to authorities such as the Qājār monarch, whom the Aga Khan refers to as the 'Shadow of God', an expression used in the Persian sources in reference to the Qājār monarch. Rather than subjecting this relationship to tortuous theological inquiries, a simpler account of it would place it within the context of the broader pattern of the Ismaili Imamate's cultivation in this period of spiritual and political constituencies outside a solely Ismaili framework. As the authority and profile of the Imamate expanded throughout the 18th and 19th centuries, the Imams developed an increasingly extensive

97 Algar, 'The Revolt of Āghā Khān Maḥallātī', p. 73.

and complex network of ties and mutually beneficial relationships with both spiritual and secular authorities. Within the context of early Qājār Iran, in which both the Niʿmatullāhīs and Ismailis faced ubiquitous threats to their safety, it should be no surprise that the two parties found occasions for mutual cooperation and regard, bound not only by a common set of opponents, but also by a shared adherence to esoteric interpretations of Shiʿism.

In the specific case of the Aga Khan's friendship with Zayn al-ʿĀbidīn Shirvānī, it would seem quite clearly that this was not perceived by the Aga Khan as a master–disciple relationship. Moreover, by the time of the Aga Khan's departure from Persia, this friendship had greatly soured. Shirvānī himself is said to have made the boast, 'I have a disciple such as the Aga Khan, who in most countries of the world has tens of thousands of disciples.' The Aga Khan himself relates this boast in his work, which some observers have taken as evidence of the Aga Khan's endorsement of this statement and his acceptance of Shirvānī as his spiritual master.[98] As the reader will see, however, when read in context, it is evident that the Aga Khan does not cite this statement for the purpose of endorsing it. In fact, the Aga Khan in his memoirs is sharply critical of Shirvānī, describing him as deceitful and power-hungry, and assigning him partial blame for the misfortunes that led to his decision to revolt. In particular, the Aga Khan recounts that while in Kirmān he had engaged Shirvānī to deliver funds to the royal court, which, according to the Aga Khan, Shirvānī inexplicably failed to do. It is in this context that the Aga Khan recounts Shirvānī's boast of his alleged 'discipleship', a pretension which the Aga Khan blames for his subsequent woes and persecution by Āqāsī, and which appears as an attempt by Shirvānī to bolster his own influence by attaching to himself some of the aura surrounding the Aga Khan's charismatic status.

Hence, rather than endorsing any particular claimant in this contest, the Aga Khan in his account instead portrays the entire affair as one of petty scheming between two power-hungry rivals, a contest in which he became unwittingly entangled and to which he subsequently fell victim. Yet despite the Aga Khan's falling out with Shirvānī, the broader relationship between the Nizārī Imams and the Niʿmatullāhiyya

98 Pourjavady and Wilson, 'Ismāʿīlīs and Niʿmatullāhīs', p. 126.

continued, even long after the transference of the Imamate to India. Both Aga Khans I and II entertained many high-ranking Niʿmatullāhīs in Bombay, among whom was the Niʿmatullāhī master Ṣafī ʿAlī Shāh, who stayed with Aga Khan II in Bombay for an entire year in 1881.[99] In addition, after the death of Raḥmat ʿAlī Shāh in 1861 Aga Khan II sent yearly funds from Bombay to pay for the recitation of the Qurʾan over this master's grave in Shīrāz.[100]

The Revolt of the Aga Khan and his Departure from Persia

As noted above, the Aga Khan in his memoirs traces the cause of the Qājār intrigues against him to the schemes of Ḥājjī Mīrzā Āqāsī and his unwitting entanglement in a contest for leadership within the Niʿmatullāhī Sufi order, while those authors writing under Qājār patronage have claimed that there was a plot on the part of the Aga Khan to assert territorial control over parts of south-eastern Persia. In this context, another factor should be mentioned that may have played a role in the events under discussion, though any evidence for it is almost entirely circumstantial. The period of the Aga Khan's besiegement in Bam coincided with a critical period in a century-long conflict between the Persian and Afghan governments over control of the city of Herat, which had formerly been a part of the Safavid empire but was later lost to Afghan control following the death of Nādir Shāh.[101] In its later years

99 On this visit, see Nile Green, 'A Persian Sufi in British India: The Travels of Mīrzā Ḥasan Ṣafī ʿAlī Shāh (1251/1835–1316/1899)', *Iran: Journal of the British Institute of Persian Studies*, 42 (2004), pp. 201–218. Another Niʿmatullāhī visitor at this time was Ḥājjī Pīrzāda, who left a rather detailed account of Aga Khan II and his household in his travelogue; see Ḥājjī Muḥammad ʿAlī Pīrzāda Nāʾīnī, *Safar-nāma-yi Ḥājjī Pīrzāda*, ed. Ḥāfiẓ Farmānfarmāʾiyān (Tehran, 1342 Sh./1963), vol. 1, pp. 132–138.

100 For more details on the relationship between the Aga Khans and the Niʿmatullāhiyya following the transference of the Imamate to India, see Pourjavady and Wilson, 'Ismāʿīlīs and Niʿmatullāhīs', pp. 130–133.

101 On this conflict, known to modern historiography as the 'Herat Problem', see G. J. Alder, 'The Key to India? Britain and the Herat Problem 1830–1863: Part I', *Middle Eastern Studies*, 10 (1974), pp. 186–209; his 'The Key to India? Britain and the Herat Problem 1830-1863: Part II', *Middle Eastern Studies*, 10 (1974), pp. 287–311; Abbas Amanat, 'Herat vi: The Herat Problem', *EIr*; Christine Noelle-Karimi, *The Pearl in its Midst: Herat and the Mapping of Khurasan (15th–19th Centuries)* (Vienna, 2014).

this conflict took on an added dimension through the involvement of European colonial powers. Following Persia's devastating defeat by Russia in the Caucasus in 1827 and the Russian imposition of the Treaty of Turkmanchay upon Persia the following year, concerns grew among British officials in India of growing Russian influence at the Qājār court. Accordingly, the launch of a new campaign to retake Herat by Muḥammad Shāh in the summer of 1837 raised fears that the fall of the city to Persian control would subsequently lead to greater Russian influence in Afghanistan.

Throughout the year-long campaign the British applied increasing diplomatic pressure on the Qājār monarch to withdraw his forces, culminating in the British occupation of the Persian island of Khārg in June 1838 in order to induce a Persian withdrawal. Finally, in August 1838 Muḥammad Shāh withdrew his forces from Herat and the city remained in Afghan hands thereafter. The coincidental timing of the Aga Khan's activities in Kirmān when viewed with hindsight and in tandem with his later close relationship with the British in India, has led to speculation that the events were driven by a British conspiracy to divert Qājār attention from Herat.[102] Yet while British officials clearly welcomed these developments for precisely this reason, there is no evidence to suggest any direct collusion between the Aga Khan and the British at this stage.[103]

The Aga Khan and his troops endured the siege of Bam for fourteen months, during which time his brother Muḥammad Bāqir Khān was seriously wounded and taken prisoner. Finally, the Imam sought the intervention of Farīdūn Mīrzā, the Qājār governor of Fārs province, who negotiated safe passage for the Aga Khan and his men in order that he might make his case directly to the monarch. In response, Farīdūn Mīrzā dispatched the Shāh's nephew, Muḥammad Ṣādiq Khān, to escort the Aga Khan and his dependents to Fārs and thence to Tehran. However, the Aga Khan reports that upon leaving the citadel he and his men were immediately taken prisoner and their possessions plundered by the

---

102 Algar, 'The Revolt of Āghā Khān Maḥallātī', p. 76. The only direct evidence that has been brought forth in support of this hypothesis is the alleged presence of several cannons with British markings in the Aga Khan's possession that were later recovered by Qājār troops.

103 On this, see further Noorally, 'The First Aga Khan and the British', pp. 21–40.

4. General view of the citadel of Bam in the 1980s.

Qājār troops. They were then sent to the city of Kirmān, where they were kept prisoner for eight months. The Imam was, however, permitted at one point during this captivity to receive a collection of tithes from his followers, which partially alleviated his circumstances. Finally, following the return of the royal retinue from Herat to Tehran, the Aga Khan and his dependents were freed in Kirmān and permitted to travel to Tehran, where he was given a royal pardon on the condition that he retire to his estates in Maḥallāt.

The Aga Khan's residence in Maḥallāt lasted just under two years, when he experienced a new set of troubles. The Aga Khan attributes these renewed troubles to the machinations of an individual named Ḥājjī 'Abd al-Muḥammad, whom he describes as 'one of the lowly peasants of Maḥallāt', who had insinuated his way into the circle of Ḥājjī Mīrzā Āqāsī's Sufi companions and, angered at the Imam's refusal to give his daughter in marriage to his son, began spreading rumours at the court that the Aga Khan was amassing an army for a revolt against the crown. Eventually Muḥammad Shāh himself set out with a body of troops for the nearby town of Dalījān to investigate these rumours. Fearing a renewal of hostilities, the Aga Khan requested permission for

5. Maḥallāt, a section of the wall encircling Aga Khan I's residential compound.

himself and his family to set out on pilgrimage to Mecca, and for the remainder of his household and retinue to travel to the Shiʿi shrine cities of Iraq (the *ʿatabāt-i ʿāliyāt*). This permission was granted, and on 1 September 1840 the Imam departed from Maḥallāt.

With the departure of the Aga Khan from Maḥallāt we once again see a divergence in the accounts of the events found in the Qājār chronicles and the Imam's *'Ibrat-afzā*. According to the *'Ibrat-afzā*, the Aga Khan discovered that an order had been given by the government to block the path of his party and to refuse them the sale of any provisions. Upon entering the province of Yazd, the Aga Khan relates, his party inexplicably came under attack by the forces of Bahman Mīrzā, the governor of Yazd. While the Aga Khan was able to temporarily repel this attack, he was nonetheless forced to abandon his plans to travel to Mecca and instead set out for the city of Shahr-i Bābak in Kirmān, where he could call upon the assistance of his many *murīd*s who resided in the region to come to his aid. According to the Aga Khan, these attacks on him and his retinue were entirely unprovoked, and fit within a broader pattern of treacherous behaviour on the part of the Qājār officials that began with the plundering and unwarranted confinement of him and his men in Kirmān two years earlier.

The official Qājār chronicles present a rather different account of the causes of the Aga Khan's revolt. As no major chronicles were produced during the reign of Muḥammad Shāh, when these events took place, the earliest accounts appear only with the histories produced during the reign of his son and successor, Nāṣir al-Dīn Shāh. The first such account was recorded by the historian and literary scholar Riḍā Qulī Khān Hidāyat, who composed his *Rawḍat al-ṣafā-yi Nāṣirī* (dedicated to Nāṣir al-Dīn Shāh) between 1854 and 1857.[104] Hidāyat, who was a close companion of Āqāsī, suggests that the Aga Khan had nurtured thoughts of revolt and independent rule from the very start of his appointment as governor of Kirmān, and continued to plot a second attempt following his pardon and return to Maḥallāt. Hidāyat claims that the Aga Khan in fact had no intention of travelling peacefully on pilgrimage to Mecca, but rather had forged documents claiming that he had been reinstated to his previous position as governor of Kirmān, intending to launch his revolt once he had arrived there and had safely ensconced himself and his men in the fortresses of the region.[105] The Aga Khan, according to Hidāyat, presented these documents to Bahman Mīrzā and other officials along the route, who at first accepted them as genuine.

104 On Hidāyat, see Paul E. Losensky, 'Hedāyat, Rezā Qolikhan', *EIr.*

105 Hidāyat, *Rawḍat al-ṣafā-yi Nāṣirī*, vol. 10, pp. 249–251. See also Vazīrī, *Tārīkh-i Kirmān*, pp. 782–786.

It was only after Bahman Mīrzā later discovered that these documents were in fact not authentic that he attacked the Aga Khan in an effort to take him and his party prisoner. The Aga Khan, for his part, mentions nothing in his memoirs of any purported reappointment as governor of Kirmān, stressing that his intention all along had been to proceed to Mecca, only diverting from his route after the unprovoked attack from Bahman Mīrzā.

The account of these events presented by Hidāyat was largely echoed, with some additional details, in the later work of his contemporary, the historian Muḥammad Taqī Sipihr, whose *Tārīkh-i Qājāriyya* was completed in 1859.[106] Later historians of the Qājār era largely relied upon the works of Hidāyat and Sipihr in relating these events, adding little new information.[107] It is difficult to reconcile the differences in the two sets of narratives concerning the origins of the revolt, that found in the Aga Khan's memoirs and that in the official Qājār accounts. Algar points to certain gaps and inconsistencies in the Aga Khan's version of events, and concludes that greater confidence may be placed in the Qājār record of events. However, it should also be noted that these gaps in the Aga Khan's account may be explained in part by the fact that his recollections of events were evidently dictated and set down in writing only a decade after the fact; a number of valuable writings in the Imam's possession were lost when his treasury and possessions were plundered by a group of Balūch tribesmen during his travels in Sindh, which apparently excluded the Imam's diaries.[108] It is not surprising, therefore, that the record of events presented in the *'Ibrat-afzā* may be incomplete, while the official patronage underpinning the Qājār sources must also be taken into account when evaluating the validity of their narrative of what happened. It is important to note here, however, that while the Qājār sources display great hostility towards the Aga Khan on account of his revolt, at no time is this hostility expressed in religious terms.

---

106 Sipihr, *Tārīkh-i Qājāriyya*, vol. 2, pp. 751–756.

107 For example, see Muḥammad Ḥasan Khān I'timād al-Salṭana, *Tārīkh-i muntaẓam-i Nāṣirī*, ed. Muḥammad Ismā'īl Riḍvānī (Tehran, 1367 Sh./1988), vol. 3, pp. 1649–1653; his *Mir'āt al-buldān*, vol. 1, pp. 927–929; Muḥammad Ja'far Khūrmūjī, *Ḥaqā'iq al-akhbār-i Nāṣirī*, ed. Ḥusayn Khadīv Jām (Tehran, 1363 Sh./1984), pp. 28–31.

108 For an account of one of these documents, see Virani, *Ismailis in the Middle Ages*, p. 49.

6. Aga Khan I in India.

On the contrary, authors such as Hidāyat and Sipihr write respectfully of the Aga Khan and his ancestors as sayyids, and while they are clearly aware of his status as the Ismaili Imam, they do not express any anti-Ismaili rhetoric in their compositions.

Regardless of his intentions prior to this time, following the conflict with Bahman Mīrzā, the Aga Khan had by now indisputably shifted into a position of open revolt against the Persian government, and the *ʿIbrat-afzā* and the Qājār chronicles do not differ substantially in their account of the subsequent chronology of events. The Imam and his supporters set out for the fortress of Shahr-i Bābak in Kirmān, which was one of his ancestral properties, to discover that it had been occupied by a number of Afghan notables from Qandahār who had been displaced by the recent British occupation of Afghanistan.[109] The Aga Khan laid siege to the fortress with the help of his local supporters and after three days succeeded in removing the Afghans from it. He then went to the nearby village of Rūmanī and dispatched his brother Muḥammad Bāqir Khān to the town of Sīrjān to obtain supplies. Four days later a messenger arrived from Sīrjān with the news that the governor of Kirmān, Faḍl ʿAlī Khān, had besieged his brother in the fortress of Zaydābād in Sīrjān. The Aga Khan immediately set out with his troops and defeated Faḍl ʿAlī Khān's forces and rescued his brother Muḥammad Bāqir Khān and his men. Subsequently, the Aga Khan's party spent the winter of 1840–1841 in the Rūdbār region in southern Kirmān, evading government troops and enjoying the protection and hospitality of local chiefs and supporters.

In the spring of 1841 (Muḥarram 1257) the Aga Khan learned that Faḍl ʿAlī Khān was assembling a new force and preparing to set out against him. The Imam sent his brother Abu'l-Ḥasan Khān to take possession of the town of Dashtāb and joined him there shortly afterwards. While the Aga Khan initially succeeded in routing the government troops, Faḍl ʿAlī Khān's army was reinforced by fresh ones from Fārs, and the Aga Khan's party was soon outnumbered and forced to retreat from Dashtāb. Over the course of the next several months the Aga Khan and his men fought a series of increasingly desperate skirmishes with government troops as they retreated from place to place. This period also saw the rapid depletion of the Imam's own forces through both casualties and desertion until, at one point, his entourage was reduced to just seven men.

The accounts of these battles are outlined in detail in the *ʿIbrat-afzā*, and hence do not merit extended elaboration here. However, it may be

109 On these events, see also Sykes, *Ten Thousand Miles in Persia*, p. 78.

mentioned that this segment of the Imam's memoirs is in many respects among the most interesting sections of the entire text. We see here the Aga Khan in the role of a military commander engaged in a desperate battle against overwhelming odds, plagued by treachery and deceit, but also bolstered by the immense bravery and unwavering loyalty of a small coterie of brothers-in-arms. It was also here, in the remote Indo-Persian borderland territories of Kirmān, Sīstān and Balūchistān, that we obtain the clearest perspective on the charismatic authority enjoyed by the Aga Khan beyond the immediate sphere of his Ismaili followers. These frontier territories had historically remained largely outside the direct control of the Persian government, and continued thus under the Qājārs at that time. This remained the case until the second half of the 19th century, when the Qājārs, relying on newly acquired forms of communication and military technology, and finding themselves increasing constrained by European colonial expansion, began a concerted effort to assert more direct control over these border regions.[110] In the Aga Khan's time, however, these regions still constituted a sort of 'wild west' of the Qājār state, a realm where politics was decided less by appeal to the rule of law than through negotiation on the basis of dynastic loyalty and spiritual charisma. Time and again, we see in these passages instances in which the Aga Khan and his men are granted shelter and aid by local notables, not on the basis of any fealty due to him as the Ismaili Imam, but rather on account of his ancestral ties to the region and his revered status as a sayyid.

These ties of affection and loyalty, coupled with the more general hostility towards the central government evidenced among many of the communities in these regions, explain why the Aga Khan and his men were able to sustain their struggles against the Qājār forces for so long, despite the overwhelming numbers arrayed against them. Yet the sheer predominance of numbers, coupled with Qājār offers of cash and rewards that drew many of the Imam's less steadfast supporters away from him, eventually took their toll, and rendered his position untenable.

---

110 On the eastern borderlands of Qājār Persia in the 19th century, see B. D. Hopkins, 'The Bounds of Identity: The Goldsmid Mission and the Delineation of the Perso-Afghan Border in the Nineteenth Century', *Journal of Global History*, 2 (2007), pp. 233–254; Firoozeh Kashani-Sabet, *Frontier Fictions: Shaping the Iranian Nation, 1804–1946* (Princeton, 1999), pp. 15–46; Pirouz Mojtahed-Zadeh, *Small Players of the Great Game: The Settlement of Iran's Eastern Borderlands and the Creation of Afghanistan* (London, 2004).

Finding no further recourse, the Aga Khan finally resolved to abandon the territory of Persia and to escape south, towards the port of Bandar ʿAbbās on the Persian Gulf, and thence to travel on by sea to either India or the Hejaz. However, finding this path also blocked by government forces, he decided instead to risk the perilous journey eastwards across the Lūt desert and towards the territory of present-day Afghanistan. The Aga Khan's forces traversed the desert unscathed and without further incident they crossed into Afghanistan in the summer of 1841. Thus, after nearly seven and a half centuries, the Ismaili Imamate's residence in Persia, where it had been based since the death of Imam Nizār in 488/1095, came to an end.

The Aga Khan and the British in Afghanistan and Sindh

The Aga Khan arrived in Afghanistan approximately two years after the occupation of the country by the ill-fated army of the British East India Company with its grandiose appellation, 'Army of the Indus'.[111] This invasion marked one of the first major developments in what was to be the decades-long contest between the British and Russian empires for control and influence in Central Asia, generally known as the Great Game. The objective of this invasion by the British was to replace the Afghan king Dūst Muḥammad, whom they feared had become susceptible to Russian intrigues, with the former king, Shāh Shujāʿ, a British protégé who had been living in exile in India. In this regard, the occupation was initially a success, as Dūst Muḥammad was forced to flee into exile before later surrendering to the British, and Shāh Shujāʿ was established in Kabul under British tutelage. Before long, however, the new regime faced a series of uprisings, both coordinated and spontaneous, across the country. By the time the Aga Khan arrived in the summer of 1841 these revolts had become widespread, although they did not yet present a serious threat to the major centres of British authority in the country, Kabul and Qandahār.

111 The literature on the First Anglo-Afghan War is rather voluminous; see in particular the recent study by William Dalrymple, *The Return of a King: The Battle for Afghanistan, 1839–42* (New York, 2013); among other recent studies, see also B. D. Hopkins, *The Making of Modern Afghanistan* (New York, 2008); and Christine Noelle, *State and Tribe in Nineteenth-Century Afghanistan: The Reign of Amir Dost Muhammad Khan (1826–1863)* (Richmond, 1997).

Whereas the question of a possible earlier relationship between the Aga Khan and the British remains mere speculation, following his arrival in Afghanistan this relationship becomes well documented. Upon arriving in the territory of Afghanistan, the Aga Khan sent word to Muḥammad Tīmūr, the son of Shāh Shujāʿ and the British-appointed governor of Qandahār, and to Henry Rawlinson, the British political agent in Qandahār. Rawlinson, who was already aware of the Aga Khan's reputation, in turn addressed a letter to William Hay Macnaghten, the head of the British mission in Afghanistan, and recommended the services of the Aga Khan on account of the support he enjoyed among his followers in the country.[112] By August 1841, the Aga Khan had become established in Qandahār and was granted a daily stipend of one hundred rupees by Rawlinson. The Aga Khan presented a proposal to Macnaghten in which he offered to capture the city of Herat, which maintained at this time a position as an independent principality, outside the control of either Kabul or Tehran, and to add it to the dominions of Shāh Shujāʿ. However, Macnaghten rejected this proposal, and the Aga Khan elected to bide his time at Qandahār, where he received a steady stream of visitors and followers from throughout Afghanistan, Central Asia and India.

In September 1841, a new revolt broke out among the Ghilzāʾī Afghans in the territories to the east of Kabul.[113] The revolt grew in intensity throughout the month of October, culminating in a major uprising in the city of Kabul in the month of Ramaḍān (early November), during which Macnaghten's chief assistant Alexander Burnes was murdered. Macnaghten himself was killed a month later in a battle with rebel forces under the leadership of Muḥammad Akbar Khān, a son of Dūst Muḥammad. Finally, in January 1842, the British commander William Elphinstone negotiated the safe withdrawal of the remaining British forces in Kabul and its surrender to Akbar Khān. During their withdrawal to India, however, the British column came under attack by Afghan forces, and nearly all of the 16,000 members of the garrison (including a large number of Indian troops) were killed.

---

112 On the Aga Khan's early relationship with the British in Afghanistan, see Noorally, 'The First Aga Khan and the British', pp. 42–51.

113 On these events, see Malcom E. Yapp, 'The Revolutions of 1841–2 in Afghanistan', *Bulletin of the School of Oriental and African Studies*, 27 (1964), pp. 333–381.

In December 1841, the revolt spread to the territories surrounding Qandahār. According to his own account, at this time the Aga Khan received an invitation from the Durrānī prince and rebel chief Ṣafdar Jung for him and his men to join them in the campaign against the British, but he declined. The Aga Khan, who had approximately one hundred horsemen under his command at this time, assisted General William Nott, the British commander at Qandahār, in a number of campaigns against the rebels in the spring of 1842. More critically, he also played an important role in British diplomacy with the rebels in this period.[114] Among other things, the Aga Khan convinced a large portion of the Twelver Shiʿi Qizilbāsh forces among the Afghan rebels to defect to the British side. As Rawlinson noted in his correspondence, while the Twelver Afghans did not recognise the Imamate of the Aga Khan, they did recognise his sayyid genealogy, which played a critical role in the decision to heed his directives.

Shāh Shujāʿ himself was assassinated in April 1842, and by the summer the situation around Qandahār had worsened to the extent that the British finally decided to evacuate the city. The British garrison left Qandahār on 9 August, with one column under the leadership of General Nott marching towards Kabul while the other, under the command of General Richard England, retreated to the city of Quetta en route to India, turning over the governing of Qandahār to Ṣafdar Jung, who had reconciled with the British and agreed to govern on their behalf. The Aga Khan and his party initially withdrew from Qandahār along with England's column. However, he soon returned after receiving an invitation from Ṣafdar Jung to stay there. The Aga Khan remained in Qandahār for another six weeks, until he found his situation there to be untenable and decided once again to depart, leaving his brother Sardār Abu'l-Ḥasan Khān to oversee matters in his stead. The Aga Khan left Qandahār in early October 1842 and initially set out to join General England's forces in Quetta.[115] He arrived in Quetta on

---

114 The published accounts of the First Anglo-Afghan War provide very little information on the Aga Khan's involvement in these events. However, more details are available from unpublished archival sources, particularly the diary of Henry Rawlinson, which contains detailed information on the Aga Khan's activities in this period. These details are summarised in Noorally, 'The First Aga Khan and the British', pp. 57–66.

115 On the Aga Khan's itinerary after departing from Afghanistan, see Noorally, 'The First Aga Khan and the British', pp. 67–73.

5 October, finding that England's party had already departed for India. From there the Aga Khan turned south and headed for the territory of Sindh, where he sought out the hospitality of Amīr Nāṣir Khān Kalātī, one of the last independent tribal chiefs of Sindh, whose ancestors had ruled over the territory since the late 18th century. The Aga Khan spent the next month in the households of Nāṣir Khān and other chiefs of Sindh.

The Sindh region had been a major centre of Ismaili communities since the Fatimid era, and the Aga Khan spent much of his time in this period attending to communal affairs.[116] In November 1842 the Aga Khan decided to part company with Nāṣir Khān and travelled to Sukkut, where he made the acquaintance of General Sir Charles Napier, the commander of British forces in Sindh. At that time, the British were pressuring Nāṣir Khān and other *amīr*s of Sindh to sign a new treaty and to accede to the British annexation of the port city of Karachi (located in present-day Pakistan) in exchange for a substantial payment.[117] The Aga Khan, once against performing his role as an intermediary, pleaded with Nāṣir Khān and the other *amīr*s, many of whom were Twelver Shiʿas, to sign the treaty. In February 1843, Napier's deputy, General Outram, organised a meeting in the city of Hyderabad of all the chiefs of Sindh, at which most of them agreed to sign the new treaty with the British. However, Nāṣir Khān and several other chiefs refused to sign, and instead resolved upon leading an armed revolt against the British. On 14 February, Nāṣir Khān launched a surprise attack against General Outram and the British residency in Hyderabad. According to the Aga Khan's own account, he had foreknowledge of this attack from Nāṣir Khān and attempted to dissuade him from it; failing that, he informed Outram of the attack in advance, thus saving the British party from annihilation.[118] Three days later, General Napier arrived with his troops

---

116 On the history of Ismailism in Sindh, see Michel Boivin, 'New Problems Related to the History and Tradition of the Agakhani Khojahs in Karachi and Sindh', *Journal of the Pakistan Historical Society*, 46 (1998), pp. 5–33; Derryl N. MacLean, *Religion and Society in Arab Sind* (Leiden, 1989), pp. 126–158; and Nanji, *The Nizārī Ismāʿīlī Tradition in the Indo-Pakistan Subcontinent*.

117 On British policy towards Sindh, see Robert A. Huttenback, *British Relations with Sind, 1799–1843: An Anatomy of Imperialism* (Berkeley, 1962).

118 This incident is described by Charles Napier's brother, the military historian William Napier, who writes: 'Amongst those who gave secret

and defeated the Sindhī *amīrs* at the Battle of Miani. Over the next several months the Aga Khan assisted the forces of Sir Charles Napier in a number of campaigns against the chiefs of Sindh, culminating in the conquest and formal annexation of the entire province to British India by August 1843.[119]

Following the British conquest of Sindh, in late 1843 the Aga Khan petitioned the British to intervene on his behalf with the Qājār government and to support his return to Persia. After much back and forth, the British declined to honour this request. In lieu of aiding him to return, the British government agreed instead to offer the Aga Khan a permanent pension of 1,000 rupees per month.[120] Following this, the Aga Khan agreed to assist the British in subduing a number of Balūch chiefs, who had been in revolt since the annexation of Sindh. The Aga Khan himself set up station in the town of Jerruck in Sindh and positioned groups of his men along the road to Karachi, while he dispatched his brother Muḥammad Bāqir Khān to join forces with Napier to combat the Balūch chief Mīr Shīr Muḥammad Khān. While stationed in Jerruck, the Aga Khan and his party suffered one of the greatest catastrophes of his career, as one night several Balūch chiefs launched simultaneous attacks on the Aga Khan's forces in Jerruck and in the village of Langar near the town of Thatta. In the ensuing exchanges, according to the Aga Khan, seventeen of his men were killed and approximately seventy of his

---

information was the Persian prince, Agha Khan, whose real title was the Emir of the Mountains, he being the lineal heir of the ancient *assassin*. Though no longer the terrible being who made kings tremble in the midst of armies, this wandering occult potentate still possessed secret but great power; and his people, spread over Asia from the Indus to the Mediterranean, supplied him with a revenue, and with information sure and varied. He had come to Scinde with a train of horsemen before the conquest, knew of the ameers' design to assail the residency, had remonstrated against it, and afterwards gave such information on that subject as to render Outram's imbecile vanity on that occasion most painfully prominent.' See William F. P. Napier, *History of General Sir Charles Napier's Administration of Scinde* (London, 1851), p. 75.

119 The Aga Khan's participation in these campaigns is recorded in the histories of the conquest composed by William Napier; see his *The History of General Sir Charles Napier's Conquest of Scinde* (2nd ed., London, 1857), pp. 224, 226, 245; and his *The Life and Opinions of General Sir Charles James Napier*, vol. 2, p. 342; vol. 3, pp. 45, 127.

120 On these negotiations, see Noorally, 'The First Aga Khan and the British', pp. 83–89.

7. General Sir Charles Napier, by Henry William Pickersgill.

*murīd*s were either killed or injured.[121] The Aga Khan himself was knocked off his horse during the battle and rendered unconscious, losing several of his teeth in the process. In addition, the Imam's treasury was plundered by the Balūch, and a great portion of his personal

121 A number of additional details and sources on this event, including some oral traditions preserved among the Ismailis of the Sindh region, are related in Noorally, 'The First Aga Khan and the British', pp. 78–80.

property, including some valuable books and documents, was stolen or lost. The Aga Khan pressed the British to assist him in recovering his treasury from the Balūch, but these efforts were rebuffed, and the British finally convinced the Aga Khan to consider the stolen treasury as a gift to the Balūch in exchange for their pacification.

Subsequently, the Aga Khan received a request from a Balūch chief named Muḥammad ʿAlī Khān, the commander of the fortress of Bamfahl (Bampūr), who was among the chiefs who had submitted to the British. Muḥammad ʿAlī Khan suggested that the Aga Khan assume possession of the fortress as a means of intimidating the other Balūch chiefs to submit to the British. The Aga Khan accepted the proposal and in March–April 1844 dispatched his brother Muḥammad Bāqir Khān to take possession of the fortress.[122] While Napier did not oppose this action, it would appear that the Aga Khan at this stage acted under his own initiative, perhaps hoping to establish himself in Balūchistān in preparation for an eventual return to Kirmān. Upon reaching the territory of Balūchistān, Muḥammad Bāqir Khān found that Muḥammad ʿAlī Khān refused to honour his initial offer, and instead insisted that the fortresses of his rival chiefs be captured first, before he surrendered Bamfahl. Muḥammad Bāqir Khān thus launched a series of campaigns against the Balūch chiefs, while the Aga Khan later dispatched his other brother, Sardār Abu'l-Ḥasan Khān, to assist him as well. The two brothers eventually succeeded in capturing a number of fortresses in the region, including Bamfahl, and Muḥammad Bāqir Khān later departed to join the Aga Khan again in India.

Despite these initial successes, this campaign once again brought the Aga Khan's family into conflict with the Qājār government, who regarded the fortress and territory of Bamfahl as theirs. Even though the territory had lain outside Persian control for some time, the government of Muḥammad Shāh Qājār evidently took the Aga Khan's activities there as a pretext to establish their control in the region.[123] After two

122 On these events, see also Sykes, *Ten Thousand Miles in Persia*, pp. 105–106, where the author claims that the campaign waged by the Aga Khan's family 'brought about the downfall of Baluchi independence'.

123 On Qājār policy towards Balūchistān in this period, see Soli Shahvar, 'Communications, Qajar Irredentism, and the Strategies of British India: The Makran Coast Telegraph and British Policy of Containing Persia in the East (Baluchistan), Part I', *Iranian Studies*, 39 (2006), pp. 329–351; Brian Spooner,

years of campaigning in the region, Sardār Abu'l-Ḥasan Khān was defeated in 1846 by an army led by Faḍl 'Alī Khān, the Qājār governor of Kirmān. Abu'l-Ḥasan Khān was taken to Tehran and held there as a prisoner for several years. However, he was later pardoned by Muḥammad Shāh's successor, Nāṣir al-Dīn Shāh, and allowed to retire to Maḥallāt. Nāṣir al-Dīn Shāh subsequently showed great favour to Sardār Abu'l-Ḥasan Khān (d. 1880), even bestowing on him a Qājār princess, Mihr-i Jahān Khānum, in marriage, and allowed him and his descendants to carry on the management of the Aga Khan's familial properties in Persia.[124]

The Aga Khan in India

Meanwhile, in October 1844 the Aga Khan left Sindh, ending the military phase of his career. He departed via the port of Karachi for the territories of Gujarat, where he spent approximately the next year and a half visiting his many *murīd*s in the region and attending to communal affairs. Beginning in the city of Jamnagar in Muḥarram 1261 (January–February 1845) the Aga Khan initiated an annual tradition of sponsoring the *ta'ziya* commemorations of Imam Ḥusayn, which he would continue annually following his settlement in Bombay, demonstrating once again his appeal to broader Muslim constituencies beyond the circle of his Ismaili followers.[125]

Early in 1846, the Aga Khan departed for Bombay, where he evidently had intended to remain for some time. However, shortly after his arrival the news came of his brother's arrest and detention in Persia, and the Qājār government began placing considerable diplomatic pressure on

---

'Who are the Baluch? A Preliminary Investigation into the Dynamics of an Ethnic Identity from Qajar Iran', in C. E. Bosworth and Carole Hillenbrand, ed., *Qajar Iran: Political, Social, and Cultural Change, 1800–1925* (Costa Mesa, 1992), pp. 93–110.

124 These details are related by Farhad Daftary, who is the great-great-grandson of Sardār Abu'l-Ḥasan Khān; see his *The Ismā'īlīs*, p. 472.

125 The *ta'ziya* is a ritual commemorating the martyrdom of the Prophet's grandson and the early Shi'i Imam Ḥusayn, which happened on 10 Muḥarram 61/680. On the Aga Khan's patronage of the Muḥarram commemorations, see James C. Masselos, 'Change and Custom in the Format of the Bombay Mohurrum during the Nineteenth and Twentieth Centuries', *South Asia: Journal of South Asian Studies*, 5 (1982), pp. 47–67.

the British to extradite the Aga Khan himself. This led to a long period of negotiations between the British and the Persians.[126] Eventually, a compromise was reached by which the Aga Khan would be permitted to remain in British India, under the condition that he remain as far away from Persian territory as possible. Consequently, a decision was taken to move the Imam to Calcutta, and in April 1847 the Aga Khan and his retinue departed Bombay for a gruelling overland journey to Bengal, during which several members of his party died from heat and sickness.[127] Upon settling in the Dum Dum district of Calcutta, the Aga Khan was surprised to learn that his new neighbours were none other than the deposed chiefs of Sindh, whom he had played a key role in overthrowing four years earlier, but with whom he now established friendly relations. While in Calcutta the Aga Khan established close relationships also with some of the Twelver Shiʿi leaders in the city, including the caretakers of the Hooghly Imāmbāra, one of the main Twelver meeting halls in Calcutta. At the same time he maintained his tradition of sponsoring the Muḥarram commemorations during his residence there.

Finally, in November 1848 the news arrived of the death of Muḥammad Shāh Qājār and the succession of his son Nāṣir al-Dīn.[128] The Aga Khan wasted no time in seeking to establish cordial relations with the new regime and arranged to have the funeral prayers read for the late king in conjunction with the Muḥarram commemorations the following month. He then dispatched yet another petition, this time to the new king, requesting once again permission to return to Persia, and without waiting for a reply immediately set sail for Bombay in December 1848. Upon arriving in Bombay later that month he composed another petition to the new king's chief minister, Mīrzā Taqī Khān, who at that time was preoccupied with a series of revolts that had sprung up across Persia on the death of Muḥammad Shāh.[129] Under these circumstances, the

126 On the details of these negotiations, see Noorally, 'The First Aga Khan and the British', pp. 110–123.

127 On the Aga Khan's residence in Calcutta and his relationship with British officials there, see Noorally, 'The First Aga Khan and the British', pp. 124–140.

128 On the reign of Nāṣir al-Dīn Shāh, see Abbas Amanat, *Pivot of the Universe: Nasir al-Din Shah Qajar and the Iranian Monarchy, 1831–1896* (Berkeley, 1997).

129 On Mīrzā Taqī Khān, known as Amīr Kabīr, see Ādamīyat, *Amīr Kabīr va Īrān*; Hamid Algar, 'Amīr-e Kabīr, Mīrzā Taqī Khan', *EIr*.

Imam's petition was not looked upon favourably by the minister, and his request was denied. Failing this, the Aga Khan began cultivating a close relationship with the newly appointed Persian consul in Bombay, Mīrzā Ḥusayn Khān, in hopes that his intercession might change the mind of the new minister, but this too came to naught.[130]

In January 1852 Mīrzā Taqī Khān was suddenly deposed and executed, and replaced by Mīrzā Āqā Khān Nūrī, with whom the Aga Khan had been long acquainted.[131] The Aga Khan began a correspondence with the new chief minister, also sending an elephant and a giraffe as gifts to the court along with his petition. This time, the Aga Khan's request met with greater success, and several of his properties that had been confiscated in the wake of his departure were restored to his family. Finally, Āqā Khān Nūrī officially granted permission for the Aga Khan and his family to return to Persia. However, the Aga Khan in the end declined the offer and did not present any further requests to return, evidently having decided to remain in India permanently. He later sent another gift of three elephants and a rhinoceros to Nāṣir al-Dīn Shāh, without any accompanying petitions or requests.[132] Later, Nāṣir al-Dīn Shāh even agreed to the marriage of one of his daughters to the Aga Khan's son, Jalāl Shāh, but the latter died before the wedding could be arranged.[133]

The account of the *ʿIbrat-afzā* concludes with the Aga Khan's final settlement in Bombay, at which time his career and the history of the Nizārī Imamate entered a new phase. A proper examination of the Aga Khan's subsequent career in India would require an entirely separate study that is beyond the scope of the present work. As these issues have been considered at length elsewhere, there will be presented here only a brief overview of some of the major developments that took place following the Aga Khan's settlement in Bombay, along with some reflections on his legacy and significance for the modern history of Ismailism.

---

130 On these negotiations, see Noorally, 'The First Aga Khan and the British', pp. 141–165.

131 On the deposition of Amīr Kabīr, see Abbas Amanat, 'The Downfall of Mirza Taqi Khan Amir Kabir and the Problem of Ministerial Authority in Qajar Iran', *International Journal of Middle East Studies*, 23 (1991), pp. 577–599.

132 Iʿtimād al-Salṭana, *Mirʾāt al-buldān*, vol. 4, p. 1567.

133 Daftary, *The Ismāʿīlīs*, p. 473.

To begin with, it is important to note that the Aga Khan's move to India entailed not simply the settlement of an individual or even one family, but rather the transfer of an entire institution, one that had grown immensely over the previous decades to include thousands of individuals from his extended family, servants, scribes, private militia forces and all manner of other affiliates. While some of these individuals initially remained behind in Persia following the Imam's departure, a great many of them joined him later in Bombay. Some sense of this substantial migration is given by the Aga Khan's grandson, Imam Sultan Muhammad Shah, Aga Khan III, who in his own 1954 memoirs reflected on the legacy of his grandfather's exile from Persia and the subsequent circumstances of his settlement in Bombay:

> My grandfather in his migration from Persia had brought with him more than a thousand relations, dependants, clients, associates, personal and political supporters, ranging from the humblest groom or servant to a man of princely stature, a direct near-descendant of Nadirshah of Delhi fame, who had taken my grandfather's side in the disputes and troubles in Persia and with him had gone into exile. With the passage of years, however, it had become no longer exile. My grandfather had been confirmed in his rights and titles by a judgment of the Bombay High Court in 1866. He was an accepted and honoured leader of the community, accorded princely status by the British Raj and its representatives in India. Aga Hall, our Bombay home, was his chief seat, but he had another palace, or group of palaces, in Poona, whither we all made seasonal migrations.... His family and his dependants, his sons and their wives, his officials, servants, and followers, were disposed in a series of houses and palaces around him, both in Bombay and Poona. In course of time many of his Persian followers married Indian wives, many of them of Ismaili families.[134]

As Imam Sultan Muhammad Shah notes here, another major development that accompanied his grandfather's settlement in Bombay was his deepening relationship with the British, which over the years evolved from a transient military alliance of convenience, as seen during the

---

134 Aga Khan III, *The Memoirs of Aga Khan: World Enough and Time* (London, 1954), pp. 9–10.

campaigns in Afghanistan and Sindh, to a deep and enduring relationship that in many ways laid the foundation for the emergence of the Ismaili Imamate as a global operator in the 20th century. The Aga Khan demonstrates genuine affection for the British in the *'Ibrat-afzā* and a clear partisanship in favour of their success during events such as the Second Anglo-Sikh War, which took place while he was residing in Calcutta. While it is true that there is no documented evidence of any collusion between the Aga Khan and the British in the conduct of his Persian campaigns, it is also true that the presence of the British in neighbouring Afghanistan at the time of these events proved to be a fortunate coincidence for the Imam, coming precisely at a moment when he was in need of new political alliances to secure his position. Yet it may also be seen, both from the *'Ibrat-afzā* and from the British archival records, that nearly ten years elapsed between the Aga Khan's first contact with the British in Afghanistan and his final decision to settle permanently in British territory, while in the interim he attempted on numerous occasions to return to Persia. Hence, it is clear that the relationship between the Aga Khan and the British was an evolving one, and not one that was necessarily based on any predetermined calculation to seek a new protector or a new seat for the Imamate.

However, it is very likely that a deepening relationship between the British government and the Imamate in the 19th century would have occurred in any case, even if the events of the Aga Khan's revolt had never taken place. This is due to the simple fact that, on account of the rapid expansion of British colonial possessions in India, by the early 19th century a significant portion of the Imam's followers had become in effect subjects of the British crown. Hence, it would have been desirable for him in any case to pursue a friendly rapport with the British, even if he had remained in Persia. Accordingly, one should regard with caution the tendency reflected in some of the scholarship on this issue to portray a direct causal relationship between the Aga Khan's failed campaigns and his subsequent relationship with the British.

Once established, the Aga Khan skilfully deployed this relationship with the British in his reorganisation and centralisation of the administration of Ismaili communities in India and elsewhere, a project which he had begun prior to his arrival in India and which he pursued with additional vigour following his settlement in Bombay. Already in 1829, while still living in Persia, the Aga Khan had filed a suit with the British court in Bombay against a group of dissident Khojas who had declined to pay the customary tithes to the Imam. While the suit was eventually withdrawn and the issue was settled out of court, the case set a precedent for the use of British courts to resolve such intra-communal matters. Following his departure for India, the Aga Khan pursued similar court cases on a number of occasions, the most famous being the 'Aga Khan Case' of 1866, which I have discussed earlier. More broadly, as Nile Green has outlined in his study, the Imamate also readily engaged with the new infrastructure and technologies introduced by the colonial presence, such as steamships and telegraph technology, which facilitated contact with distant Ismaili communities, as well as the printing press, which was employed to produce and distribute communal literature, and the *'Ibrat-afzā* itself.

Finally, there is the question of the manner in which the relationship with the British government allowed the Aga Khan to continue and expand his role as a patron and advocate for broader Muslim constituencies beyond the Ismaili community. The Aga Khan's patronage of a number of pan-Shi'i activities in India during his Imamate has already been discussed. This patronage was expanded by his son and successor, Āqā 'Alī Shāh, Aga Khan II, whose Imamate was relatively short, lasting only four years from 1881 until his premature death from pneumonia in 1885. During his brief Imamate, however, Aga Khan II took an increasingly active role in politics, serving on the Bombay Legislative Council and as president of the Muhammadan National Association, and was a major patron of educational schemes for Indian Muslims. In this, the Aga Khans adopted a role exemplified by other sayyids in British India (among the most famous being Sayyid Aḥmad Khān, the founder of the Muhammadan Anglo-Oriental College), who used their position of prestige and influence to advocate with the British for the causes of education and political representation for the Indian Muslim community. This role was expanded even further by Sultan Muhammad Shah, Aga Khan III, who during his long Imamate from 1885 to 1957 served in many roles, including as the first president of the All-India Muslim League and, later, as president of the League of Nations from 1937 to 1938, at a time of profound international crisis.[135] In all cases,

---

135 On the Imamate of Aga Khan II and III, see Daftary, *The Ismāʿīlīs*, pp. 477–497. The latter's long political career is also chronicled in his memoirs and in the collection of his speeches and writings published as *Selected Speeches and Writings of Sir Sultan Muhammad Shah*, ed. K. K. Aziz (London, 1998).

8. Aga Khan I and Aga Khan II.

it may be argued that the assumption by the Aga Khans of these positions as political advocates and intermediaries was taken not in spite of their role as Ismaili Imams, but rather because they reflected precisely the sort of political and social roles that had been adopted by sayyids and holy men in the Islamic tradition for centuries.

9. Mausoleum of Aga Khan I in Hasanabad, Bombay.

Part IV: The *'Ibrat-afzā*

The Authorship

The *'Ibrat-afzā* covers the period from the Aga Khan's birth in 1219/1804 down to the year 1852, when he abandoned his final attempt to return to Persia and settled permanently in Bombay. However, the first thirty years of the Aga Khan's life are covered only very briefly in this work, with the bulk of the text focusing on the eventful period beginning with the Aga Khan's appointment as governor of Kirmān in 1834. While I have referred to the *'Ibrat-afzā* throughout this introduction as the work of Imam Ḥasan 'Alī Shāh (Aga Khan I), it should be noted that the text was actually composed on his behalf by an individual named Mīrzā Aḥmad Viqār-i Shīrāzī (1817–1881), the eldest son of the celebrated Persian poet and calligrapher Viṣāl-i Shīrāzī.[136] In 1850, Viqār-i Shīrāzī

136 On Viqār-i Shīrāzī, see Riḍā Qulī Khān Hidāyat, *Majma' al-fuṣahā*, ed. Maẓāhir Muṣaffā (Tehran, 1336–1340 Sh./1957–1961), vol. 6, pp. 1676–1708; Paul Losensky, 'Waḳār, Mīrzā Aḥmad Shīrāzī', *EI2*; Māhyār Navvābī, *Khāndān-i*

travelled to India and spent some time in the company of the Aga Khan in Bombay, during which he composed a collection of poetry and a number of works under the Imam's patronage. The question of Viqār-i Shīrāzī's role in the compilation of the *'Ibrat-afzā* has long been a matter of dispute, although this uncertainty may be attributed only to the inaccessibility of the original lithograph printing of the text, rather than any ambiguity to be found in the text itself. Viqār-i Shīrāzī's role as the author of this text was first noted by Wladimir Ivanow. However, Ivanow offered no direct evidence at that time in support of his assertion, which was evidently based on oral reports by his Ismaili informants, as Ivanow had not been able to access the text itself.[137] Hamid Algar later challenged this claim, citing the lack of evidence presented by Ivanow and the absence of any evidence to that effect within the text itself.[138] However, Algar admittedly had access only to Kūhī Kirmānī's edition of the text, which inexplicably omitted any information attesting to Viqār-i Shīrāzī's authorship, and also did not have access to the original printing of the *'Ibrat-afzā*. With reference to the original lithograph of the work, there remains no question that the *'Ibrat-afzā* was indeed composed on the Aga Khan's behalf by Mīrzā Aḥmad Viqār-i Shīrāzī.

The *'Ibrat-afzā* in its original form appeared alongside two other works by Viqār-i Shīrāzī, a poetic work titled *Bahrām ū Bihrūz*, which is a *mathnavī* modelled on the *Khusraw ū Shīrīn* of Niẓāmī Ganjavī, and a short untitled work in prose and verse on the topic of Sufi gnosis (*ma'rifat*).[139] The colophon appended to the *Bahrām ū Bihrūz* records that the text was produced by Viqār-i Shīrāzī 'on the orders'

Viṣāl-i Shīrāzī (Tehran, 1335 Sh./1956), pp. 51–120; Ma'ṣūm 'Alī Shāh, *Ṭarā'iq al-ḥaqā'iq*, vol. 3, pp. 372–373. On the Viṣāl family, see also Maryam Ekhtiar, 'Innovation and Revivalism in Later Persian Calligraphy: The Visal Family of Shiraz', in Doris Behrens-Abouseif and Stephen Vernoit, ed., *Islamic Art in the 19th Century: Tradition, Innovation, and Eclecticism* (Leiden, 2006), pp. 257–280.

137 Wladimir Ivanow, *Ismaili Literature: A Biographical Survey* (Tehran, 1963), pp. 148–149. Viqār-i Shīrāzī's role in producing the text is also noted in Daftary, *Ismaili Literature*, p. 108.

138 Algar, 'Āqā Khan', pp. 170–175. The *'Ibrat-afzā* is not mentioned in Ismail K. Poonawala, *Biobibliography of Ismā'īlī Literature* (Malibu, CA, 1977).

139 This latter text is presumably the same work referred to by Ivanow as either the *Risāla dar insān-i kāmil* or *Risāla dar 'irfān*, although neither title appears in the work itself; see Ivanow, *Ismaili Literature*, p. 149.

(*ḥasb al-farma'ish*) of the Aga Khan,[140] while the introduction and conclusion to the text include many verses in praise of the Aga Khan (referred to in them by his sobriquet in the Niʿmatullāhiyya, ʿAṭā' Shāh). A slightly abbreviated colophon at the conclusion of the *ʿIbrat-afzā* likewise reiterates the point that the text was composed 'on the orders' of the Aga Khan. Moreover, in a final poem appended to the end of the volume containing the *Bahrām ū Bihrūz* and the *ʿIbrat-afzā*, Viqār-i Shīrāzī directly refers to his composition of the *ʿIbrat-afzā*, recounting how he presented the text of the *Bahrām ū Bihrūz* to the Aga Khan, who was greatly pleased with it and then asked Viqār to compose his biography.[141] Viqār carried out this task, he writes, 'having neither added nor subtracted anything'.

To this, we may add some new evidence from a previously unstudied text. Later in his life, in 1870, Viqār-i Shīrāzī evidently made a second trip to India, this time to the princely state of Hyderabad in the Deccan, at the invitation of its prime minister, Sālār Jang. While there, Viqār composed a text entitled *Tadhkirat al-vāṣilīn*, the unique autograph copy of which is held in the archives of the Salar Jung Museum.[142] The *Tadhkirat al-vāṣilīn* is a hagiographical compendium focused on various Shiʿi holy men who had lived in the century before its composition. The majority of the biographies included in the work are of Sufis of the Niʿmatullāhī order, but it also includes accounts of the Aga Khan and his father, Imam Khalīlullāh; the respect shown in the text to these two figures, moreover, is such that theirs are the second and third biographies, respectively,

---

140 The text of the colophon to *Bahrām ū Bihrūz* is included in the notes to the edition of the *ʿIbrat-afzā*. Mūsā Khān Khurāsānī, the continuator of Fidā'ī Khurāsānī's *Hidāyat al-mu'minīn al-ṭālibīn* (discussed further below), refers in his work to the *Bahrām ū Bihrūz* when citing the *ʿIbrat-afzā*, indicating the inseparable link in the identity of these two texts; see Fidā'ī Khurāsānī, *Hidāyat al-mu'minīn*, p. 154.

141 This concluding section of the book is unpaginated.

142 For the description of this manuscript, see Muhammad Ashraf, *A Catalogue of Persian Manuscripts in the Salar Jung Museum & Library* (Hyderabad, 1965), vol. 2, pp. 67–70 (MS T-S. 7). The biography of Viqār composed by Māhyār Navvābī (*op cit.*) does not mention either his stay in Hyderabad or the *Tadhkirat al-vāṣilīn*. However, a brief account of the author and the text appended to the manuscript, evidently composed by one of the collection's archivists, notes that Viqār undertook a second journey to India in 1287/1870, at which time the text was written.

10. Title Page of the lithographic edition of *ʿIbrat-afzā*, 1278/1862.

coming only after an account of the Shiʿi justice minister of Hyderabad. In his account of the Aga Khan, the author reiterates his high praise of him and mentions his previous visit to him in Bombay, and presents several newly authored *qaṣīda*s in praise of the Ismaili Imam.[143]

Therefore, it would appear that the *ʿIbrat-afzā* was indeed composed by Viqār-i Shīrāzī on the request of the Aga Khan, in a manner that is akin to the role of a modern-day 'ghostwriter'. Notwithstanding Viqār's claims to have faithfully rendered the Aga Khan's biography, it is almost certain that his role constituted more than merely a verbatim rendering of the Aga Khan's own words; after all, it was undoubtedly on the basis of his talents as an author, and not merely his ability to hold a pen, that the Aga Khan commissioned him. Yet, whatever Viqār-i Shīrāzī's exact role may have been in the composition of the *ʿIbrat-afzā*, there should be no doubt that the text constitutes substantially, if not literally, the words and thoughts of the Aga Khan as he chose to have them presented to the public, since it was composed and distributed with his sanction. Accordingly, the text may be appropriately considered to lie within the genre of autobiography or memoir, and not that of biography written by a third party.

Manuscripts and Editions

The *ʿIbrat-afzā* was evidently composed before the year 1267/1850, at the conclusion of Viqār-i Shīrāzī's visit with the Imam in Bombay,

143 *Tadhkirat al-vāṣilīn* ff. 8b–11a.

as the narrative of the text substantially concludes in this year. However, for reasons that are not clear, it was not published until a decade later, in 1861, with a paragraph at the end of the text briefly accounting for the intervening period.[144] Two manuscripts of the codex containing the *Bahrām ū Bihrūz* and the *'Ibrat-afzā* were prepared by Āqā Muḥammad Ibrāhīm 'Ṣafā', son of Muḥammad Ḥusayn Khān Awliyā'-samī' Shīrāzī, for the Dāwūd Miyān printing house in Bombay. The first of these was the basis of a lithograph edition dated Ramaḍān 1278 (1862). Despite its continuous pagination, a significant section of the text is missing in this edition.[145] This copy is cited as ب in the notes here. A Gujarati translation of the *'Ibrat-afzā* was reportedly also lithographed concurrently with this Persian edition, although copies of this are extremely rare today and were not available for consultation. A second manuscript by the same copyist, dated slightly later in Sha'bān 1278 (January–February 1862), includes the pages omitted from the Bombay edition. This manuscript is preserved today in the National Library of Iran in Tehran as MS 1316 and is cited in the notes as ت. This copy is not foliated, and consequently, while it was consulted in the preparation of this edition the pages are not cross-referenced in the notes.

To date all of the copies of the lithographed edition of the text of which I am aware have been copies of ب and reflect the missing pages found in that copy. However, some later copyists of the text, as noted below, evidently had access to the complete text, including the pages missing from ب. Therefore, it is possible that a second, corrected lithograph version may have been published at some point (possibly based on ت), although it has not been possible to determine any record of such a printing. Ivanow, who by the 1930s had already found copies of the *'Ibrat-afzā* to be exceedingly rare, even in Ismaili circles, produced his own handwritten copy of the text in May 1931 'from an old lithograph

---

144 There are several possible reasons that may account for the evident gap between the completion and publication of the text. It is possible that the text was only completed by Viqār-i Shīrāzī upon his return to Persia, based on notes he took while in Bombay, and later sent to the Aga Khan. An alternative and more likely possibility is that the text was initially composed specifically in support of an effort to petition for the Imam's return to Persia, but then put aside once that objective was abandoned, and that the decision to publish it by way of a general memoir was taken later.

145 The omitted section falls between pages 44 and 45 of the text.

copy' of the text. This copy is currently held in the archives of the Institute of Ismaili Studies in London as MS 917. While Ivanow evidently relied on ب for his copy, he also appears to have had access to an additional version as well (possibly ت), as his text includes the pages missing from the Bombay lithograph and he refers to the missing section in his marginal notes. While Ivanow's copy was on occasion consulted in order to confirm readings of certain passages, since it is a direct copy of ب and ت it is not referenced in the notes.

Three previous printed editions of the *'Ibrat-afzā* have been produced, the first two of which are highly flawed and unreliable. The first was a publication by the journalist Ḥusayn Kūhī Kirmānī, published in Tehran in 1325 Sh./1946. Since his publication contains no references to the original text, it cannot be considered a critical edition. Moreover, it contains numerous errors, omissions and uncited modifications to the original text, which have been a source of immense frustration to previous scholars who have been obliged to rely on it. Kirmānī's text was later reproduced *in toto* in a book by Muḥsin Sā'ī, published to mark the occasion of the visit of Aga Khan III to Iran in 1951. This version not only reproduces all the errors found in Kirmānī's edition, but, furthermore, introduces a number of additional errors and unwarranted modifications to the text.[146] Finally, while the present publication was in preparation, a new edition of the *'Ibrat-afzā* by Muḥsin Mūsavī Garmārūdī appeared in Iran.[147] This new edition corrects the errors and misreadings found in the previous editions by Kirmānī and Sā'ī. More importantly, the new edition by Garmārūdī includes an extensive apparatus of notes which have proved immensely useful in the preparation of the translation of the text.

The Fate and Significance of the 'Ibrat-afzā

The *'Ibrat-afzā* served as an important source for several later works of Ismaili historiography that were produced in the late 19th and early 20th centuries. Among these is the *Khiṭābāt-i 'āliya* of Pīr Shihāb al-Dīn Shāh Ḥusaynī, the grandson of Aga Khan I and elder brother of

---

146 Muḥsin Sā'ī, *Āqā Khān Maḥallātī va firqa-yi Ismā'īliyya* (Tehran, 1329 Sh./1950).

147 *'Ibrat-afzā: khāṭirāt-i Āqā Khān Maḥallātī*, ed. Sayyid Muḥsin Mūsavī Garmārūdī (Mashhad, 1393 Sh./2015).

Aga Khan III, composed sometime before the former's death in 1298/1881,[148] and the *Hidāyat al-muʾminīn al-ṭālibīn* of Fidāʾī Khurāsānī, which was composed around the turn of the 20th century under the patronage of Aga Khan III.[149] Both of these works also include a substantial number of oral traditions concerning the Aga Khan, supplementing the information found in the *ʿIbrat-afzā*.[150] However, for a number of reasons, the *ʿIbrat-afzā* had already begun to fall into obscurity by the early 20th century. As the reader will soon discover, the *ʿIbrat-afzā* is not simply a straightforward autobiographical account of the Imam's life and career, such as the memoirs of his grandson, Aga Khan III, whose English-language autobiography, published in 1954, remains popular among both Ismaili and non-Ismaili readers down to the present. Rather, the *ʿIbrat-afzā* was clearly composed with a specific agenda in mind, that is, to defend the Aga Khan's actions in Persia and to clear his record from accusations of rebellion against the Qājār regime. Yet this agenda had already started to become anachronistic by the time of the work's publication, given that by this time the Imamate had become firmly established in Bombay and the Aga Khan had abandoned any aspiration of returning to Persia. In the decades

148 The text has been published as Sayyid Shihāb al-Dīn Shāh al-Ḥusaynī, *Khiṭābāt-i ʿāliya*, ed. Hūshang Ujāqī (Bombay, 1963). On this work, see also Daftary, *Ismaili Literature*, p. 152.

149 Muḥammad b. Zayn al-ʿĀbidīn Fidāʾī Khurāsānī, *Hidāyat al-muʾminīn al-ṭālibīn*, ed. A. A. Semenov (Moscow, 1959). On this work and its author, see Farhad Daftary, 'Fedāʾī Khorāsānī', *EIr*; Daftary, *Ismaili Literature*, p. 112. A number of later copies of this work are preserved by the Nizārīs of Central Asia. According to Daftary, these copies, which formed the basis for Semenov's edition, demonstrate numerous corruptions from the original text of Fidāʾī Khurāsānī's work preserved in Iran, which remains unpublished. On this, see Farhad Daftary, 'Kitābī na-chandān muhim dar tārīkh-i Ismāʿīliyya', *Nashr-i Dānish*, 4 (1984), pp. 32–37.

150 Another important source to mention here is the *Āthār-i Muḥammadī*, which is a history of the Ismaili Imams written by Muḥammad Taqī b. ʿAlī Riḍā Maḥallātī in 1310/1893 for Aga Khan III. The author came from the town of Maḥallāt, from a family who had long been in the service of the Nizārī Imams, although it is not clear if he himself was an Ismaili. Unfortunately, the copy of the text available (IIS MS 919) is incomplete and breaks off during the account of the life of Imam Khalīlullāh, the father of Aga Khan I. On this text, see Ivanow, *Ismaili Literature*, pp. 152–153. As this project was nearing completion a complete copy of the *Āthār-i Muḥammadī* was made available to us from a collection in Bombay, which will be considered further in a later study.

following the publication of the *'Ibrat-afzā* the orientation of the Imamate turned increasingly towards India and the British Empire, as the events surrounding the Aga Khan's campaigns in Persia receded further into historical memory.

From the Iranian side, the memory of the Aga Khan's rebellion would soon become eclipsed by the increasingly severe political crises faced by the Qājārs in the late 19th and early 20th centuries. As noted above, the relationship between the Ismaili Imamate and Persia was already restored partially during the reign of Nāṣir al-Dīn Shāh, and was later fully restored under the Pahlavi dynasty, which supplanted the Qājārs in 1925, culminating in an important visit to Iran by Aga Khan III in 1951. This close relationship was continued under his successor, the current Imam, Aga Khan IV, who competed for the Iranian ski team at the 1964 Olympics. Accordingly, the immediate purpose underpinning the production of the *'Ibrat-afzā* had become obviated within a generation of its composition, contributing significantly to its subsequent obscurity.

It is natural that many general readers, who may be familiar with the memoirs of Aga Khan III, may expect to find a similar reading experience with the present work. Of such readers, I would ask their patience and for them to keep the context and purpose of the work in mind as they approach it. The notion that a biography, or even autobiography, should provide a complete and accurate rendering of the subject's life is a distinctly modern one that does not inform the contents of the *'Ibrat-afzā*. As I have noted, the *'Ibrat-afzā*, rather than offering a general autobiographical account of the Imam, was instead intended for a more specific purpose, that is, to present the Aga Khan's own narrative of the events leading to his conflict with the government of Persia and his subsequent emigration to India. Moreover, it is clear that the text was not composed foremost with an Ismaili audience in mind: while the text contains ubiquitous references to the author's role as the Imam, it nonetheless contains little in terms of Ismaili teachings. Instead, it appears to have been composed primarily with aristocratic Iranian and Twelver Shiʿi audiences in mind (including the Persian diaspora in India), to whom the Aga Khan appeals on the basis of his fealty to the Qājār throne and with reference to his own status as an 'Alid sayyid and a descendent of the early Shiʿi Imams. When approached with this context in mind, the work will no doubt hold enormous interest for both researchers and a general readership, offering a rare specimen of autobiographical writing by an Ismaili Imam and presenting a unique window into the history of the Ismaili Imamate at the dawn of its transition to the modern era.

Note on the Text and Translation

Although the text of the *ʿIbrat-afzā* is composed for the most part in a relatively plain and straightforward language, it does preserve elements of a classical Persian style, such as the repeated use of synonyms, which may lend a poetic quality to the text in the original but tend to appear tedious when rendered into English. Accordingly, we have at times taken minor liberties with the text in order to simplify the narrative for the general reader, while endeavouring to preserve the original meaning. Those consulting the work for scholarly purposes may, of course, refer to the original Persian text. Commentary and notes on the text are given with the translation, the notes to the Persian text referring only to textual matters. With the exception of the insertion of paragraph breaks, we have eschewed any punctuation to the Persian text that is not authorised by the manuscript record.

Garmārūdī's edition has proved to be immensely useful in identifying the sources of verses and other quotations; all identifications of quoted sources should be credited to his edition, unless otherwise noted. For identification of individuals, the notes to Garmārūdī's edition along with the reference work by Mahdī Bāmdād and the *Encyclopedia Iranica* were utilised,[151] in addition to the previous studies by Hamid Algar and Farhad Daftary. While not all individuals mentioned in the *ʿIbrat-afzā* could be identified, we have endeavoured to identify at least those more prominent and significant figures who were necessary for understanding the historical context of the narrative. For identification of places, the notes to Garmārūdī's edition once again provided an important resource for locations in Iran, along with the *Jughrāfiyā-yi Kirmān* of Aḥmad ʿAlī Khān Vazīrī. The author or scribe of the work appears to have been less familiar with the place names of the Indian subcontinent, and accordingly, several locations mentioned in this section of the narrative could not be identified with absolute certainty. Locations with a standardised anglicised spelling

151 Mahdī Bāmdād, *Sharḥ-i ḥāl-i rijāl-i Īrān* (Tehran, 1347 Sh./1968).

have been given in the text in their commonly known form in English (e.g. Tehran, Herat, Bombay), while the names of lesser-known places have been transliterated.

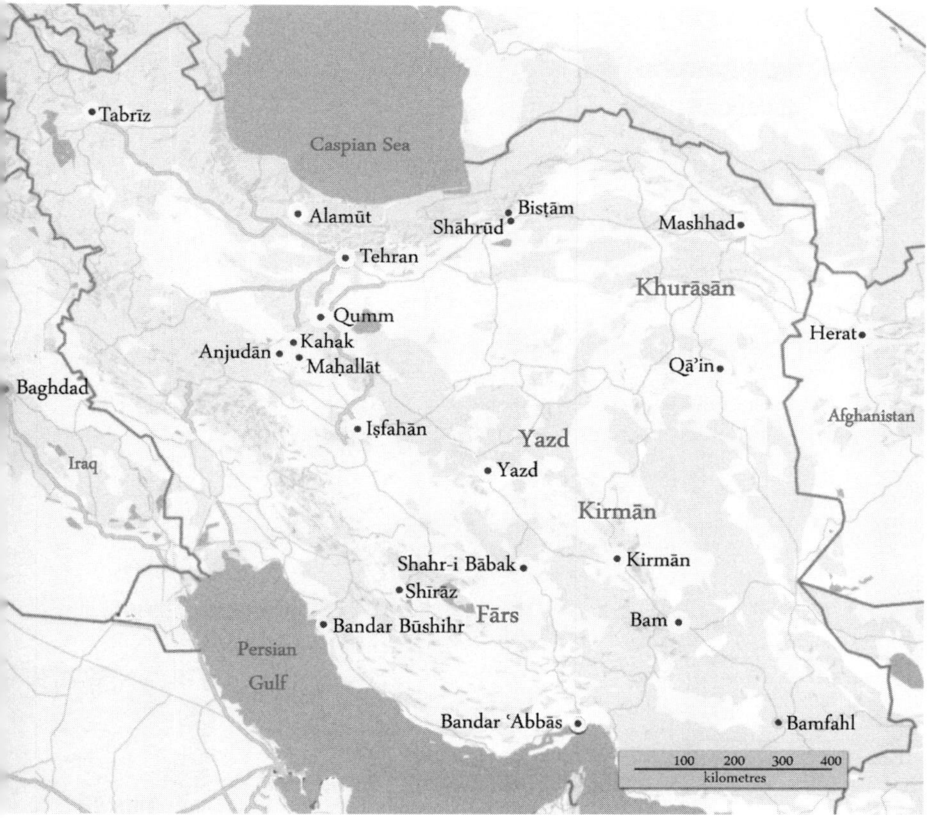

ıp 1. Persia (Iran) showing sites associated with the Nizārī Ismailis.

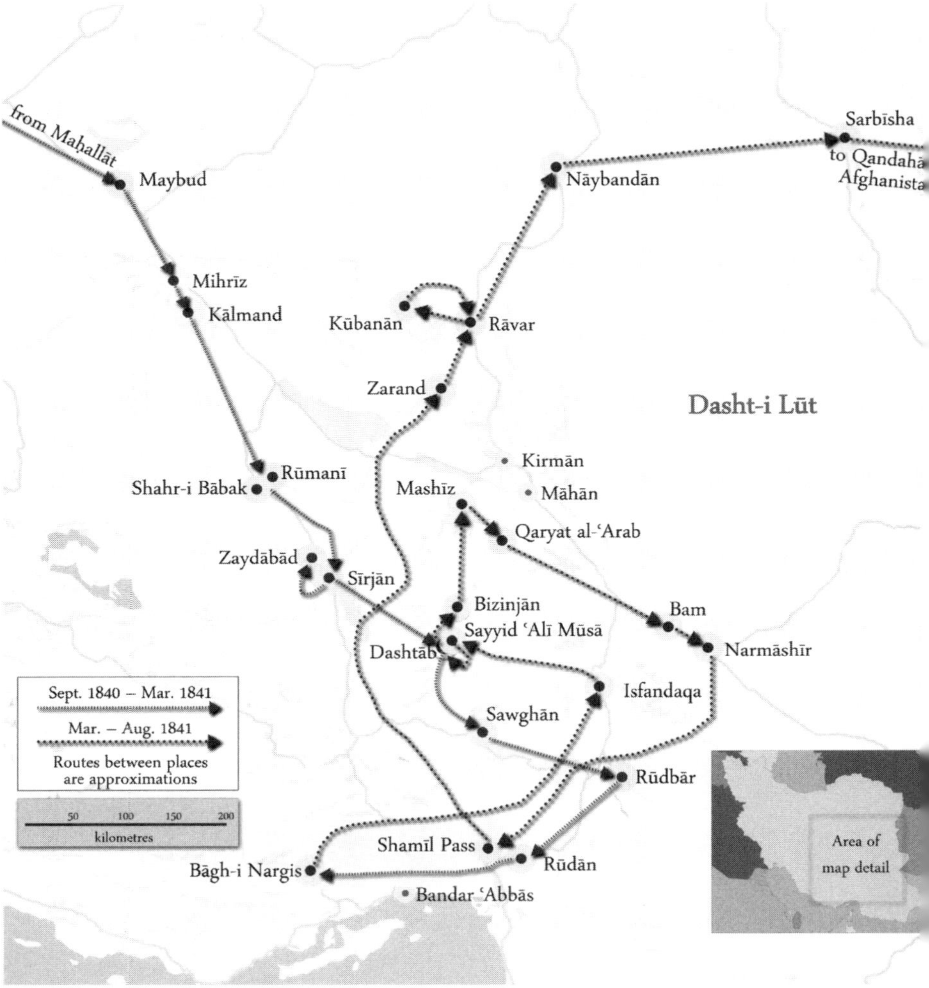

Map 2. South-eastern Persia showing the routes taken by Aga Khan I in 1840–1841.

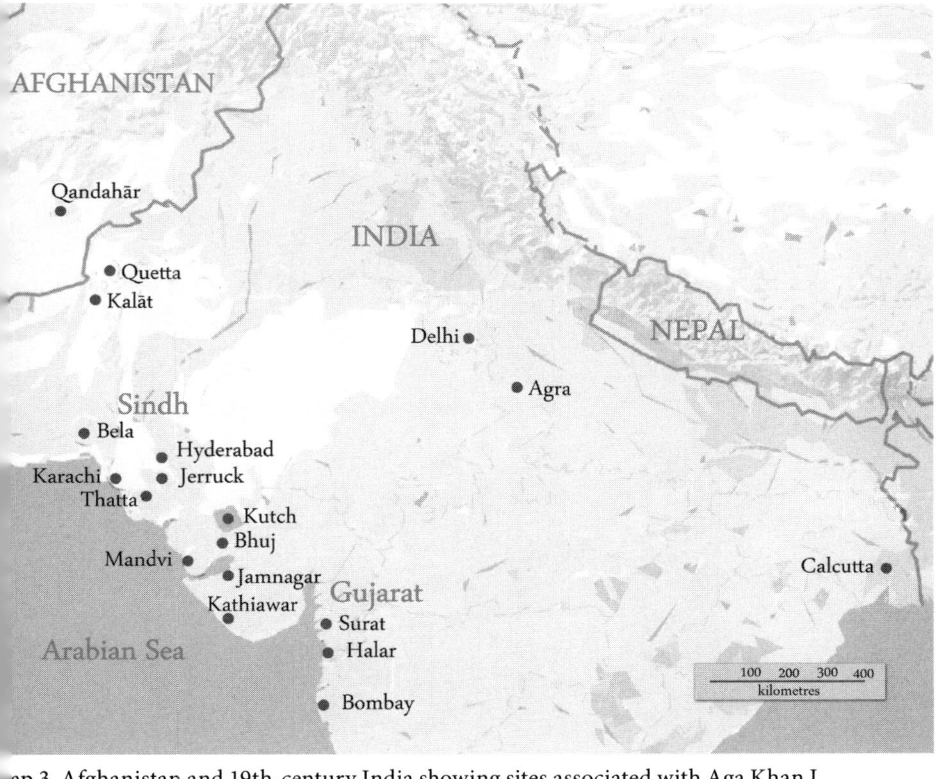

ap 3. Afghanistan and 19th-century India showing sites associated with Aga Khan I.

ʿIbrat-afzā

of

Muḥammad Ḥasan al-Ḥusaynī,
also known as Ḥasan ʿAlī Shāh

Translated by

Daniel Beben
and
Daryoush Mohammad Poor

In the name of God, the Most Beneficent, the Most Merciful.

Praise and salutations are due to the one creator, whose uniqueness is reflected in the entire world and in the denizens of the world.

> But language does not have the capacity to express praises to Him
> Or to describe the perfection of His majesty[1]
> 'I am incapable of praising you; rather, it is you who praises
> you'[2]

And praise is due to His Prophet, whose uniqueness is described in 'Were it not for your sake, I would not have created the universe'.[3]

> The garden of the soul is a reflection of his face
> And the elegant cypress came into being following his shadow[4]
> He reached glory through his perfection and all darkness was
> removed through his beauty[5]
> He is the centre, the circle and the compass, altogether.

Blessings be on the rightful executors and the true saints, generation after generation, who are in every one of the ages and eras, the referents of this blessed verse: 'Oh you who believe! Obey God, and obey the Apostle, and those among you who possess authority';[6] and the content of the ḥadīth: 'Verily I am leaving among you two weighty things, and if you hold on to them you will not go astray after me: the book of God and my progeny. They are two outstretched ropes and they will not break and will not be cut until the Day of Judgment, when the two shall join me at the pool [of Kawthar]', a tradition applying specifically to their generous existence.

---

1 Verse by Ḥazīn Lāhījī (d. 1178/1766).
2 This is a saying attributed to Imam ʿAlī.
3 This is a *ḥadīth qudsī*.
4 Verse by Ḥazīn Lāhījī.
5 Verse by Saʿdī Shīrāzī (d. ca. 691/1292).
6 Qur'an 4:59.

And then, since in the workshop of creation humankind has the most worthy temperament and vision for learning lessons [by experience], therefore this vagrant figure in the circles of contingencies, crippled in the circulation of time, reflected through contemplation of his past conditions and composed a summary of the details of his fate, the transformations of the conditions and an approximation of the events which have befallen him, so that this account might become the beginning of the narration of the conditions of others, and so that they may use it to weigh their own experiences. For whom is the grace of mistakes and confusion impossible in the elaboration of their biography?

> Therefore, there will be nothing else here other than silence, and
> the truth speaks
> And here there is none other than God as the creator
> And thus his creation bears testimony to our vision
> Leading us to him in the existence of truths
> So whoever so wishes may believe and whoever else wishes
> otherwise
> To claim contrary to what we said, then God is the most
> truthful one.[7]
> 'But ye shall not will except as God wills.'[8]

At the same time, I endeavour to be brief so that the reader is not bored by verbosity.

> This alley of life is a terrifying path,
> Wherever someone is sober, he is perplexed,
> The actor of the universe has all kinds of artifices,
> The arena of the world is a wondrous theatre.[9]

I, Muḥammad Ḥasan al-Ḥusaynī, known as Āqā Khān, son of Shāh Khalīlullāh, spent my life from the moment of birth until I was five years old as it befits the behaviour of young children, and this does not require any explanation.

---

7 Verse by Ibn 'Arabī (d. 638/1240), here slightly modified.
8 Qur'an 81:29.
9 Verse by Ḥazīn Lāhījī.

I was six years old when I was taken to school and put under the care of a certain Mullā Muḥammad ʿAlī Adīb. His knowledge was such that he easily rendered difficult the discernment of black from white, such that when he taught the *Gulistān* of Saʿdī, when he reached the phrase: 'The Arabian horse (*asb-i tāzī*) that gallops fast', he explained it as referring to a hound instead of a horse.[10] And when he was instructing me using the *Nisāb al-ṣibyān*,[11] upon reaching the meaning of *ḥusida ḥāfida* ('the offspring were envied'), he would angrily say it is not the business of children to ask about the nonsense of the Sufis and that delving into the meaning of such things would lead to the destruction of religion and the corruption of tradition. May God have mercy on him.

Anyway, I was at the age of seven when my martyred father was taken to Yazd and Īmānī Khān Farāhānī[12] was deputised to oversee some villages belonging to us. These villages were given to us by the late Āghā Muḥammad Khān[13] in exchange for some properties in Kirmān at the time when my father and my relatives were moved from Kirmān. There was a certain Muḥammad ʿAlī who was the chief of the village of Rīvkān of Maḥallāt.[14] He did not submit to Īmānī Khān's directive. Therefore, in order to get some peace of mind, he wrote a letter to my late mother[15] making solemn promises and vows. When my late mother felt confident that nothing would happen to him, she sent him to Farāhān, but Īmānī Khān broke his vows and imprisoned him. He also sent bailiffs who looted his home and furniture, even the women's dresses. My mother went to Farāhān[16] in order to vouch for him and intercede on his behalf,

---

10 The term *tāzī* in Persian may refer both to an adjective meaning 'Arab' (as it is intended in the cited verse by Sāʿdī) and a noun meaning 'hunting dog'.

11 *Nisāb al-ṣibyān* was a popular Persian-Arabic primer by Abū Naṣr al-Farāhī, composed ca. 640/1242.

12 Īmānī Khān Farāhānī was the Imam's brother-in-law and husband to his sister Shāh Bībī.

13 Āghā Muḥammad Khān Qājār (r. 1789–1797) was the founder of the Qājār dynasty in Iran.

14 Maḥallāt is the capital of Maḥallāt county in the province of Markazī in west-central Iran. The Aga Khan's ancestors had lived in the nearby village of Kahak since the late 11th/17th century and held a large number of properties in the area and in surrounding regions.

15 The mother of the Aga Khan, Bībī Sarkāra, accompanied him to India and died there in 1267/1851.

16 Farāhān is another city in Markazī.

but Īmānī Khān left Mashkābād, which was his residence, for another village and hid himself.

Because of these things we were compelled to leave our home and residence in Maḥallāt and settle perforce in Qumm at the age of eight. In Qumm, due to the abundance of hypocrites and the absence of any loyal companion, life became so hard and we were so poor that we could barely obtain even yoghurt and bread. Any assistance either from relatives or strangers was entirely inconceivable until I was thirteen years old. It was in this year that my late father was martyred in Yazd.

After this incident, relatives and strangers all unanimously opposed me. The encouragement of the royal officials in support of those who opposed me exacerbated the situation, such that my late mother finally lost patience and departed for the royal capital in Tehran and sat there in the majestic royal court seeking justice:

> To seek purity from the soil of purity;
> And to get blessed omens from the beauty of Marwa[17]

And she was honourably received with great respect in the exclusive royal apartments and she made a petition seeking justice in such a manner that is described in this verse:

> The fire temple of our heart is not empty,
> The idol house of Ādhar has a Khalīl.[18]

The passionate petition of my late mother touched the heart of His Majesty,[19] such that he drew his knife from his belt and set upon the late Ẓill al-Sulṭān,[20] moving towards him and addressing him in abusive language, saying: 'These few ruined villages were given to them in return

---

17 Verse by Khāqānī (d. 586/1190); al-Marwa is a hill in Mecca and is one of two hills between which the pilgrims run back and forth seven times as one of the rituals associated with the *ḥajj*.

18 Verse by Ḥazīn Lāhījī; Ādhar was the name of the father of the Prophet Ibrāhīm, while Khalīl (or Khalīlullāh, meaning 'Friend of God') is one of Ibrāhīm's chief epithets.

19 This refers to Fatḥ 'Alī Shāh (r. 1797–1834), the second King of the Qājār dynasty.

20 'Alī Khān Ẓill al-Sulṭān was the tenth son of Fatḥ 'Alī Shāh and the governor of Qumm at this time; see Hamid Algar, 'The Revolt of Āghā Khān

for the estates of Kirmān by the late Āghā Muḥammad Khān. How dare you and with what authority have you interfered with them?' And indeed, if my late mother had not intervened, Ẓill al-Sulṭān would have certainly received a thorough drubbing.

Therefore, His Majesty, through his fairness, began compensating for what had been lost and rectifying all the damages we had sustained over the years and in past times. Having a virtuous character and compassion, he initiated the arrangement of a marriage bond and of friendship. His Majesty, therefore, obligated my mother with my marriage to his own noble daughter[21] to me. My mother demurred in diplomatic terms, saying: 'What does the royal tent have to do with the milieu of poverty?' Nonetheless, despite all these frustrations, since in the mind of His Majesty the decision had become set, he paid an equivalent of 23,000 *tūmāns* in cash from the royal treasury for the expenses of the marriage. Out of all the people he raised me up in distinction to become his son-in-law. As long as he was alive, he paid such great respect to me, even greater than the respect he gave to senior princes. He always accepted my intercession between the great ones and the lesser. In many gatherings, he proudly spoke of me as his son-in-law, may God let him rest in the vicinity of Paradise.

> The heart which seeks the manifestation of the sun
> Shall become a disciple of every particle in the universe.[22]

Since the purpose here is to give a general account of my biography, I will avoid verbosity and loquaciousness. Following the demise of the late King, terror gained a grip on both the leaders and the led, near and far, with chaos prevailing in the land. As the entourage of the late King, Muḥammad Shāh, may his soul rest in paradise, approached Tehran, from every territory, princes, governors and agents headed to the capital. As a result of the pillage and plunder which took place in between the demise of the previous King and the enthronement of the next one, many people fell prey to punishment. As is the manner of friends,

---

Maḥallātī and the Transference of the Ismā'īlī Imāmate to India', *Studia Islamica*, 29 (1969), p. 62.

21 This refers to Sarv-i Jahān Khānum, with whom the Aga Khan later had three children, including the future Aga Khan II.

22 Verse by Qāsim-i Anvār (d. 836/1433).

I entered the royal court in the company of Ghulām Ḥusayn Khān Sipahdār[23] to express felicitations on the King ascending the throne. In the land of ʿIrāq and elsewhere, mobs plundered and pillaged the property of neighbours and travellers, and caravan-drivers from all directions took refuge within the boundaries of my domains, staying in peace in order to arrive safely at their destinations.

As the news of such protection and goodwill reached the King, he was greatly satisfied. However, the realm of Kirmān had been ruined as a result of the repeated invasions of the Balūch and the Afghāns, and the land had been occupied by the sons of the late Shujāʿ al-Salṭana.[24] The fortresses there were impenetrable, the citadel of Bam[25] is renowned for its strength, and the number of enemies there was also enormous. These considerations disturbed his peace of mind. Therefore, the late King sought the advice of Mīrzā Abu'l-Qāsim[26] (may God grant him mercy), who had complete knowledge of the life, deeds and words of this dynasty throughout its history. Therefore, I was summoned and commanded thus: 'Since the government of Kirmān belonged to your ancestors, it belongs to you now. Go to the treasury and receive the funds necessary to prepare an army and quickly get ready to depart.' Out of consideration for this sort of kindness and the necessities of time, I said: 'Even though at this time the realm of Kirmān has been conquered by others, and at the time when Luṭf ʿAlī Khān[27] was in Kirmān, the late Āghā Muḥammad Khān personally made a considerable effort by expending

---

23 Ghulām Ḥusayn Khān Sipahdār was the son-in-law of Fatḥ ʿAlī Shāh Qājār and the governor of Iṣfahān at this time.

24 Ḥasan ʿAlī Mīrzā Shujāʿ al-Salṭana was the sixth son of Fatḥ ʿAlī Shāh and former governor of Khurāsān, and later a rival of Muḥammad Shāh in the succession to the Qājār throne.

25 The Citadel of Bam (*Arg-i Bam*) is a famous fortification and UNESCO Heritage site (see http://whc.unesco.org/en/list/1208) located in the north-east quarter of the city of Bam. This site, parts of which date back to the Achaemenid era (6th–4th centuries BC), is renowned as one of the largest standing mud-brick structures in the world. The site was devastated by an earthquake in 2003 but is currently undergoing renovation.

26 Mīrzā Abu'l-Qāsim Qā'im-maqām Farāhānī briefly served as chief minister (*vazīr*) under Muḥammad Shāh between 1834 and 1835.

27 Luṭf ʿAlī Khān (d. 1208/1794) was the last ruler of the Zand dynasty which preceded the Qājārs in Iran. The author alludes here to the efforts of his grandfather, Abu'l-Ḥasan ʿAlī, during his governorship of Kirmān to repel an invasion of the province by Luṭf ʿAlī Khān.

enormous funds and preparing a large army to liberate the city, since you have charged me with this duty, by the grace of God and the royal good fortune, I will not ask for a penny from the royal treasury until I have taken the land out of foreign occupation, from the sons of Shujāʿ, and have secured it. Upon the completion of this service, you may reward me with any blessing as you see fit.'

After receiving the permits and orders from the King, I left for Maḥallāt and stayed there for a few days in order to prepare and then I set out for Kirmān. Before I entered Kirmān,[28] the children of Shujāʿ al-Salṭana had evacuated the city and headed towards Bam and Narmāshīr.[29] I took over the city upon my arrival and stayed there for some time in order to organise affairs. I dispatched my brother, Sardār Abu'l-Ḥasan Khān, along with the chiefs and khāns of the faithful 'Aṭā'ullāhī and Khurāsānī tribes[30] towards Bam and Narmāshīr. The sons of Shujāʿ had turned over the fortresses of Narmāshīr and Bam to the Afghāns and the Balūch from Sīstān and fled in haste with all their servants and retinue, turning their backs on us.

The Afghāns and the Sistānīs had become presumptuous and defiant, because annually for eleven years during the reign of the late King, not only the taxes of Kirmān, but an additional 40,000 *tūmān*s had been spent on troops that had failed to dispel them. They had fortified the castles that they had captured with enormous reserves and fighting men. They resisted through their steadfastness and by the use of firearms and swords, and they displayed great courage. Finally, after I had brought order to the affairs of the city [of Kirmān], I determined to move towards Narmāshīr, Īwār and Shabgīr to fight them. For a year and more, rest was denied to me. I gave one Tabrīzī *man*[31] of grain and 5,000 *dīnār*s to each of my men. Despite the shortage of food, the strength of the castles and the multitude of enemies among the Balūch and the Afghāns, I did not rest until I had slain or captured all of them in battle.

---

28 The author refers here to the city Kirmān, the capital of the province.

29 Bam and Narmāshīr (the latter formerly known as Rustamābād) are cities in the province of Kirmān in south-eastern Iran, and are the capitals of their respective counties.

30 The 'Aṭā'ullāhī and Khurāsānī were two of the main tribal communities among the followers of the Nizārī Imams in this period. See further the discussion of these communities in the Introduction.

31 A Tabrīzī *man* is equal to approximately 5 kilograms.

After I had released the prisoners, I began an assessment of the funds spent on subjugating the outlaws and the rebels, for catering for the troops and the peasantry and for increasing the funds of the royal offices. Once I was done, I sent Mīrzā ʿAli Riḍā Mustawfī[32] to the capital to settle the account of the royal expenditures and income, and to secure praises for the services detailed above. I myself rested with a tranquil heart, awaiting the outcome of the agreement made between the late King and myself, and I recited this verse to myself:

> O Cup-bearer! Bring the wine, and take no heed of friend or foe
> Since our heart's desire has arrived![33]

Because I was loyal to my promise and had rendered my services as per the requests of the officials of the government, I was constantly thinking joyful thoughts awaiting the outcomes of the royal commands. After some time, a messenger came on behalf of someone who was a confidant both of the royal court and this dervish [i.e., the Aga Khan], bringing a message with these contents:

You know that the laws of the government of Iran are such that upon a change of ministers, inevitably the rules and officials of the previous minister change during the time of the next minister so as to consolidate the independence of the ministry. Since your services were clearly considerable, and since the government of Kirmān was granted to you at a time when it had been captured by powerful enemies and the government was still weak, it was not possible to remove you for no cause without breaking the royal oath. Therefore, in the reasons that are contained in the report given by the carrier of this message, you will perceive the details of the issue as follows: During the lifetime of the late King, Ḥājjī Mīrzā Zayn al-ʿĀbidīn Shirvānī[34] delightedly propagated his spiritual leadership and quietly raised the flag of the Niʿmatullāhī path in each quarter. He had also made secret promises to a number of senior princes, including the late King, to elevate them to the throne of the

32 Mīrzā ʿAlī Riḍā Mustawfī was a local political figure who served as an administrator for several of the governors of Kirmān in this period.

33 Verse by Ḥāfiẓ Shīrāzī (d. 792/1390).

34 Zayn al-ʿĀbidīn Shirvānī (d. 1253/1838) was the contemporary master (*quṭb*) of the Niʿmatullāhī Sufi order. This figure and his relationship with the Aga Khan are discussed at length in the Introduction.

kingdom of Iran. Even though the late King had given his allegiance and devotion to the guidance of Ḥājjī Mīrzā Āqāsī,[35] due to his immense integrity and certainty, he placed faith in the invocation of the recitations (*awrād*) taught by the late Ḥājjī Shirvānī on his journey to Khurāsān.[36]

As soon as the renowned and pure-natured King ascended to the throne, the aforementioned Ḥājjī [Shirvānī] lifted himself from a position of seclusion to a lofty status, and he raised the flag of greatness to the melody of 'Is there any more?'[37] He received the trust of the servants of the kingdom and some of the confidants of the government sincerely believed in his cause and thus he obtained the utmost dignity and respect. At the time of the late King, when the aforementioned [Shirvānī] was fleeing for his life from Fārs and 'Irāq, he sought refuge in my care and I gave him lodging in Dawlatābād,[38] which was my recently acquired property. I sheltered him for a time until he was safe, and he returned to his homeland. During these times he expressed affection and trust for me.

Therefore, after returning from Kirmān and joining with the royal camp, he rose up in a position of reward in the service of the late King. As a kind of boast, it was made public that 'I have a disciple like the Aga Khan, who in most countries of the world has tens of thousands of disciples.' Meanwhile, I had determined to give, from my own lawful monthly income, 500 *tūmān*s for the provision of the Paradise-residing King and 100 *tūmān*s expenditure for the table of Ḥājjī Mīrzā Āqāsī. When the aforementioned Ḥājjī [Shirvānī] set out from Kirmān for the royal camp, I sent him to Jurjān with the aforementioned six-month supply of funds in the company of His Excellency Shāhrukh Khān.[39]

---

35 Ḥājjī Mīrzā 'Abbās Īravānī Āqāsī (d. 1265/1848) was chief minister under Muḥammad Shāh and a senior member of the Ni'matullāhī Sufi order, who is also discussed at length in the introduction.

36 The author refers here to the Qājār campaign to retake Herat from the Afghans in 1837–1838, on which Shirvānī accompanied the royal camp. See further the discussion of these events in the Introduction.

37 Qur'an 50:30.

38 Dawlatābād is a village situated 36 kilometres north of Maḥallāt.

39 Shāhrukh Khān was a son of Ibrāhīm Khān Qājār Ẓahīr al-Dawla, who was a stepson and son-in-law of Fatḥ 'Alī Shāh Qājār and a former governor of the province of Kirmān.

During this period, Ḥājjī Zayn al-ʿĀbidīn had decided to order the affairs of the kingdom and was making every effort to remove Ḥājjī [Āqāsī] from his ministerial position. With the help of a number of the royal confidants and officials, such as Mīrzā Naṣrullāh Ṣadr al-Mamālik,[40] Mīrzā Masʿūd, the foreign minister,[41] Mīrzā Bāqir Malik al-Kuttāb, and some of his other comrades and companions, he [Shirvānī] had assembled a list, accusing Ḥājjī Vazīr of numerous crimes the details of which are beyond the scope of this account, and had enumerated them. With absolute confidence he sought an opportunity for his overthrow in Shāhrūd and Bisṭām,[42] and with all that support he assumed that succeeding in his intention would be a trifling matter.

He showed the list to the late King, and in his moments of arrogance he had not delivered the six months' payment that I had sent to the late King and Ḥājjī Vazīr. As a result, the late King summoned Ḥājjī Mīrzā Āqāsī there and then and gave him the list. The minister considered the list and only replied: 'They did not record my biggest error, which was giving the daughter of His Excellency Ḍiyā' al-Salṭana[43] to Mīrzā Masʿūd.' In summary, on the same night, the Ḥājjī Murshid [Shirvānī], who was then at the peak of his glory, was expelled from the camp and the realm in utter humiliation. Despite the presence of a hundred horses and both pack and riding mules, he was given only a single draught pony and sent wandering into the valley of bewilderment saying, 'Where is my refuge?' After that, no one referred to him at all and he laid out his bedroll in the desert of the silent ones. May God have mercy upon him.

40 Naṣrullāh Ardabīlī, known also by the *ṭarīqa* title of Nuṣrat ʿAlī, held the position of Ṣadr al-Mamālik, or chief religious officer, of Tehran in the early years of the reign of Muḥammad Shāh. On him, see further Mansur Sefatgol, 'From *Dār al-Salṭana-yi Iṣfahān* to *Dār al-Khilāfa-yi Ṭihrān*: Continuity and Change in the Safavid Model of State-Religious Administration during the Qājārs (1795–1895/1209–1313)', in Robert Gleave, ed., *Religion and Society in Qajar Iran* (London, 2005), pp. 78–79.

41 Ḥājjī Mīrzā Masʿūd Khān Garmārūdī Anṣārī served as the foreign minister under Muḥammad Shāh Qājār.

42 Both Shāhrūd and Bisṭām are cities in the province of Simnān in northern Iran. The author is most likely refering to events that took place when the Qājār camp passed through these locations during the Herat campaign.

43 Nawwāb Ḍiyā' al-Salṭana was the daughter of Fatḥ ʿAlī Shāh Qājār, who was married to Mīrzā Masʿūd, the foreign minister (see note 41 above), who was a supporter of Shirvānī.

The sun raised its flag on top of the mountains and departed,
The beloved knocked on the door of the lovers and departed,
The nightingale sang the song of spring and departed,
The flower laughed at the conditions of the world and departed,[44]
Indeed, with the service of a noble intellect and right counsel,
One can conquer the heavens.

Ḥājjī Vazīr, remembering the boast, 'The Aga Khan is my disciple', made by the Ḥājjī Murshid [Shirvānī] in the presence of the King, and also that he had not received the six-months' worth of dues either, thereby resolved on disgracing me and prepared to do his utmost for my destruction. When the royal camp was moving to Jurjān,[45] I sent a petition to the late King and said: 'Considering the agony and pain of the royal foot, it is not necessary for you to put yourself through the hardship of travelling. If you order five armies to be put under my charge I will, God willing, conquer Herat in a short time and annex it to the royal territories.' Beside the conquests of Kirmān, Bam and Narmāshīr, these comments were highly effective and pleased the King immensely, such that he proclaimed publicly: 'I wish I had a brother like the Aga Khan, so that I could then rest in peace and spend my days in tranquility.' For these reasons, Ḥājjī Vazīr had become my enemy and decided to destroy me, awaiting any opportunity. But because of the King's kindness to me, he could not implement his agenda without an excuse. Therefore, he enticed my messenger, Mīrzā 'Alī Riḍā Mustawfī, with a promise of enormous rewards, to accuse me before the King. Thus they began their scheme to put an end to my endeavours. When I was in Bam and had dispatched my brother, Sardār Abu'l-Ḥasan Khān, to conquer Bamfahl[46] and Balūchistān, I heard about Suhrāb Khān's[47] move towards Kirmān. I was not able to return to Kirmān immediately, fearing the danger to the realm from the Balūch and others, although

---

44 Verse by Ḥazīn Lāhījī.

45 Jurjān is the capital of the province of Gulistān in north-eastern Iran. The events referred to here were part of the campaign to retake Herat from the Afghans in 1837–1838. See further the discussion of these events in the Introduction.

46 Bamfahl (or Bampūr) is one of the main fortresses of Balūchistān and is discussed at greater length later in the text.

47 Suhrāb Khān Gurjī was a military commander and the son-in-law and former treasurer of Fatḥ 'Alī Shāh.

through messengers and letters I tried to dispel any allegations against me and to seek respite until Sardār [Abu'l-Ḥasan Khān] had returned from Bamfahl. All of these efforts failed and what happened, happened. Indeed,

> It is not appropriate in religious law and in reason
> For the King to order something without evidence,
> Because his decree is like the signature of Fate,
> Which sometimes takes away and sometimes gives life.[48]

In short, it became evident that Divine providence was directed to a different end. I said to myself:

> I know that there is none omnipotent other than God,
> I have no ill will because of anyone's injustice towards me.
> It is not the nature of creatures to be victorious,
> Being defeated by God is not a disgrace to me,[49]
> And all command belongs to the one omnipotent God,
> If I suffer in seeking him, it is all befitting.
> Because when love is the destination of your pilgrimage,
> traversing deserts is easy.[50]

In these preliminary accounts, it is evident to all people of knowledge and insight that, were it not for their short-sightedness and lack of judgement, nothing could prevent the friends of the majestic court from ascertaining the truth. If they were not following their whims and evil deceptions, they would have taken into account the interests of the government and the dignity of the kingdom. This way, someone such as I, who had not failed in giving my property and life in the royal service, would not have been destroyed and turned out, nor would all those losses of property, life and reputation have been incurred by His Majesty the King. Instead, in addition to the lands of Balūchistān and Sīstān, other lands would also be part of the royal territories without any conflict. In the same manner that I expelled the sons of the late Shujāʿ

---

48 Verse from the *Jawhār al-akhlāq* of Sayyid Maḥmūd Amīnī (cited in Garmārūdī's edition of *ʿIbrat Afza*, p. 52, n. 154).
49 Verse by Ḥazīn Lahījī.
50 Verse by Saʿdī Shīrāzī.

al-Salṭana along with the Afghāns and the Balūch from Kirmān, Bam and Narmāshīr, and sent them fleeing to Balūchistān, Afghanistan and Herat, I would have pursued the matter and secured other lands for the kingdom too. But alas:

Have you heard that the patient friend,
Once united with a foe, becomes like a snake?[51]
Therefore, O you who have eyes to see, take heed!

That hypocritical old man, and that incompetent minister, and those nurtured by the government and its benevolence, and that power and glory and conqueror of lands, His Royal Majesty, as mentioned in the introduction to these reports, with splendour and dignity set out for Herat. In the same manner, due to evil whims, selfish desires and arrogance, the interests of the government, the reputation of the King, and the majesty of the kingdom were disregarded. As is clear to the whole world, after thousands of failures in those troublesome undertakings, all of them were left disappointed and rejected even by the basest of servants without obtaining their desires.

See the difference in the path and where it leads[52]

And the consequences of ungratefulness, as seen, befell them all. And goodness lies in what occurred.

The entire world, new and old,
Is not worth a grain because it all passes away.[53]

In summary, in the midst of these disturbances I chose to remain composed and dignified, and I remained patient and stayed firm. I gave up all desires and cut off the thread of hope from all the past occurrences, seeking infinite divine blessings, and I sang this melody:

If I die with a good reputation, then so be it!
A good name is what is needed and the body is predisposed to death.[54]

---

51 Verse by Jalāl al-Dīn Rūmī (d. 672/1273).
52 Verse by Ḥāfiẓ Shīrāzī.
53 These verses are omitted in Garmārūdī's edition.
54 Verse by Abu'l-Qāsim Firdawsī (d. ca. 411/1020).

If I do not have a triumphant future in my horoscope, who cares?
If nature does not learn to be congenial, who cares?
If you must cut off your ties with your companions,
Then who cares if today you do not have a confidant?[55]

It is known to God and His shadow, His Majesty the King, that I have not had nor do I have any desire to rule Kirmān, much less Iran and Tūrān.[56] I only took up the royal command and carried out the imperial wishes and decrees. All know that, with the divine grace and the blessing of my ancestors and my pure forebears, I find rulership contemptible when compared to the vast and lofty realm of my dervish-hood. God be praised:

The earth is our throne, scars are our signet, and a lack of
headdress is our crown,
Jamshīd envies our royal glory![57]

And it is evident to all that the material and spiritual kingdom has belonged to my ancestors and forebears since time immemorial, and will belong to them for eternity. Despite the fact that my great forefathers were the firm handle of religion and the strong cord of God, 'in which there is no split',[58] as is recorded in the Qur'an, and 'there is no splitting the twain and no cutting the twain', in the famous tradition of my ancestor, the Master of the Messengers, peace be upon him and upon his family, I am not attached to the slightest detail of this world and what is in it. Yes, as far as is possible, I have endeavoured to spread the faith and the religious law of the final Messenger, following the example of my pure ancestors and forebears. Likewise, it is evident that in Egypt several generations of my ancestors held the positions of kingship and the caliphate,[59] and they conjoined the Ja'farī path[60] and the law of the

55 Verse by Ḥazīn Lāhījī.

56 The term Tūrān is generally evoked in Persian literature to refer to the lands to the east of Iran, sometimes equated with the territories of Central Asia across the Amu Darya river.

57 Verse by Abu'l-Ḥasan Yaghmā-yi Jandaqī (d. 1275/1859).

58 Qur'an 2:256.

59 The author refers here to the Fatimid dynasty of Egypt.

60 A reference to Ja'far al-Ṣādiq (d. 148/765), the fifth Imam of the Ismaili tradition and the sixth of the Ithnā'asharīs.

Ithnāʿasharī, which today is attributed to Shāh Ismāʿīl Ṣafavī.[61] I am the descendant of that same dynasty. And if any observers do not lack depth of reflection and contemplation, they will know that:

> Those with a prominent heritage are the servants of my progeny,
> Those who are true lovers are drinkers of my wine,
> In our realm, our kingship is ancient,
> The Magian sages are those born in the service of my house.[62]

Praise be to the benevolent and beneficent God, who has spread and extended the domain of my dervish-hood across the realms of the earth. Whilst the kings of the land extract taxes from the common people by force and coercion, my fortune reaches me unsolicited through an abundance of insufficiency and abject humility. If the permitted and the forbidden are weighed through the firmly established commands of the Most Learned and the path of the Master of Mankind,[63] the criterion for [judging] truth and falsehood will be our dervish-hood and our kingdom.

In summary, when word came of the arrival of Suhrāb Khān and there was little time to make a defence against my accusations, I summoned my brothers Sardār Abu'l-Ḥasan Khān from Balūchistān and Sardār Muḥammad Bāqir Khān from Rāvar.[64] Because the battlefield was narrow and the enemy was quite prepared for battle, Sardār Muḥammad Bāqir Khān was therefore hit in his leg by a bullet and was captured with all of his troops and retinue. And they were imprisoned along with my nephew, Muḥammad Jaʿfar Khān, whom I had appointed my deputy in Kirmān. They surrounded Bam with a fully equipped army led by Shāhrukh Khān, the son of Ibrāhīm Khān Qājār.[65] I was forced to endure the siege to protect my life and family. The siege went on for fourteen months.

---

61 Shāh Ismāʿīl Ṣafavī (d. 930/1524) was the founder of the Safavid empire of Iran and is credited with the wide-scale conversion of much of the population of Iran to Twelver Shiʿism in the 10th/16th century. On this passage and its significance, see further Daniel Beben, 'The Fatimid Legacy and the Foundation of the Modern Nizārī Ismaili Imamate', in Farhad Daftary and Shainool Jiwa, ed., *The Fatimid Caliphate: Diversity of Traditions* (London, 2018), pp. 192–216.

62 Verse by Ḥazīn Lāhījī.

63 This is a reference to the Prophet Muḥammad.

64 Rāvar is a town 140 kilometres from the city of Kirmān.

65 See note 39 above.

Since my intention was to remove the accusations hanging over me, I repeatedly wrote to them and requested: 'Give me safe passage to go to the court of the King. And if that is not permitted, then allow me to leave the land of Iran with all of my unhappy family and go to another land.' Yet however much I repeated these entreaties, I received no reply except the sound of cannon and gunfire. Day in and day out, on account of their numbers and exertions, the difficulty of our siege increased, even though I repeatedly and visibly defeated them and captured their artillery. If I had wished, I could have completely destroyed them all. But since I did not want all ties of friendship to be cut off and to let the accusation of my enemies be proved right, I refrained.

Following this affliction, I sent my brother Sardār Abu'l-Ḥasan Khān with a petition to His Excellency Farīdūn Mīrzā[66] in Shīrāz to seek assistance. He dispatched Muḥammad Ṣādiq Khān, the nephew of the late King, to escort me to Fārs. The aforementioned khān entered the citadel in the company of 'Abbās Qulī Khān Lārījānī,[67] who had laid siege to the citadel on behalf of the late King, carrying a copy of the Holy Qur'an, pledging that they would not violate my property, my retainers and my dignity in the slightest degree if I evacuated the citadel and set out for Fārs with my retinue and family. After receiving these pledges I prepared to evacuate the citadel and I ordered my retainers to leave the citadel and to allow them to enter. Suddenly, a commotion arose among my retainers. It transpired that every one of them was seized, stripped and bound. The situation was hopeless. They seized every single item at their disposal, even the clothing of the young and the old. We were dispatched as captives to Kirmān. Since disasters such as this are a part of my inheritance, I therefore surrendered myself to Divine fate and expressed thanks to God:

There are so many wonders under this ethereal wheel
This ancient universe is a place to learn from
See the soul imprisoned in the chains of the body
And the Sīmurgh trapped in the spider's web.[68]

---

66 Nawwāb Farīdūn Mīrzā (d. 1272/1856) was the brother of Muḥammad Shāh Qājār and the governor of the province of Shīrāz.

67 'Abbās Qulī Khān Lārījānī was one of the leading generals of Muḥammad Shāh Qājār.

68 Verse by Ḥazīn Lāhījī.

They sent the glad tidings of this victory to Herat. His Excellency Muḥammad Riḍā Mīrzā[69] was a close companion of Ḥājjī Zayn al-'Ābidīn and one of his disciples. He was aware that the Ḥājjī had confiscated the six months of payments I had sent for the expenses of the late King's table and that of Ḥājjī Vazīr. So, he briefed the Ḥājjī [Āqāsī] about what had happened and the late Ḥājjī regretted what he had done to me.

In summary, I remained in Kirmān for eight months in captivity. But since Divine grace has blessed this dervish at every moment, one after the other, on the day that I had arrived in Kirmān, so many dues in cash arrived from India, Khurāsān, Turkistān[70] and Badakhshān[71] for me that they compensated for everything they had stolen from me and my retainers many times over. After the royal retinue arrived in the capital from Herat, in light of the words of Muḥammad Riḍā Mīrzā, I was summoned and sent after to go to the capital. Since my innocence had now been proved to the Ḥājjī [Āqāsī] – may God forgive him – he accompanied me respectfully, but during the journey he did not enquire at all about what I had done and what he had done. He did not say a single word about why he had broken his promise and what had happened to the compensation for my services.

After encountering this level of audacity, I was given leave to spend some time in Wishnāvah[72] near Qumm to take the air there and then

---

69 Nawwāb Muḥammad Riḍā Mīrzā was one of the sons of Fatḥ 'Alī Shāh and the governor of the province of Gīlān in northern Iran.

70 Turkistān is a rather imprecise geographical term that may refer variously to either the name of a city near the Syr Darya river in the south of present-day Kazakhstan, more generally to the territories south of the Qazaq steppe along the Syr Darya or, in some contexts, even more broadly to Central Asia as a whole. It is probably in the latter sense that the term is intended here. While the bulk of the Ismaili communities of Central Asia have historically been centred in the Badakhshān region (referred to next in the author's list), there are scattered reports from 19th-century sources suggesting the presence of small communities in the major urban areas of Central Asia, such as Samarqand and Bukhārā.

71 Badakhshān is a historical region comprised of the mountain territories of present-day eastern Tajikistan and north-eastern Afghanistan. It has been a major centre of Ismailism since it was first introduced there in the 5th/11th century by the Iranian poet, philosopher and *dā'ī*, Nāṣir-i Khusraw (d. after 462/1070).

72 Wishnāvah is a mountain village approximately 60 kilometres south-west of Qumm.

I set out for Maḥallāt to rest. There was a certain Ḥājjī ʿAbd al-Muḥammad, who was a lowly subject of Maḥallāt and had become a companion of Ḥājjī Vazīr, using my name and practising the usual ways of the dervishes, during the time when Ḥājjī Vazīr had no power. When the Ḥājjī became vizier, he gradually became his confidant and through him he had become a friend and confidant of the King too, being accorded great credit. He came to Maḥallāt from Tehran. Conceited as a result of the temporary power that he had, he claimed a daughter of mine in marriage. Because he was not of the rank of our family, I declined his request and after this claim I no longer received him in my presence. After he was disappointed, he went back to Tehran and insisted repeatedly to the King and the Ḥājjī that the Aga Khan was preparing troops and intended to go on the rampage. Yes,

> Whoever by origin has an evil nature
> Never expect any goodness from him
> Because you can never forcibly change
> the black raven into a white falcon.[73]

This accusation gradually became widespread and on a daily basis I received all kinds of letters and messengers from some of the government officials and princes of ʿIrāq and Khurāsān and the scholars of the realm (*ʿulamāʾ-i millat*), inviting me to proceed, promising that they would not forbear to give up their life and property for this cause. I declined all these requests giving them all sorts of excuses, until I was left without recourse. At that time, the royal retinue departed from Tehran heading for Dilījān, which is 5 *farsangs*[74] away from Maḥallāt. Then the King came to Āb-i Garm, which is 1 *farsang* away from Maḥallāt. At that time I was away on a hunting expedition. The King stayed in Āb-i Garm for three days and after his return from there, the royal retinue departed from Dilījān. Then I wrote a letter to the Ḥājjī and told him: 'If the intention is that I do not stay in this land, then grant me permission to

73 Verse by Ibn Yamīn Faryūmadī (d. 769/1368).

74 The *farsang* is a Persian unit of distance roughly equivalent to the English 'league', or the distance a man can cover on foot in one hour. Dalījān is 23 kilometres from Maḥallāt, yielding a *farsang* of approximately 4.6 kilometres in the author's usage.

send my family to the holy shrines (*'atabāt*)[75] and let me travel to Mecca, so that the People of God (*khalq Allāh*) and I will be assuaged.' He wrote in response: 'I know what numbers you have and what you have in mind, but you are free to go wherever you wish.'

Thus, I was forced to part from my homeland and my family. I bid farewell to my late mother, to the Illustrious Princess[76] and the children, sending them with their retinue and their servants to the *'Atabāt*. Then I began making preparations for my journey to Mecca along with my brothers, nephews and various other members of my family. On the fourth day of Rajab 1256 (1 September 1840), I set out from Maḥallāt.

I was unaware that all the governors, officials and police in the towns along the way had been ordered not to sell us any grain or provisions, and everyone had been ordered on the way to make every attempt to capture us or murder us in whatever way they could. Thus, in [the territory of] Maybud,[77] of Yazd, they ambushed us at night, relentlessly attacking with forays and volleys of gunfire. But since Divine assistance was aiding my innocence, we prevailed and left there safely. Likewise, we entered the town of Mihrīz[78] in Yazd, and we were utterly exhausted. My servants and retinue found lodgings to take some rest. It was around midday that I was struck with a Divine inspiration that we had to leave this town, for as it is said:

> Do not rush towards crumbs out of greed,
> Be careful, because there is a snare under every morsel.[79]

---

75 The *'ātabāt-i 'āliyāt* are the Shi'i shrine cities of southern 'Irāq, including Najaf and Karbalā, where many of the early Shi'i Imams are buried. Pilgrimage to the *'ātabāt* from Iran became increasingly popular in the Qājār era; on this, see Tomoko Morikawa, 'Pilgrimages to the Iraqi 'Atabāt from Qajar Era Iran', in Pedram Khosronejad, ed., *Saints and Their Pilgrims in Iran and Neighbouring Countries* (Wantage, 2012), pp. 41–60.

76 This is a reference to the Aga Khan's wife, Sarv-i Jahān Khānum, the daughter of Fatḥ 'Alī Shāh.

77 Maybud refers both to a county in the province of Yazd and to the county seat.

78 This is the capital of the county of Mihrīz in the province of Yazd.

79 The author of this verse is unknown, but Garmārūdī (p. 71, n. 226) notes that it is also cited in the *Anvār-i suhaylī* of Kamāl al-Dīn Vā'iẓ-i Kāshifī (d. 910/1505), whose poetry is quoted elsewhere in the *'Ibrat-afzā*.

At once, I ordered everyone to leave the aforementioned town and to remain outside it. It later became clear that at the same time, His Excellency Bahman Mīrzā,[80] the governor of Yazd, had entered the town of Mihrīz from the other side with two detachments of infantry and 2,000 horsemen, hurrying to capture us. But since God was assisting us, they had no chance of success. After performing the evening and night prayers, we mounted our horses and rode off. Since the villages near Mihrīz were all located near the main road, they kept shooting at us through the night until midnight. When I felt that they were becoming really arrogant, I ordered my troops to shoot back at them. Within half an hour they captured the village and the fortress, arresting some of them and bringing them to me. I released them all and we set out.

We entered Kālmand[81] at dawn, bereft of supplies and food. Kālmand was a small village located in a depression, containing only two households and two ruined gardens. In the morning, a convoy arrived and offered to sell their supplies for a high price. It was around midday that it occurred to me that we should leave this low plain of Kālmand. So I ordered all the baggage to be loaded up and the servants to be mounted and set out. My brothers and servants presented excuses saying that since the men and the horses were tired, it were best if we waited till evening, when the horses could be fed, and then we could ride out. I did not concur and ordered that we depart at once. I myself asked for a horse and mounted it. Then all the supplies were loaded up and everyone was mounted, and we climbed out of the plain of Kālmand.

Suddenly, we saw that the plain was filled with soldiers. I told Sardār Muḥammad Bāqir Khān to go and find out who they were and what they wanted. I set out with a few horsemen. Before he reached them, a volley of cannon and gunfire came from their side. Then, Sardār Abu'l-Ḥasan Khān and some of the cavalry rode out and confronted them. Even though they numbered more than 4,000 soldiers, musketeers and cavalry, they were mostly untrained mercenaries. They did not get the chance to fire more than twice before, with Divine assistance, they were defeated. About 500 of them were seized, along with 200 of their camels,

---

80 Bahman Mīrzā Bahā' al-Dawla, who led the military campaign against Aga Khan and his supporters for the next several months, was the thirty-seventh son of Fatḥ 'Alī Shāh and was the governor of Yazd.

81 Kālmand is a village located approximately 20 kilometres from Mihrīz.

horses and mules with their loads. Our cavalry surrounded them and we kept fighting until an hour before sunset. One of my retainers was killed and Naṣrullāh Khān 'Aṭā'ullāhī and four other people were injured. Then they all cried out for mercy and collapsed through thirst. Then I ordered that the captives and their baggage be released.

At that same moment, 'Alī Muḥammad Khān, who was a nephew of Mīrzā Ḥusayn-i Vazīr, the governor of the lands of Dashtāb,[82] arrived. After the departure of the enemy troops, we set out and near morning we dismounted near a well. I ordered Mīrzā 'Abd al-Ghanī to go to Anār[83] with some cavalry and buy supplies and to have them ready, so that once we arrived there, no time would be wasted and we could move from one stage to the next in proper order.

Four days later, one of the horsemen who had been sent to Anār met us on the way and said: 'We went there and bought all the necessary supplies and stockpiled them. The second night a group of people ambushed us and fought with us. I fled and they killed the rest of us.' After I heard these reports, I became certain that they would not allow us to reach our destination. Therefore, we changed our course and, trusting in the grace of Almighty God, set out for Shahr-i Bābak.[84]

Once we entered Shahr-i Bābak, the chiefs of Qandahār, Kuhandil Khān, Khudāraḥm Khān and Mirhdil Khān,[85] who were stationed in the fortress of Shahr-i Bābak, which was my inherited home and property, closed the gates of the fortress on us and started shooting at us from the battlements and the towers. I was left with no choice but to

---

82 Dashtāb is a rural district in the county of Bāft in the province of Kirmān.

83 Anār is the capital of the county of Anār in the province of Kirmān.

84 Shahr-i Bābak is the capital of the county of Shahr-i Bābak in the province of Kirmān, which had previously served as the headquarters of Imam Ḥasan 'Alī in the 18th century and where the Aga Khan's family still owned a number of properties.

85 These brothers, relatives of the *amīr* of Afghanistan, Dūst Muḥammad Khān, had controlled Qandahār and its surrounding territories as largely autonomous rulers for the past two decades, but had recently been displaced as a result of the British invasion of Afghanistan and the capture of Qandahār in April 1839. See further Christine Noelle, *State and Tribe in Nineteenth-Century Afghanistan: The Reign of Amir Dost Muhammad Khan (1826–1863)* (Richmond, 1997), pp. 235–245. The brothers were later reinstalled in their position in Qandahār, in part on the Aga Khan's insistence, as is mentioned later in the text.

order a siege of the fortress. They had no supplies in the fortress, so after three days of siege, they sent an old man suing for mercy and declaring their submission. The old man reported Kuhandil Khān saying, 'I committed this inappropriate act because my son, Muḥammad 'Umar Khān, is in Tehran and I was assigned by the royal officials to block your passage. So, for this reason, I can neither come to you to apologise, nor dare to give up the fortress to you, nor to fight with you. I know that this place is your estate and it belongs to you. I am also your guest, but since I have taken refuge in your home and have left my homeland, I hope that you will abandon the siege and consider me a loyal friend. So leave me and go.'

I accepted their excuse and ordered my retainers to put an end to the siege of the fortress. Then I sent my brother, Muḥammad Bāqir Khān, with Mīrzā Isḥāq, Āqā Muḥammad Bāqir Anārī, Khān Bābā Khān and 'Abbās Qulī Khān, along with some cavalry, to Sīrjān[86] to purchase whatever supplies were available there. I myself left for Rūmanī[87] with my family. After four days, a messenger from Muḥammad Bāqir Khān arrived saying, 'Faḍl 'Alī Khān[88] has surrounded us with five detachments of soldiers and cavalry and five cannon. If you do not come to our aid, they will capture us.'

So, I ordered all the cavalry to mount their steeds and the musketeers and arquebusiers (*shamkhālchiyān*) to ride out as well, and commanded everyone else, the family, the supplies and the treasury to stay put, until they receive a second order from me. With four hours remaining before sunset we set out, fully armed and equipped. Since the distance was a mere 15 *farsang*s we therefore arrived at the fortress of Zaydābād in Sīrjān[89] at dawn. At that moment, from the enemy's side there came

86 Sīrjān is the capital of the county of Sīrjān in the province of Kirmān.

87 Rūmanī is a village in the vicinity of Shahr-i Bābak.

88 Faḍl 'Ali Khān Qarābāghī was the governor (*beglarbegī*) of the province of Kirmān.

89 The fortress of Zaydābād is a famous citadel in the region, which at that time was in the possession of a local notable named Yūsuf 'Alī, popularly known as Ḥājj Darvīsh. According to an oral tradition reported to me by Houchang Chehabi, a great-great-grandson of Ḥājj Darvīsh, he was later imprisoned by the Qājār government for having offered shelter to the Aga Khan's brother but, according to the tradition, was set free after Muḥammad Shāh had a dream in which Imam 'Alī commanded his release (email communication, 28 December 2017).

forth soldiers, cavalry and artillery, ready to fight, and the battle began. Our horsemen sallied forth and defeated their soldiers. Muḥammad Bāqir Khān seized the opportunity, left the fortress and joined us. In order to rescue the others, I placed my trust in Divine protection and ventured to attack the fortress, because after Muḥammad Bāqir Khān had left the fortress, their soldiers had rushed into it. They fired so many cannon and guns at us that were it not for Divine protection, not a single one of us would have survived. Nonetheless, my nephew, Muḥammad Ja'far Khān, and some of the other retainers were injured.

Since our cavalrymen and our horses had been galloping for 15 *farsang*s and our arsenal had not yet arrived, and four hours of fierce battle had taken place, we were therefore forced to retreat. They pursued us for about 4 *farsang*s but they were unable to overtake us and went back. Yes,

> Were all the particles of the world to roll over and spin together,
> They would be unable to do anything in the face of Divine fate.
> When Fate reveals its countenance from Heaven
> All wise men turn blind and deaf,
> Fish will fall out of the sea
> And the snare will grasp the flying bird in misery[90]
> This Fate is a fierce and ferocious wind
> People are as helpless straws before it.[91]

Since we and our horses were tired, we dismounted near an oasis next to a fortress.[92] We sent some people to the door of the fortress to buy supplies. The residents of the fortress closed its gates on us. Again, we sent requests to them to sell us supplies at any price they wished and [offered] to pay the price in cash, but they did not agree. So I ordered the capture of the fortress by force, seizing their supplies. After performing the evening and night prayers, for the comfort of the wounded we changed our course and set out towards the frontier of Fārs.

Ḥājjī Faḍlullāh Kīshkū'ī invited us into his fortress and performed all the obligations of hospitality. We stayed there for a few days and sent the

---

90 Verse by Jalāl al-Dīn Rūmī.

91 Verse by Kamāl al-Dīn Ḥusayn Vā'iẓ-i Kāshifī.

92 This refers to the fortress of Akbarābād in the central region of Sīrjān in Kirmān.

wounded to Bandar ʿAbbās.[93] For the sake of rest and recuperation, we assumed the fortress of Sawghān[94] to be safe and departed from Kīshkū.[95]

Once we arrived near Sawghān, we received word that Ḥaydar Khān had closed the gates with a large number of musketeers and would not let us in. I had no choice but to order the seizure of the place by force. After the fortress was captured, I took command of the battlements and forgave Ḥaydar Khān with kindliness. From every corner, we started receiving provisions through the grace of God, even though an order was sent to all regions and towns not to let us in or sell us water and bread, or anything else. Faḍl ʿAlī Khān was camped two stages away from us with detachments of cavalry and infantry. Divine protection helped us in moments of distress, until obtaining supplies became difficult for us.

In the midst of this, a few horsemen arrived on behalf of Saʿīd Khān Balūch Rūdbārī,[96] inviting us to come to his land. I regarded this opportunity favourably and the next day we left Sawghān. For three months we stayed in the villages of Kahnūpanchirt, Bulūk and Nawsārī.[97] Our supplies and our treasury being in Rūmanī with my family, after the Zaydābād incident Faḍl ʿAlī Khān sent troops there and pillaged everything while my family were in the mountains.

During these few months, I sent letters in every direction to make necessary arrangements and to bring provisions via ports and from Masqaṭ.[98] Then I ordered the people to go to Bāgh-i Nargis, which is near

93 Bandar ʿAbbās is an important port city on the Persian Gulf and the capital of the province of Hurmuzgān in southern Iran.

94 Sawghān is a fortress in the Bāft region of the province of Kirmān.

95 Kīshkū is a village in the Dashtāb district of Kirmān.

96 Saʿīd Khān Balūch Rūdbārī was the son of Madat Khān, the governor of the district of Rūdbār (now Rūdbār-i Junūb) in Kirmān.

97 These are villages in the area of Rūdbār and the neighbouring district of ʿAnbarābād.

98 The author refers here to the port city of Muscat, the present-day capital of Oman, which historically served as a major transit point for trade entering the Persian Gulf. The 18th-century historian Muḥammad Kāẓim Marvī noted that the port of Muscat served as a transit point for pilgrims and tithes that came to Imam Sayyid Ḥasan Beg from India; see Muḥammad Kāẓim Marvī, *ʿĀlamārā-yi Nādirī*, ed. Muḥammad Amīn Riyāḥī (Tehran, 1364 Sh./1985), vol. 3, p. 1182.

the border of Fārs and adjacent to Rūdbār. For each of them, as befitting their status, wooden dwellings were made and I myself set out for Rūdān.[99] I sojourned there for some time and then I sent word for the family to be brought to Bāgh-i Nargis. I too went and took up residence in Bāgh-i Nargis in peace of mind.

Since ancient times, it has been the rule of our family, in the manner of dervishes, that wherever I am, people with demands and requests arrive from every land. They stay until their demand is met and then they leave. Accordingly, our sundry population was large and we had little grain, while being surrounded by the enemy on all four sides. Therefore, staying there became a challenge. Lacking any resort, I sent all the family and the children to the mountains, where they took up residence, and I myself set out towards Kahnūpanchirt and Bulūk with two cannon,[100] determined to defeat the enemy and to protect my life.

After Muḥarram 1257 (March–April 1841), I received news of the massing of enemy troops and the movement of 'Alī Khān Lārī[101] towards Fārs, aided by Faḍl 'Alī Khān, the governor of Kirmān. I lost hope and was under severe pressure.

I dispatched my brother, Mīrzā Abu'l-Ḥasan Khān, with a hundred cavalry to seize Dashtāb by force. 'Alī Muḥammad Khān had previously received me before all the other khāns in Kālmand, but had since preceded all others in audacity and declared his enmity for me. Therefore, the land of Dashtāb, which was his land and his territory, was seized from him. After I received word that Dashtāb had been conquered, I moved from Kahnūpanchirt to Isfandaqa,[102] which is the land of Fatḥ 'Alī Khān Mahīnī, and the aforementioned person fled.

I stayed for a couple of days in a garden near his fortress and I sent people in every direction in an effort to reconcile with him, but to no avail. Then I got word that 4,000 cavalry and infantry had set out for Dashtāb led by Isfandīyār Khān, Faḍl 'Alī Khān's brother, to

---

99 Formerly known as Rūdkān, this is one of the towns of the province of Hurmuzgān in the south of Iran.

100 These cannons were evidently of British manufacture and were alleged by the Aga Khan's opponents to have been provided to him by the British as a means of undermining the Iranian forces during the Herat campaign; see Algar, 'The Revolt of Āghā Khān Maḥallātī', p. 76.

101 'Alī Khān Lārī was the ruler of the district of Lāristān in the province of Fārs.

102 Isfandaqa is one of the towns in the district of Jīruft in Kirmān.

conquer the place. So I set out in order to push them back and to assist Mīrzā Abu'l-Ḥasan Khān. I spent the night in a mountain valley and set out in haste at dawn with forty cavalry, and I ordered the rest of the cavalry and the infantry to follow us with supplies.

It was four hours after sunrise when we entered the Sayyid 'Alī Mūsā pass.[103] This is a narrow passage abutting a high mountain overlooking an *imāmzāda*[104] with the mausoleum placed at the centre of it. The passage is restricted to two very narrow paths. I was unaware that Isfandiyār Khān had taken strongholds around the mountain, ready to seize anyone who passed through.

As soon as I realised this, I chose death over captivity, and so we rode up the mountain with our companions. Isfandiyār Khān had captured the top of the mountain, where they had room to manoeuvre their horses. It was difficult for us to ascend and therefore by the time we reached there to confront them, they had attacked and we had encountered gunfire five times. Naṣrullāh Khān 'Aṭā'ullāhī, Imāmqulī Khān Qājār and some of my other horsemen were killed. My brother Muḥammad Bāqir Khān was also gravely wounded. Finally, we reached the top of the mountain to confront them.

Although their numbers were large and we were only thirty-two men, we abandoned any concern for our lives and plunged into their troops. Their leader, Isfandiyār Khān, was knocked from his horse by a gunshot. What was left of his men piled him onto a horse and fled down the mountain. Some of their horses and men were hit and we pursued them until they reached their large stronghold at the foot of the mountain. I laid in wait above them, standing ready until my cavalry, musketeers and cannons arrived. They were 4,000 strong. I therefore ordered the cannons to be pointed towards their stronghold from above on the mountain and for the gunpowder cases to be filled.

Four hours after sunset, I ordered the attack and let loose the cannon fire. Then some of their cavalry who were on the alert picked up Isfandiyār Khān and fled. The rest of the chiefs and khāns, such as Walī Muḥammad Khān Sartīp, Muḥammad Salīm Khān Mashīzī and

---

103 This is an area in the Dashtāb region of Kirmān.

104 An *imāmzāda* is the shrine of a descendant of a Shi'i Imam. The *imāmzāda* mentioned here belongs to an individual named Sayyid 'Alī Mūsā, who is believed to have been a descendant of Mūsā Kāẓim (d. 183/799), the seventh Ithnā'asharī Imam.

Ḥusayn Khān Qaryat al-'Arabī,[105] along with some others, were captured along with a mass of troops, and the khāns were brought to me tied up. I thanked God and at once rode out for Dashtāb, taking the khāns along with me. I ordered that the rest of their retainers and the captives be transported with all their equipment and weapons and to depart in peace.

The next day, we held a celebration.[106] I summoned Walī Muḥammad Khān Sartīp with the other khāns to the party and I placated them to make them comfortable. Then I gave rewards to my retainers as befitting their rank and merit. I also conciliated the captives and they pledged their sincere service.

After a few days of rest, we received word that 'Alī Khān Lārī was approaching with the army of Fārs. I decided to engage 'Abdullāh Khān Ṣamṣām al-Dawla Qarākūzlū Sartīp,[107] who was camped in Bizinjān[108] with soldiers and artillery, before he could join up with 'Alī Khān. Since my brother Muḥammad Bāqir Khān was injured, I appointed him to the defence of Dashtāb along with my nephew, Mīrzā Ḥusayn Khān, Muḥammad Salīm Khān Mashīzī, and fifty riflemen, and with the body of the newly pledged bondmen I departed for Bizinjān. After we reached the vicinity of the aforementioned fortress, I stationed each of the khāns and their soldiers at intervals in the surrounding hills, and ordered them not to move or engage in battle until I order them to, for:

> Hoping for renewed friendship from old foes
> Is like seeking a flower in a rubbish heap.[109]

I dismounted in front of the fortress with my retainers. Then I divided the cavalry and the musketeers into three sections and ordered them to charge towards the fortress from three directions. From 'Abdullāh

---

105 These individuals were local chiefs from across the Kirmān region.

106 Given the time of year, this was probably the celebration of Nawrūz, the Persian New Year.

107 Garmārūdī (p. 90, n. 284) suggests that the name given here is an error and that the individual intended is a Qājār military commander named 'Abdullāh Khān Qarāgūzlū Ṣārim al-Dawla.

108 Bizinjān is a mountain town in the Bāft district of Kirmān.

109 According to Garmārūdī (p. 91, n. 287), the author of this verse is unknown but it is quoted in the *Safīna-yi majma' al-baḥrayn*, composed by the Mughal prince, Dārā Shikūh (d. 1069/1659).

Khān's side, a detachment of cavalry and artillery came forward fully prepared, and the battle began. The combat was fierce, but since they were unjustly attempting my destruction, God gave aid, and despite all the bullets and cannon fire I charged forward. Suddenly, my retainers charged forward on three sides and ʿAbdullāh Khān's artillery and cavalry turned tail. Some soldiers were captured and the rest were surrounded in the fortress.

The next day, ʿAbdullāh Khān wrote a letter to me with the following contents: 'I have no quarrel with you. I pledge that I will resolve this rancour between you and the pillars of the kingdom in such a manner that both parties are satisfied.'

Finally, the next day, Muḥammad ʿAlī Beg Fārghānī came on behalf of ʿAlī Khān Lārī, carrying a copy of the Holy Qurʾan, to which he had appended a letter signed and sealed in his own hand that read as such:

> At the time when my father abandoned his estate and household, wandering about with his family and with nomads, he sought refuge with your family, who gave him full board and lodging for five years with the utmost honour. My brother Naṣīr Khān and I were born in your house. We are your servants and grateful to you, and we have always sought for an opportunity in which God might create a cause whereby, rendering some service to you, we might make compensation for all your benevolence. Now is that time. And I ask you to go to Mashīz[110] and rest there, so that I can make preparations to resolve this dispute within two months, and dispel all these accusations against you, and acquire the decree returning the governorship of Kirmān to you as before. And the witness and the judge between you and me is Almighty God and his word. Peace.

And all those verbal promises were repeated so often by Muḥammad ʿAlī Beg that I became certain of his honesty. Therefore, the next day, I sent Mīrzā Aḥmad to respond to ʿAlī Khān. At the same time I sent Muḥammad ʿAlī Beg to Dashtāb to collect my nephew, Mīrzā Ḥusayn Khān, and to go to ʿAlī Khān to explain the truth of what had happened, to find out what he truly had in mind, and come back. I myself settled matters with ʿAbdullāh Khān and moved towards Mashīz with my party.

---

110 Mashīz is a district in the county of Bardsīr in Kirmān.

However, after Sayyid Ḥusayn Khān[111] and Mīrzā Aḥmad had arrived at 'Alī Khān's camp, and after private conversations and discussions with him, in the morning the bugle was sounded in his camp calling the troops to action. Mīrzā Aḥmad asked 'Alī Khān the reason for this call, and he replied that they were setting out. When asked in which direction they were going, he replied that they were going to Dashtāb. Mīrzā Aḥmad told him: 'Muḥammad Bāqir Khān is stationed in Dashtāb with a large body of troops, and they are well prepared. If you go there, as long as they live they will not let you pass without a fight. They will fight until large numbers on both sides are killed, and even then it is not clear which side will win and which side lose. Moreover, what happened to your pledge of assurance to the Aga Khan?' He replied, 'I have no choice in this matter. The decision lies with Aḥmad Beg Yūzbāshī.' Mīrzā Aḥmad decided that 'Alī Khān was making excuses. The troops of 'Alī Khān were 6,000 infantry and cavalry with six cannon. Aḥmad Beg's men were also 6,000 infantry and cavalry. So Mīrzā Aḥmad gave assurances to 'Alī Khān and sought permission to leave. 'Alī Khān dispatched Muḥammad 'Alī Beg Fārghānī with 1,000 musketeers to evacuate Dashtāb and take up position in Mashīz. Since the wound in Muḥammad Bāqir Khān's leg had rendered him immobile, after [Muḥammad 'Alī Beg] arrived in Dashtāb they decamped and set out.

'Alī Khān's forces entered Dashtāb immediately. Ten days later, Muḥammad Bāqir Khān and the others entered Mashīz. I was infuriated at what they had done, asking them, 'Why did you evacuate Dashtāb?' Mīrzā Aḥmad answered, 'Because I became certain that 'Alī Khān was deceiving you and making excuses, and with that many men would have captured Dashtāb, and we would have had no chance to give you aid.'

Given the pledges that 'Alī Khān had appended to the Word of God, I thought that Mīrzā Aḥmad was imagining things. The next day, Zulf 'Alī Sulṭān, who had lost a leg from cannon fire at the time of the siege of Bam, intercepted two riders carrying letters with them.

After reading the letters, it became clear that Aḥmad Beg and 'Alī Khān had written to Faḍl 'Alī Khān saying: 'We have assured the Aga Khan and his people that they will be fine and they are resting unaware in Mashīz. You, 'Abdullāh Khān, and the chiefs of Qandahār should

111 This is evidently the same Mīrzā Ḥusayn Khān mentioned previously.

make haste and arrive here from three directions, as tomorrow we will set up camp 2 *farsangs* away from Mashīz. Even if they turned into birds, we would not let a single one of them flee away from here. With the royal good fortune, the entire lot of them will be seized.' After reading this, I was in awe of 'Alī Khān's degree of manhood and integrity. So I said, 'To God belongs the command.'

Then I sent out messengers, and that evening after supper I ordered everyone to depart. I mounted my horse intending to invade 'Alī Khān's camp at night. But my brothers and Mīrzā Hādī Khān advised against it and said, 'Now that the situation has changed, we should go and capture Bam and wait to see what God decides.' After that decision was revoked, we set out towards Qaryat al-'Arab.[112]

The next day at noon we arrived in Qaryat al-'Arab, which was 24 *farsangs* away. We stayed there for one day and from there stage by stage we moved towards Bam, until we were 2 *farsangs* away. From there, I sent Mīrzā Abu'l-Ḥasan Khān[113] with fifty horsemen to capture Bam. The next day, we set out and entered [the town of] Bam. The citadel of Bam was equipped with a plethora of cannon in the hands of artillerymen from many lands.

We stayed in Bam for twenty-two days and launched numerous raids against the citadel, but without success. Then reliable news arrived that four camps had joined forces and that very day were arriving with 24,000 troops to make camp 2 *farsangs* away from us.

I saw no wisdom in confronting them, so we departed for Narmāshir. I aimed for the fortress of Rīgān, which was the biggest castle in Narmāshīr. After we arrived there, since the fortress was full of artillery our path was blocked. So we approached on foot and at midday I gave the order to attack. Six of my men were killed or wounded. After the victory we took the fortress and then I sent my brother Muḥammad Bāqir Khān to Āzād Khān Balūch[114] to bring him with his musketeers to help us in protecting our lives.

---

112 This is the present-day town of Gulzār in the Bardsīr district of Kirmān.

113 The Aga Khan's brother is referred to throughout the text variously with the titles Sardār or Mīrzā.

114 Āzād Khān Balūch was the ruler of the district of Khārān in Balūchistān, now in Pakistan.

The enemy troops arrived fourteen days later. At first light I gave orders to load up the supplies and the baggage, and I rode out with the cavalry to confront the enemy. Because the area was forested and there was no field for battle, the khāns said, 'We should ride out slowly behind the baggage, and these people will come as well. Wherever we find a field for battle, we will turn back and fight them.' I followed their advice and we moved about half a *farsang* away from the fortress.

As we moved away, the enemy became confident and gained speed in pursuing us, such that we were in range of their bullets. I turned back and shot at them, ordering everyone to turn back and shoot. Suddenly, our cavalry and Mīrzā Abu'l-Ḥasan Khān loosed their reins and fled. They also took my spare horses with them. It also happened that my horse took a bullet and there were no more than seven people left with me: Muḥammad Ja'far Khān, my nephew, Mīrzā Hādī Khān Khurāsānī, Muḥammad Raḥīm Muhrdār, Mīrzā Aḥmad, Mīrzā Ḥusayn Pīshkhidmat, Najaf 'Alī Beg and Malik Muḥammad Beg. And clearly what could seven people do against 24,000 infantry and cavalry, without Divine protection? Bullets and cannon fire showered down upon us from left and right, with the flags of the enemy raised up at all four corners around us.

Anyway, we continued to resist through fight and flight, until we reached a high hill in the afternoon, where Mīrzā Abu'l-Ḥasan Khān and other cavalrymen had taken up positions. I changed my horse there and we set out.

By a bizarre set of coincidences, amidst the fighting and retreating, two donkeys that had been tied together came to the front and the horse of Muḥammad Raḥīm [Muhrdār] became entangled in their rope. Najaf 'Alī Khān Beg rode up and cut the rope. At that moment, a bullet pierced the gunpowder magazine tied to his waist and his clothes caught fire. The entire body of that unfortunate man was burned all over, but he did not fall from his horse and he survived.

In summary, it was sunset when we reached a narrow defile where the enemy troops could not pursue us any further. They remained behind us at a distance of a *farsang*. We alighted there, performed the prayer, had our meal, and fed the horses. Then we rode out. It was dark and stormy, and there were difficult valleys to traverse on our way. As a result our people became separated. Half of them took one path and the other half took another. The next day, around noon, we met up at the foot of a high hill. At every stage, we were in the lead and the enemy kept following us.

I thought to myself and decided that proceeding in this manner would be of no use and would be a mere waste of life, even if I fought with these people like this for ten years. So I resolved to go to Bandar ʿAbbās through the Shamīl pass,[115] and from there I could board a ship to go to India or Arabia.

The next day, therefore, we entered the Shamīl pass with this purpose. The enemy troops stayed on the other side of the pass and it was 6 *farsangs* long. We had almost reached the end of the pass, when the cavalry who were at the front came back and said that there was a large number of musketeers who had blocked the pass on both sides and would not allow anyone to pass. I rode forward myself. It became evident that these musketeers had been stationed here well equipped for some time in order to defend the territories of Mīnāb[116] and Bandar ʿAbbās. I made every effort to negotiate with them and made promises of rewards for them, but it did not work. We had no choice but to turn back. We dismounted near a stream in the middle of the pass. We had no supplies at all and there was no oasis in the midst of those mountains, but only one peak after another. So I said to myself, 'The command belongs to God, the Unique, the Almighty.'

It was half an hour to sundown when, by Divine grace, a certain Darvīsh Nūrī showed up and said, 'Make a list of anything you need and I will bring it for you.' So, Mīrzā Aḥmad gave him a list of the supplies we required. He left and came back two hours later with all the necessary supplies, along with a few sheep. We stayed there for a few days next to the stream and the aforementioned dervish regularly brought us the supplies we needed.

On the third day, my brothers and two of my senior retainers came. I asked them, 'What is it you want?' Mīrzā Abu'l-Ḥasan Khān came forward and said, 'What we have in mind is that you either order us to break out of this pass, or give us leave to disperse in these mountains, so that each person can go his own way.' I said, 'If I order you to break through the pass, some people will be killed. If I tell you to scatter in the mountains, all of you will be killed. Be patient, with God's grace there will be a way out.'

---

115 This is a region in the Takht district of Bandar ʿAbbās in the province of Hurmuzgān.

116 Mīnāb is the capital of the county of Mīnāb in Hurmuzgān.

Abu'l-Ḥasan Khān said, 'It is impossible to find a way out of this predicament any longer. It will never happen.' I joked with him and said, 'What will you give me if we find a way out?' He said, 'I will pay you 100,000 *tūmāns*.' I said, 'That is wrong. Where would you get that money?' He said, 'I will charge towards an army of 50,000 people right in front of you.' I said, 'This is also wrong. You will be killed.' He said, 'I will confess that you are a prophet.' I said, 'This is also wrong. The Prophet was our ancestor. But I had a dream last night that the day after tomorrow, one and a half hours before sunset, two riders will come our way with papers. As soon as they arrive, we will depart.'

They returned to their positions. Two days later, at the hour that I had said, Mīrzā Abu'l-Ḥasan Khān approached me holding the reins of his horse. I said: 'Abu'l-Ḥasan Khān! It seems you have come at the promised hour!' So I told 'Alī Beg, the musketeer, 'Go up the hill and check if anyone is coming our way.' He climbed up further and said, 'I can see two riders approaching.' After a few minutes, they arrived and gave us their papers. I ordered the baggage and the horses to be prepared and we rode off.

The khāns of Kirmān and others had written altogether: 'We all pledge ourselves together in service. Come quickly, so that together we can attack the camp of Faḍl 'Alī Khān and 'Alī Khān.' But I did not trust them. I had made up my mind to go to Khurāsān but I did not reveal my resolve to anyone. We left the Shamīl pass and we reached Zarand[117] in seven days. We stayed there for a few days for the horses to rest and then moved towards Rāvar. I sent a few riders to tell 'Alī Riḍā Khān Rāvarī,[118] in case he was fearful. He sent his representative, Mullā Ḥusayn, in the company of my people, asking me to halt in Kūbanān.[119] As he requested, I stopped at Kūbanān and rested there.

The commander of artillery had set out from Tehran fully prepared to support Faḍl 'Alī Khān and had arrived in Yazd. 'Alī Riḍā Khān, like the other khāns, had become fearful. He therefore sent the 3,000 musketeers that he had stationed to protect Rāvar to Kūbanān to join my retainers. And he wrote to me, 'Within ten days, I will provide 10,000 musketeers

117 Zarand is the capital of the county of Zarand in Kirmān.

118 'Alī Riḍā Khān Rāvarī was the son of Mīrzā Shafī' Khān, the chief of the Rāvar region.

119 Also known as Kūhbanān, this is the capital of the present county of Kūhbanān in Kirmān and previously was in the county of Zarand.

in your service.' Thenceforth every day, four or five hundred of his musketeers arrived in Kūbanān and joined my troops.

Mīrzā Abu'l-Ḥasan Khān and some of my senior retainers began imagining things and repeatedly claimed: "Alī Riḍā Khān wishes to seize you by trickery in order to gain some credit in the eyes of government officials.' They kept repeating these claims, so much so that I had no choice but to order our departure. So I left 'Alī Riḍā Khān's musketeers and we departed.

The next day, we arrived at the foot of a hill that was adjacent to the territory of Yazd. Suddenly, Mullā Ḥusayn, the representative of 'Alī Riḍā Khān, arrived, yelling and tearing at his collar, asking, 'Why did you leave?' I felt deeply embarrassed and I told my brothers and all the troops: 'If there is any risk of being seized or killed, it is mine. And I will of course return. So anyone of you who wishes to accompany me, can come with me. And anyone who fears for his life can go, as they wish.'

So, I returned and all of them accompanied me, except my brother, Mīrzā Abu'l-Ḥasan Khān, and some other people whom I trusted. I said, 'Let them go under the protection of God,' and I told the troops: 'They will come back within ten days. Some of them will be injured and some of them will be captured. Some of them will come back with Abu'l-Ḥasan Khān in embarrassment.'

After entering Kūbanān, I stayed for one night. The next day, at the request of 'Alī Riḍā Khān, we moved to go to the renovated garden of Mīrzā Shafī' Khān, his father, which was close to Rāvar. We stayed there in utter tranquility for a few days. 'Alī Riḍā Khān did everything in his power to provide the best of service. Incidentally, on the tenth day, Mīrzā Abu'l-Ḥasan Khān arrived with four companions, the rest of them having been wounded or captured by the royal troops.

In summary, since I had made up my mind to go to Khurāsān, during the time that I spent in Rāvar I gave reassuring advice to 'Alī Riḍā Khān and made him feel comfortable. Then I informed my retainers of my intention and I gave them the choice either to accompany me or go back to their homelands.

The next day, we departed from there and set up camp near the Dasht-i Lūt.[120] Most of my companions left at night without giving notice and in

120 The Dasht-i Lūt is a large salt desert in eastern Iran which stretches across portions of Kirmān, Sīstān and Balūchistān.

the morning we rode out, placing our trust in God. Ismāʿīl Khān Ṭabasī was leading the way with some local guides. Since the Dasht-i Lūt was waterless, we moved quickly. Nonetheless, some of the animals such as ponies, falcons and hunting hounds died, until we had passed through the Dasht-i Lūt in the afternoon and waterskins sent for us from Nāybandān[121] arrived. I testify to God that it was the water of life which revived all the people and animals. Thank God that no man died, because Nādir Shāh was taken along the same route by the khāns of Ṭabas and two-thirds of his troops were either buried there in the sand or died of thirst.[122] Thank God, we all arrived in good health and that evening we arrived in Nāybandān. Since this place had pleasant air and water, we stayed there for two or three days.

From there, we decided to go to Qāʾin.[123] I sent Mīrzā Hādī Khān to Amīr Asadullāh Khān[124] to inform him. We travelled in a leisurely fashion, stage by stage, until we were one stage away from Qāʾin. Mīrzā Hādī Khān came back with apologies from the *amīr* as follows: 'Āṣaf al-Dawla[125] is my enemy and intends to ruin me, such that he has instigated the Nakhaʿī tribe[126] against me, and we are now in the middle of a dispute. If you come to Qāʾin, they will use it as a pretext to defame me before the King and put an end to my career.'

I found his apology reasonable and changed my course towards Sarbīsha.[127] There, the aunt of Amīr Asadullāh Khān insisted on entertaining us for eleven days and extended the highest degree of respect and service to me. I also reciprocated the respect as befitted her and her son. From there I decided to move to Qandahār, in order to be closer to my *murīd*s from every land.

---

121 Nāybandān is a large park and present-day wildlife sanctuary located in South Khurāsān.

122 On these events, which occurred in the last months of Nādir Shāh's life, see Michael Axworthy, *The Sword of Persia: Nader Shah, from Tribal Warrior to Conquering Tyrant* (London, 2006), p. 277.

123 This is the capital of the county of Qāʾin in South Khurāsān (formerly known as the province of Quhistān).

124 Amīr Asadullāh Khān was the governor of Qāʾin.

125 Allāhyār Āṣaf al-Dawla was a powerful chief of the Davlū clan of the Qājār tribe and the governor of Khurāsān under Muḥammad Shāh Qājār.

126 The Nakhaʿī are a major tribal community in eastern Iran who trace their origins back to Arabs who settled in Khurāsān in the early Islamic period.

127 This is the capital of the county of Sarbīsha in South Khurāsān.

I travelled stage by stage completely relaxed, until we reached Lāsh and Juwayn,[128] which are the first territories of Afghanistan. When I was about two stages away I sent a rider to Shāh Pasand Khān, who was the lord of the territory, to inform him of our arrival. We were one stage away when we received a reply from him, insisting that we halt 4 *farsang*s away from there to meet and then continue our journey. Many of my companions had all sorts of suspicions and rightly so, as there were many possible outcomes and the result could only be imagined. But I placed my trust in God and relied on my Protector. I rested peacefully, relying on fate and surrendering without worries, for 'God suffices as a guardian and God suffices as a witness.'

The next morning we rode out from our stopping point. At every mile and every *farsang* piles of fruit and good food reached us, as befitted his hospitality, until we reached a place 4 *farsang*s away from there, which was a very pleasant location with much fruit, such as melons, watermelons, cucumbers and other produce stockpiled there. We therefore dismounted there. On that day, in the utmost simplicity, I donned my plain wool robe and dervish headgear with its thread, and took up position at the appointed location. My retainers also took places in the vicinity to rest.

An hour later, Shāh Pasand Khān arrived with his children, grandchildren and relatives with all the luxury at his disposal, following proper protocol and extending the greatest respect. We met and after partaking of sweets, fruit and tea, we mounted our horses and moved slowly to the foot of the magnificent castle of Lāsh. We wanted to dismount from our horses but he stopped us and asked us to go up to the castle and stay in his residence. So, we all moved up to the citadel and dismounted there. This incident led to much affection and friendship on his side, because he had not let Kāmrān Shāh in,[129] who was his lord, along with four others, nor did he accord the same respect to his son, except by command. Therefore, this moment marked a fortuitous change in circumstances.

He obliged us to stay there for twelve days and spared no expense in hospitality. Then he agreed to let us leave and he himself accompanied

---

128 Lāsh and Juwayn refers to a district in the province of Farāh in present-day western Afghanistan.

129 Shāh Kāmrān Sadūzā'ī was the governor of Herat and son of the former ruler Shāh Maḥmūd Durrānī.

us to Juwayn. We observed all the formalities, as befitted me and him, and he sent 'Abd al-Qādir Khān, one of his relatives, and some riders with us and himself went back.

We then travelled stage by stage until we reached Girishk.[130] From there, I sent a rider to inform Prince Muḥammad Tīmūr,[131] the governor and Sir Major Rawlinson,[132] the collector of Qandahār. The khāns and a large number of nobles came to welcome us when we were 4 *farsang*s away from Qandahār. We entered Qandahār on 17 Dhu'l-Qa'da 1257 (30 December 1841) with great dignity.[133] We went to a house that had been appointed for us and the chief became our host.

After three days, we were allocated a stipend of 100 rupees a day for our accommodation and meals. After a few meetings, the prince and Sir Rawlinson wrote an account of the events that had befallen me and read them out to me too. I wrote a letter to Lord Macnaghten[134] and Shāh

---

130 Girishk is a town in the province of Helmand.

131 Shāhzāda Muḥammad Tīmūr was the son of the Afghan ruler Shāh Shujā' and British-appointed governor of Qandahār.

132 Henry Rawlinson (d. 1895) was a British officer and accomplished orientalist who served for many years in India, Iran and the Middle East. During the First Anglo-Afghan War, Rawlinson served as the British political agent in Qandahār. Rawlinson briefly mentions the Aga Khan in his *England and Russia in the East: A Series of Papers on the Political and Geographical Condition of Central Asia* (London, 1875), p. 67, in which he denies the allegations that the British provided support to the Aga Khan during his military actions in Kirmān. Rawlinson provides many additional notices on the Aga Khan and the Ismailis during this period in his unpublished papers, which have been examined at length in Zawahir Noorally, 'The First Agha Khan and the British, 1838–1868: A Study in British Indian Diplomacy and Legal History' (MA thesis, School of Oriental and African Studies, University of London, 1964).

133 The date given here is clearly an error. It is most likely that the Aga Khan arrived in Afghanistan not in December but sometime in the summer of 1841. The revolts against the British occupation of Kabul, which the Aga Khan indicates arose only after his arrival in Afghanistan, and which forced the British withdrawal from Kabul in January 1842, had already begun in September of 1841, while William Macnaghten, to whom the Aga Khan addressed a letter after arriving in Qandahār, was killed by the Afghan rebels on 23 December 1841 (see below note 134). Complicating matters further, Kirmānī misrepresents the date as Dhu'l-Qa'da 1258 (20 December 1842), which is followed without comment by Algar (p. 77), despite the obvious problems in chronology.

134 Sir William Hay Macnaghten was a civil servant with the British East India Company and one of the chief architects of the British invasion of

Shujāʿ,[135] and received very kind replies. Thus it was decided that I would capture Herat with their assistance and then reside there. But all these plans were not meant to be, because the disturbances in Kabul arose and the position of the British became precarious. Gradually these disturbance spread to Qandahār. The chiefs and khāns of Qandahār rebelled and chaos reigned. The Afghans of the city lost any credit they had had and most of them were expelled. The gates were turned into trenches and the roads were blocked to all traffic. Repeated battles took place and I was present in all of them, and in so far as I could help, I took care of the People of God (*khalq Allāh*).[136] Since the details of all these battles are recorded in the books of the English, this brief narrative suffices here. But by Divine grace, our *murīd*s from Peshawar, Kabul, Balkh, Bukhārā, Badakhshān and Sindh all reached Qandahār safely, despite the blocked roads.

When the siege had become prolonged, Prince Ṣafdar Jang,[137] Sardār Muḥammad ʿUmar Khān, and the other chiefs and rebelling khāns wrote a sealed letter to me, forcibly threatening me with the message, 'If you come out and join us then all will be well; otherwise, the first chance we get we will murder you and your men, and then all the English.'

Afghanistan, otherwise known as the First Anglo-Afghan War (1839–1842). During the war Macnaghten served as the British political agent in Kabul and was captured and killed on 23 December 1841 in the course of the uprisings that resulted in the British withdrawal from Kabul and their disastrous retreat through the Khyber Pass.

135 Shāh Shujāʿ (d. 1258/1842) was the son of the Afghan Durrānī *amīr* Tīmūr Shāh and ruled his father's kingdom from 1803 to 1809, when he was overthrown by his half-brother Maḥmūd Shāh. Shāh Shujāʿ was eventually granted asylum in British India and later selected to replace the Afghan ruler Dūst Muḥammad, effectively serving as the British puppet ruler in Kabul during the First Anglo-Afghan War. Shāh Shujāʿ was assassinated by Afghan rebels following the British retreat from Kabul.

136 Contrary to the claim by Hamid Algar ('The Revolt of Āghā Khān Maḥallātī', p. 77), the term *khalq Allāh* is not used in the text specifically in reference to the British. It appears a total of three times in the text, the first of which appears (see p. 95 above) in a context before the Aga Khan made contact with the British. In all three cases in which the term is used in the text, it is within a context in which the Aga Khan is exercising some sort of mediational role, with the term seemingly intended to refer generally to the people under his care and on whose behalf he sought to intercede.

137 Shāhzāda Ṣafdar Jang was a son of the Durrānī ruler Shāh Shujāʿ and one of the leaders of the rebel party who later reconciled with the British.

Then the news arrived that Shāh Shujā' has been killed. The British lords decided to evacuate Qandahār and they set fire to their excess stocks of gunpowder.[138] Then they summoned Prince Ṣafdar Jang and appointed him governor there and left the city. I also departed in the company of the British lords. The British remained outside the city for several days sorting out the business of Ṣafdar Jang, when Karīm Khān, the prince's retainer, came and said: 'The chiefs regret that the Aga Khan has left, for if he had stayed they could have dealt with him.' This report made me change my mind and I told Sir General Nott[139] and Major Rawlinson that I would return to Qandahār. They tried to dissuade me but I did not agree. So the next day, they left for Kābul and I returned to Qandahār.

I took up residence in the house of Mihrdil Khān,[140] which was situated amidst the houses of the other Afghans. Praise be to the True Protector, who instilled so much affection in the hearts of the prince and other chiefs that they would not grant me a moment's rest, day or night. Since I had decided that, given their position, the situation was beyond their ability to control, I did not find it appropriate to reside there any longer. On account of their affection, the prince and other chiefs did not want me to depart, and I therefore left Sardār Abu'l-Ḥasan Khān, my brother, in Qandahār. Out of consideration for the impoverished common folk, I wrote a letter to Kuhandil Khān,[141] saying: 'Come quickly to Qandahār, so that its people may find peace.' Then I departed.

Ṣafdar Jang divulged, 'A rebel, Ṣālū Khān Achakzā'ī, has blocked the road. You should wait for a couple of days, until I send some riders with you to assist you.' I did not agree and I set out. Even though the aforementioned person [Ṣālū Khān] had closed the roads and passes with 3,000 troops, I travelled without any issues. As soon as we met, he extended great courtesy to me and took us to his home, according us hospitality. I left on the third day and travelled until I arrived in

138 This occurred in August 1842.

139 General William Nott (d. 1845) was the British military commander in Qandahār.

140 Mihrdil Khān was one of the Afghan chiefs whom the Aga Khan had previously encountered occupying the fortress at Shahr-i Bābak.

141 Kuhandil Khān was another of the Afghan chiefs that the Aga Khan had previously fought at Shahr-i Bābak.

Shālkūt,[142] which was the territory of Malik Naṣīr Khān Kalātī.[143] From there, I sent a rider to inform Naṣīr Khān. He sent his deputy, Muḥammad Ḥasan, and the elders of his land to welcome us and extended great courtesy to us and hosted us with great honour.

From there I departed for Baylū[144] on the road to Sindh, and the late Mīr Naṣīr Khān extended great respect to us and gave us a few houses next to his citadel to accommodate me and my servants. After holding banquets for us, he allocated 100 rupees a day for the expenses of my people.

At that time, Sir General Charles Napier[145] and Sir Outram[146] were in Sindh. Their objective was that Mīr Naṣīr Khān would relinquish Karachi to them, but the aforementioned mīr would not submit to them. Mīr ʿAlī Murād Khān Khayrpūrī[147] agreed with the general and gradually the conflict became prolonged. Out of goodwill, I urged the mīrs: 'Turn over Karachi to the British and be satisfied with it, for whatever annual profit you receive from Karachi, the government of the British will grant more.' But they did not agree. They assembled their troops and set up camps outside Hyderabad. I also rode my horse and went to the camp of the aforementioned mīr. I first offered my counsel and goodwill, and

---

142 This is another name for the city of Quetta, the capital of Balūchistān in present-day Pakistan; see Edward Thornton, *A Gazetteer of the Countries Adjacent to India on the North-West; including Sinde, Afghanistan, Beloochistan, the Punjab, and the Neighbouring States* (London, 1844), vol. 2, pp. 187–188.

143 Mīr Muḥammad Naṣīr Khān Kalātī (d. 1261/1845) was the last independent ruler of Sindh whose ancestors had ruled over the territory since the late 18th century. This figure and the Aga Khan's relationship with the mīrs of Sindh is discussed further in the Introduction.

144 The identification of this place is uncertain, but it most likely refers to the present-day town of Bela in Balūchistān.

145 Major-General Sir Charles James Napier (d. 1853) was a British military officer known most famously for his conquest of Sindh in 1843. See further the discussion of this figure in the Introduction.

146 Major Sir James Outram (d. 1863) was a British military officer who served under Charles Napier during the Sindh campaign. Outram later wrote a history of the campaign that was highly critical of Napier's conduct towards the Sindhi *amīrs*, *The Conquest of Scinde: A Commentary* (Edinburgh, 1846).

147 Mīr ʿAlī Murād Khān Khayrpūrī was the ruler of the city and territory of Khaypūr in the province of Sindh, and he initially resisted the British but later cooperated with them.

tried to dissuade him from combat and encouraged him to leave Karachi, but to no avail.

Finally, he responded saying, 'Tomorrow, you will see the swords of the Tālpūr.'[148] I told him, 'In this case, it is contrary to the law of Islam for my servants and I not to assist you, but since all my servants have Persian garments, the Balūch of your army may not recognise them and confusion will result. Please give them some Sindhī garments to accompany you in battle.' He did not agree and said, 'You are our guest and I would never impose such an obligation upon you.'

So I arose and returned. They had plans to ambush Chahāvanī[149] at night and kill Sir Outram and all those present there. So that God might be content, I sent word at night and informed them about the scheme. They evacuated Chahāvanī at night and rode out on their mounts unharmed.[150]

The next day, when their forces were moving to confront the British army, I left Hyderabad[151] for Jerruck.[152] After the mīrs of Sindh were defeated and Hyderabad was conquered, and following the riot of the Balūch chiefs and the corruption created by Mīr Shīr Muḥammad Khān,[153] the British lords recognised me as a friend of the People of God (*khalq Allāh*). As befitting Muslim custom, they asked me to send some people to placate Mīr Shīr Muḥammad Khān and the other Balūch chiefs in order to put an end to the conflict without rancour.

I agreed to fulfil their request. Some people listened to my advice, but most of them did not accept it. Mīr Shīr Muḥammad Khān killed my messenger and made up his mind to fight the British army with guns and cannon. Sir General [Napier] made up his mind too and took my brother Muḥammad Bāqir Khān with him.

---

148 Tālpūr was the name of Naṣīr Khān's tribe.

149 This refers to the British cantonment near the city of Hyderabad in Sindh.

150 The author refers here to the events leading to the Battle of Miani on 14–17 February 1843.

151 References to Hyderabad refer to the city of this name in the Sindh province of present-day Pakistan, not to be confused with the city of the same name in present-day India.

152 Jerruck is a town along the Indus river in the Thatta district of Sindh.

153 Mīr Shīr Muḥammad Khān was another member of the Tālpūr tribe and the last chief of Sindh to offer military resistance to Napier's conquest of the province.

As per the request of the aforementioned Sir [Napier], the defence of the roads and the peace of the common people and residents from Jerruck to Karachi were turned over to my troops. I stationed my men in Langar of Thatta,[154] Karachi and at other points along the way. Then I took up position in Jerruck with twenty cavalry. Nearly 1,000 men and women of my *murīd*s from every land were in Jerruck and I was engaged in their affairs. Upon the movement of Mīr Shīr Muḥammad Khān, all the Balūch of Sindh and the vicinity rose up in his support and followed him. Some of them joined him and some did not get there. Altogether, there was Shīr Muḥammad Khān Nūmlī,[155] with 4,000 soldiers, and Muḥammad Khān Khushk[156] with 2,000 soldiers. Shīr Muḥammad Khān ambushed us one night in Jerruck, and in Langar of Thatta, Muḥammad Khān [Khushk] attacked my people and ten of my men were killed there. In Jerruck, seven of my men and seventy of my *murīd*s were killed or wounded. I rode out with several horsemen wearing only a single tunic and fought as long as I was conscious. In the midst of the battle my horse tripped over and rolled over on me. Four of my teeth broke and I was knocked unconscious. My brothers-in-arms lifted me up and carried me out of the battle.

During that incursion, an equivalent of 23 *lakhs*[157] were pillaged from my treasury and from my people, and the same amount was looted from my *murīd*s from every land and those living in Jerruck. Since Mīr

---

154 The term *langar*, meaning 'hostel', is found in the name of a number of locations in this region. It is not clear exactly which place is intended here, but it evidently refers to a village or camp in the vicinity of the city of Thatta in Sindh. Garmārūdī (p. 126, n. 358) suggests that it refers to a city by this name in the province of Punjab, but this is clearly not so. In the record of Napier's conquest of Sindh compiled by his brother, William Napier, he mentions the Aga Khan's posting at this time in Jerruck and at other unspecified sites along the road to Karachi; see William F. P. Napier, *The Life and Opinions of General Sir Charles James Napier* (London, 1857), vol. 2, p. 342.

155 As Garmārūdī notes (p. 127, n. 361), the *nisba* of this individual has probably been rendered incorrectly. The correct reading is likely to be either Nūmrī or Nūmirī, referring to a tribe of Rajput or possibly Arab origin who lived in the territory of Jerruck, of whom this individual was evidently one of their chiefs. See A. W. Hughes, *A Gazetteer of the Province of Sindh* (London, 1874), pp. 290–293.

156 This individual was evidently a chief of the Khushk tribe of the Balūch who lived in the Sindh region.

157 A *lakh* is a unit equal to 100,000.

Muḥammad Khān [Khushk] had been defeated and had already fled, Shīr Muḥammad Khān had given control of Jerruck to his guards and musketeers, and had left with all the furniture and the property he had pillaged.

The same night I entered Chahāvanī and spent several days making arrangements concerning the property until Sir General [Napier] returned. I sent my nephew, Muḥammad Ja'far Khān, along with Mīrzā Aḥmad and some retainers to Jerruck to bring the rest of the community members (*jamā'at*) and the wounded. They set out and took Jerruck back from the Balūch who had occupied the place. Then they brought the *jamā'at* and the wounded back to Chahāvanī in Hyderabad to attend to their treatment. Sir General [Napier] asked for an inventory of our plundered properties so as to demand them from the Balūch. But he advised that I should leave what they had plundered with the Balūch to pacify them and to bring peace to the land, and in return they would pay us from the office of the Company. After a while, when all the Balūch were pacified and peace was made, we were told that the Company office had not agreed to pay for my plundered property and had asked, 'Why did you not protect it yourself?' I said, 'My brother Sardār Muḥammad Bāqir Khān with all his cavalry accompanied you in battle with Shīr Muḥammad Khān at your request, some of my retainers were guarding the roads in Langar and Thatta, as per your order, and I myself was in Jerruck with twenty servants and my personal forces when this suddenly happened. How could I have fought 4,000 troops?' I did not receive any reasonably acceptable response. So I had no choice but to keep quiet and then I was also busy making preparations for my own affairs and those of my servants.

In the meantime, a certain Faqīr Muḥammad from Bamfahl arrived as the deputy of Muḥammad 'Alī Khān Balūch and brought some papers for Sir Charles Napier, the governor, and for me on behalf of Muḥammad 'Alī Khān.[158] The papers stated: 'The land of Sindh and Balūchistān is conquered by the officers of the British troops. I consider myself and my territory to belong to Britain and for this reason, Dīn Muḥammad Khān, Mīr Aḥmad Khān and the other khāns and chiefs of the Balūch are

---

158 Muḥammad 'Alī Khān Bampūrī was the son of the Balūch chief Miḥrāb Khān, with whom the British had signed a treaty in 1839. See Brian Spooner, 'Baluchistan i. Geography, History and Ethnography', *EIr.*

opposed to me and fight with me. If one of your brothers were to come here, I would hand over the fortress of Bamfahl and enter his service.'

I thought to myself that, even though Bamfahl was indeed on the border of Iran, it had always been in possession of Miḥrāb Khān Balūch,[159] the father of Muḥammad 'Alī Khān, and after him it will belong to his son. For some time now he had declined to acknowledge the authority of Iran. Even though, at the time when I was in Kirmān, I had sent my brother, Sardār Abu'l-Ḥasan Khān, to conquer that land [for the government of Iran], as I have mentioned previously, the officials of the government did not allow this to take place and I had to summon him before he could prevail and conquer the place. Now, in light of the request of Muḥammad 'Alī Khān, although it would not be necessary for me to inform the governor and there would be no harm if I sent [my brother] to conquer the land, nonetheless it would help to rectify things between us.

Therefore, in the month of Rabī' I 1260 (March–April 1844), I sent my brother, Sardār Muḥammad Bāqir Khān, fully equipped. After he arrived near Bamfahl he encountered Muḥammad 'Alī Khān and the latter voiced some disagreement, saying, 'First capture the forts of the khāns opposed to me and hand them over, and then I will surrender the fortress of Bamfahl to you.'

For this reason, they returned from Bamfahl, with Sālār Mulūk and Mīr Aḥmad Khān following them. Mīr Aḥmad Khān had evacuated the fortress of Payp, which was his residence, and turned it over. He pledged his service and sent an account of himself to me. I therefore allocated rewards and payments for the chiefs who had submitted. I provided all necessary support to my brother and appointed two of my *murīds* as agents there. One of them was in the port of Karachi and the other in the service of Sardār Muḥammad Bāqir Khān. I gave orders that even if it cost 10 *lakhs*, not to hold back but to make every effort to conquer Bamfahl.

On Thursday 26 Ramaḍān 1260 (9 October 1844), I set out by sea from Karachi to visit the *jamā'at* of my *murīds* living in Kutch and Bhuj.[160] It was the first time I had ever boarded a ship and the sea was stormy, but we arrived safely at Maddā'ī.[161] The ruler of the land was Maharaj Rao

159 See the previous note.

160 These are two cities of the Gujarat region of western India where there are large Ismaili Khoja communities.

161 This most likely refers to the present-day port city of Mandvi in Gujarat.

Desalji,[162] who was quite wise, chivalrous and mature, despite his young age. He came to the port of Maddā'ī and we had a meeting. Meanwhile, he asked that I go to Bhuj, which was his capital. I accepted the invitation and after visiting the *jamāʿat*s in the towns along the way, I changed course towards Bhuj. All arrangements were made to extend every courtesy to me on behalf of the maharaj, and he allocated a stately place as a lodging and everything else. I stayed in Bhuj for a month, attending to the affairs of the *jamāʿat* and the ruler extended his royal salutations and I proffered my humble ones. Then I moved towards Anjār.[163] After I finished attending to the business of the *jamāʿat* of that region, I departed for Hālār and Kathiawar.[164]

In Muḥarram 1261 (January–February 1845) I carried out the Muḥarram commemorations (*taʿziya*)[165] in honour of my ancestor Abū ʿAbdullāh[166] in Jamnagar.[167] I spent approximately one year in the territory of Kathiawar, Hālār and its environs, attending to the *jamāʿat* of those lands. Then I left for Daman from the port of Surat.[168] After carrying out the *taʿziya* in Muḥarram 1262 (December 1845–January 1846), at the end of the month of Ṣafar of the same year (January–February 1846) I departed for Bombay. After entering the aforementioned port I gave praise to God and to my glorious ancestors, from Adam to the Seal of the Prophets and His family, past and present.

And praise be to God, a permanent, primordial and eternal praise from this dervish who is descended from the fruit of the renowned, visible and pure tree, and is a remnant of the honoured luminescent one.[169] He was brought into this ruined tavern from the retreat cell of non-existence to the manifestation of the events embedded in past times, with a fate written for him in lightness and in dark, in difficulty

---

162 Maharaj Rao Desalji was the ruler of the Princely State of Cutch from 1819 until his death in 1860.

163 This is a city in the Cutch district of Gujarat of western India.

164 These are places along the Saurashtra peninsula in Gujarat.

165 The *taʿziya* is a ritual commemorating the martyrdom of the Prophet's grandson and the early Shiʿi Imam Ḥusayn on the tenth day (ʿĀshūrā) of the month of Muḥarram 61/680.

166 A reference to Imam Ḥusayn.

167 Jamnagar is a major city on the Saurashtra peninsula in Gujarat.

168 This is a port city on the western coast of India north of Bombay.

169 This is a reference to Fāṭima (known as al-Zahrā, 'The Luminescent'), the Prophet's daughter and the spouse of Imam ʿAlī.

and ease, in moments when I was neither forced nor in control of affairs, when I neither was nor was not in non-existence, and then through a single command I was blessed with the robe of the epiphany of His grace. Thereupon may praise be to Him at all times.

Sometimes in the company of dust
And sometimes dealing with the wind
Sometimes accompanying the sky
And sometimes face to face with the air.[170]
It doesn't matter if the body is ruined, since the soul is there.
It doesn't matter if a bubble has burst, as the Sea of 'Ummān is
still there.
Loss in the business of love is profit.
It doesn't matter if the soul perishes, since the beloved is there.[171]

And among the bounties inherited from my ancestors is the verse 'He is nearer to me than the jugular vein'[172] and 'We are closer to Him than ye.'[173] And by addressing us through the verse 'O Soul, at peace!'[174] he granted us an exalted tranquility. There is no deity but God and blessed is the Creator of all contingent individuals, who are described by existence and non-existence at the time of establishment, and are described at the time of negation by being neither existent or non-existent, but somewhere in between, who is the Creator of the contradiction and the ruler of the two paths. For, 'there is no will other than through God, the Almighty, the Great'. It is absurd that existence may be characterised by absence, and impossible that absence may be characterised by existence.

The man with a torn drum beautifully described this point:
A gnostic has no God and he is not created![175]
In this world, never be polluted by transient things.
Never let yourself be polluted by Winter and Spring.

---

170 Verse by Mujīr al-Dīn Baylqānī (d. 586/1190), here slightly modified.
171 Verse by Ḥazīn Lāhījī.
172 Qur'an 50:16: 'For We are nearer to him than his jugular vein.'
173 Qur'an 56:85.
174 Qur'an 89:27.
175 Verse by Qāsim-i Anvār.

O friend! For you this body is just a handful of dust.
Beware! Do not be polluted by this dust![176]

And it is evident that the Truth is pure light and pure darkness, even though light is never touched by darkness and darkness is never touched by light. Creation is a purgatory between light and darkness, because in His essence He is neither described by darkness nor by light, and 'God is the light of the heavens and the earth'[177] is the exaltation of the Creator, who is the protector of the protected and the contingent, 'that they should be in confused doubt about a new creation?'[178]

What was lost is in the past and where is what will come to you?
So arise and embrace the opportunity between two non-existents[179]
Let me not go astray, so that no one can tell me to return to the right path
Let me leave the path, so that they do not say of me that he misled others[180]
There was God and there was none with him
God is a witness that wherever I am, I am with him[181]
Nay, nay, I am wrong. I did not compose this song in time[182]
'And he is with us wherever we are'[183]
The beloved is the mirror of his majestic beauty
He is totally engrossed in gazing upon his own beauty
This jealous beauty does not tolerate love
He is Moses and his staff and Sinai and its mountain[184]
Glory be to God!
I know not whether I am awake or asleep.
I know not with whom I exchange these questions and answers.

---

176 Verse by Ḥazīn Lāhījī.
177 Qur'an 24:35.
178 Qur'an 50:15: 'Were We then weary with the first creation, that they should be in confused doubt about a new creation?'
179 Verse attributed to Imam 'Alī by Bahā' al-Dīn al-'Āmulī (d. after 787/1385).
180 Verse by Abu'l-Ḥasan 'Alī Āghājī Bukhārī (fl. 4th/10th century).
181 Verse by Ḥāfiẓ Shīrāzī.
182 Verse by 'Urfī Shīrāzī (d. 999/1591).
183 Qur'an 58:7.
184 Verse by Ḥazīn Lāhījī.

Surely, all these ravings are results of madness or consequences of the connivings of the artful, because he gave me ears to hear with and eyes to see with. Nay, nay, 'There is nothing like Him and He is the all-Hearing, the all-Seeing.'[185] What association does a mere silent one have with a speaking one?[186]

I have a heart filled with gems of secrets
But my lips are sealed[187]
With all that proximity and this much distance
How can I dream of placing tulips in my turban?
I do not remember what I was talking about,
Where I stopped, and why I stopped,
O friend! You are the light of the wakeful eye!
You are the beloved! You are the lover of encounter!
You are the chaos in the world, the disturbance in the market!
You are Joseph the Egyptian and his purchaser![188]

In summary, since no one is capable of describing the Truth, it is better to return to the original account. I have already related my dispatch of Sardār Muḥammad Bāqir Khān, as per the request and demand of Muḥammad ʿAlī Khān, to Bamfahl, and the disagreement of the latter with my brother and his excuses, and my order that even 10 *lakh*s should not be spared until Bamfahl was conquered. After some time, in order to strengthen the forces there and to consolidate endeavours to conquer the aforementioned land, I sent my other brother, Sardār Abu'l-Ḥasan Khān, fully equipped, to make every necessary effort to conquer Bamfahl. After the brothers were reunited, as is customary among the people of the time, some of the men gathered around the elder brother, Abu'l-Ḥasan Khān, and some others joined Muḥammad Bāqir Khān, and gradually they turned the unity of the brothers into enmity.

---

185 Qur'an 42:11.

186 The author evidently alludes here to the conception in Ismaili theology of the Imam as the 'silent' (*ṣāmiṭ*) successor to the 'speaking' (*nāṭiq*) Prophet and as the transmitter of the esoteric meaning of the scripture. On this, see further Wilferd Madelung, 'Aspects of Ismāʿīlī Theology: The Prophetic Chain and the God beyond Being', in Seyyed Hossein Nasr, ed., *Ismāʿīlī Contributions to Islamic Culture* (Tehran, 1398/1977), pp. 54–55.

187 Verse by Farīd al-Dīn ʿAṭṭār Nīshāpūrī (d. 618/1221).

188 Verse by Ḥazīn Lāhījī.

This news arrived after my entrance into the port of Bombay. I summoned my brother Muḥammad Bāqir Khān and I appointed Abu'l-Ḥasan Khān as commander separately. Gradually, Bamfahl and the other areas of Balūchistān were conquered and some peace of mind was achieved.

Suddenly, the ministers of the late King[189] requested through their foreign agents that I be not permitted to remain in Bombay and, by corrupting and persuading officials, they requested that I be moved to the port of Calcutta in Bengal. Simultaneously, they sent an army led by Faḍl 'Alī Khān[190] to Balūchistān against Abu'l-Ḥasan Khān. The capture of Bamfahl by conquest and military force would have been impossible, except through a blockade of food and provisions, and in the fortress of Bamfahl there were stockpiles to last for a year, and the Iranian forces could not have continued their siege of Bamfahl for longer than a month. Nonetheless, on account of discord among my perfidious servants, one night when the forces of Faḍl 'Alī Khān had despaired of victory and had decided to leave, 'Abd al-Raḥīm Khān, Muḥammad Qāsim Khān and Fatḥullāh Khān, who were among my trusted servants, along with several men, separately went with Mīrzā Abu'l-Ḥasan Khān to launch a night attack against the enemy's camp from one side, and then Sālār Mulūk and a group of riflemen emerged from the other side of the fortress. Abu'l-Ḥasan Khān's disloyal servants became lost and wandered about until close to morning, and had by morning wandered 7 or 8 *farsangs* away from the enemy's camp. Abu'l-Ḥasan Khān was rendered helpless. The next day at noon his horse collapsed and the remainder of his troops stayed in the rear. The traitorous 'Abd al-Raḥīm Khān passed by him and rode off. Then Abu'l-Ḥasan Khān and the fortress of Bamfahl were captured and conquered in a single day.

> 'So learn lessons, O you who have eyes to see!'[191]
> 'And to God, the one, the omnipotent belongs the Kingdom!'[192]
> The affairs of the world do not deserve regard
> There is no task better than disregarding them.

---

189 Muḥammad Shāh Qājār.

190 This refers to the same Faḍl 'Ali Khān Qarābāghī, the governor of Kirmān, who earlier fought against the Aga Khan and his men in Persia.

191 Qur'an 59:2.

192 Qur'an 40:16.

Do you know why I have chosen seclusion?
Because the world is so narrow there is no space to move![193]

In summary, my dispatch of Muḥammad Bāqir Khān to Bamfahl was entirely at the wishes and request of Muḥammad Khān Balūch. After the breaking of his promise and the manifestation of his treason, which was worthy of retaliation, out of two considerations I gave an order that the territory be removed from his control. The first was the punishment of Muḥammad ʿAlī Khān and the other for the amelioration of my brothers and servants. For Balūchistān is a land that has never been under the control of a single ruler, except for the brigand Balūch, whose life and wealth subsisted on plundering and pillaging wayfarers. Approximately 5 *lakh*s had been spent on capturing the territory, and Muḥammad ʿAlī Khān absconded and fled to the safety of the officials of Iran.

After two years, Faḍl ʿAlī Khān with a worthy army captured the territory in the manner that has been described. However, it is clear that there was no cause for this, apart from reversing my orders and the discord between the Balūch chiefs and my retainers. Following this, some of the chieftains of the border region opposed to Madad Khān Sarḥad,[194] who had been faithful in the service of my dear brother, were incited to plunder the environs of Bam and Narmāshīr. This was the consequence reaped by the ungratefulness and ingratitude for the blessings that each of them had received and the cause of the reversal of events.

Everyone will only reap what they sow.[195]
O Lord! what happens when your generosity assists us!
And your grace nurses the broken!
I have seen all the care that the people of the world can give,
Do not let my affairs be left to the care of any other than
yourself![196]

In Jamādī I 1263 (April–May 1847) I left Bombay for Bengal and travelled overland, in accordance with the wishes of both governments.

---

193 Verse by Ḥazīn Lāhījī.

194 Madad Khān Sarḥad was a local chief of the region along the border between Sīstān and the province of Balūchistān.

195 Verse by Ḥāfiẓ Shīrāzī.

196 Verse by Ḥazīn Lāhījī.

While I enjoyed an outpouring of respect and honour from the British officials and the rajas of every city and township along the way, according to their means and aptitude, nonetheless the intensity of the heat and the malodorous and pestilential wind brought much suffering, and several of my party perished before we reached Akbarābād.[197]

From there we set out by sail and steamship along the Ganga and Yamuna rivers towards Calcutta. After twenty days we reached Calcutta. We took up residence in the neighbourhood of Dum Dum, which the governor had designated for us. Indeed, despite the vastness of the territory, it was so well maintained that one could not imagine anything better. In short, from Akbarābād to Calcutta on both sides of the river, as far as the eyes could see, there were villages next to one another.

In total, we spent a year and eight months living in Dum Dum. During this time I lived near the [former] mīrs of Sindh, and I had good relations with them.[198] I carried out the customs of Shiʿism and I provided all the necessary support for the performance of the *taʿziya* commemorations during the days of ʿĀshūrā.

Although the late Mīr Naṣīr Khān was in the prime of his youth and at the beginning of his reign, he was a wayfarer on the path of the Jaʿfarī and the stages of the road of the Ithnāʿasharī. While this belief was in opposition to those of his relatives and family members, the candle of the friends of the Ahl-i Bayt has cast a ray of light upon the darkness of many of their hearts and changed them. His Excellency Captain Cavenagh,[199] who was a true gentleman, displayed no shortcomings in meeting all the requirements of affection and hospitality.

And Sir Maddock,[200] who was the deputy of the governor, made every effort to extend courtesy to us, showing us great hospitality. This was done despite the enormous pressure brought by the uprisings of the Singh

---

197 This is the former name of the city of Agra.

198 Following the annexation of Sindh, some of the former chiefs of Sindh who had fought against the British were exiled to Calcutta, including Naṣīr Khān. Thus, the Aga Khan found himself the neighbour of the same men whom he had fought against during his service with General Napier several years previously.

199 William Orfeur Cavenagh (d. 1891) was a British official who at that time served as superintendent of the former *amīrs* of Sindh. Cavenagh recounts his association with the Aga Khan in his *Reminiscences of an Indian Official* (London, 1884), pp. 74–77.

200 Sir Thomas Herbert Maddock (d. 1870) was the deputy-governor of Bengal from 1845 to 1849.

and Afghān tribes near Peshawar, Multan, Lahore and Punjab,[201] which, along with the support and provocations of Muḥammad Akbar Khān[202] and the masses of rioting crowds, gave the British lords not a moment's rest. For, after the events in Afghanistan and the efforts to remedy to some degree the losses that were suffered there, other incidents took place which did not leave them much peace. In addition to this, there took place a major event, during which, had [the British] not been agile and courageous, they could hardly have managed to stand against the cavalry, infantry and artillery of the Singh,[203] who were known for their courage and fighting skills throughout the world.[204] They fought hard and suffered enormous hardships, with many senior chiefs and lords killed in the process, but in the end the enemy was completely routed, and the wealth, property and inhabitants of the realm, both young and old, were secured.

Finally, after staying for twenty months in Dum Dum, I tired of living there and in Shawwāl 1264 (August–September 1848), I moved from Dum Dum to the town of Chinsura.[205] This town lies on the banks of the Ganges and the Yamuna. Its climate was quite moderate and its population, whether Persian or Indian or otherwise, made for agreeable company. Ḥājjī ʿAlī Lavāsānī, who was truly distinct among his peers in virtue, perfection, origin and nobility, and his brother, Āqā Kamāl, accompanied us at all times and became steadfast companions. Likewise, His Excellency Mīr Karāmat ʿAlī, who was the custodian of the Hooghly Imāmbāra,[206] was one of our close neighbours, and we spent a great deal

---

201 This refers to the events of the Second Anglo-Sikh War, fought from April 1848 to March 1849.

202 Muḥammad Akbar Khān became the *amīr* of Afghanistan following the death of Shāh Shujāʿ and the British retreat from Afghanistan, and ruled until his death in 1845. The author appears to have confused this figure with his successor, Dūst Muḥammad Khān, who had previously ruled Afghanistan until his overthrow by the British in 1839 and who supported the Sikhs in their conflict with the British.

203 This is a reference to the Sikhs.

204 The author is most likely referring here to the Battle of Chillianwala of January 1849, during which the British East India Company forces suffered enormous losses, although they were nonetheless victorious over the Sikh forces at the conclusion of the war.

205 Chinsura is a city in Bengal about 35 kilometres north of Calcutta.

206 An *imāmbāra* is an assembly building in the Twelver Shiʿi tradition used primarily for the performance of the Muḥarram ceremonies. The Hooghly Imāmbāra was founded in 1841 by the Shiʿi philanthropist Muḥammad Muḥsin.

of time in his company. His Excellency excelled in the virtues of the age and surpassed the scholars and *'ulamā'* of the day in his learning. My association and friendship with him brought much cheer.

At the end of the month of Dhu'l-Ḥijja 1264 (late November 1848) the dreadful news came of the inevitable event, that the King Muḥammad Shāh had attained Eternity, may he rest in peace.[207] Truly, this was the cause of much grief and sorrow, and having no recourse except through weeping and mourning, I therefore carried out the *ta'ziya* according to custom and I had the *Fātiḥa* read in his name in conjunction with the commemoration of the calamity of my great ancestor, the Master of the Martyrs, a thousand prayers and blessings be upon him.[208]

After the time of 'Āshūrā 1265 (6 December 1848), I sent my felicitations for the auspicious ascension of the new King, Nāṣir al-Dīn Shāh, and on the twelfth of Muḥarram (8 December 1848) I set out by steamship with great confidence for Bombay. After I had entered Bombay, the news of the Bābī uprising in Māzandarān and the Sālār insurrection in Khurāsān spread far and wide.[209] I thought to myself that if I were to set out for Iran unannounced and without seeking the approval of the government, then I would once again fall prey to the designs of the scheming officials, as yet again the events of the past would be recalled and a simple affair would be rendered difficult. It would be better to remain patient and composed for some time, and to settle here until the thorn of corrupt and defiant enemies was removed from the garden of the government and then irrigated with Divine grace. Then I would dispatch a petition with an announcement of partnership and collegiality, and at that time I would set off to perform the pilgrimage to the Ka'ba. Amidst all this, I composed a sincere letter to the late Chief Minister Mīrzā Taqī Khān.[210] But since I had addressed the letter to the 'August Master' (*makhdūm-i mukarram*), he was apparently displeased.

---

207 Muḥammad Shāh in fact died in September 1848 but the news evidently did not reach the Aga Khan in Calcutta until two months later.

208 This is a reference to Imam Ḥusayn.

209 The author refers here to two major revolts that broke out in Iran upon the ascension of Nāṣir al-Dīn Shāh to the Qājār throne in late 1848; on these events, see further Abbas Amanat, *Pivot of the Universe: Nasir al-Din Shah Qajar and the Iranian Monarchy, 1831–1896* (Berkeley, 1997), pp. 109–116.

210 Mīrzā Taqī Khān, known as Amīr Kabīr, served as the first chief minister under Nāṣir al-Dīn Shāh from 1848 until his sudden dismissal and execution in 1852. Despite his relatively short time in office, he was nonetheless

In the meantime, Mīrzā Ḥusayn Khān,[211] son of the late Mīrzā Nabī Khān, was appointed to the Iranian consulate of Bombay and entered the city. Upon his arrival, I extended all kinds of courtesies to him, as befitted officials of the royal government. I was the foremost in the purchasing of gifts for him and the first to offer my prayers for him and to pledge my vows of support. My relatives, retainers and the rest of the businessmen, merchants, and Iranian immigrants there followed me in proffering their services.

In summary, day by day, I expressed my agreement and devotion to His Excellency and I hoped that they would reciprocate and accord me due respect, showing me kindness. I imagined that after all the losses I had sustained during the time of the late King, they would now restore me and allow me to return to my homeland, along with my family and children who had fled. But suddenly, the reed flute of fate began to play a different melody, and I once again encountered the meaning of the tradition, 'I came to know God through the revocation of decisions.'[212] I received word through the messenger of the Chief Minister, who had sought after me, offering promises on the condition that I would return via the port of Būshihr.[213]

I said to myself, 'To God be Glory! With all this prominence, why should I choose servitude? The wise do not put themselves in the shackles of enemies while they are free by their own will. Even though Divine fate sometimes agrees with the calculations of the true servants, yet it will never agree with hypocrisy.'

Then, once again I assessed the situation and found the heart of His Majesty the King to be kind and pure towards me. So, I realised that this was also a result of the actions of selfish and conceited

---

one of the most powerful and influential figures of the Qājār era and was responsible for initiating a number of critical modernising reforms. See further Hamid Algar, 'Amīr-e Kabīr, Mīrzā Taqī Khan', *EIr.*

211 Mīrzā Ḥusayn Khān was from a prominent family of Iranian bureaucrats and a son-in-law of Fatḥ 'Alī Shāh. He later also became a riding companion of the Aga Khan.

212 This is a saying attributed to Imam 'Alī.

213 Būshihr is a major port city on the Persian Gulf. As the author alludes in the following lines, Amīr Kabīr also stipulated that the Aga Khan would be required to surrender as a fugitive upon his arrival in Iran; see Algar, 'The Revolt of Āghā Khān Maḥallātī', p. 80.

ministers. Therefore, I reverted the issue to the justice of the Universal Judge. Yes,

> The people of our age would not give dregs to the Pure Ones
> And never would they give up straw for amber.
> These people are lords of the ones like themselves,
> As long as they have a dog around, they would not give the bone to Humā![214]

In summary, my sincerity and inner affection towards His Majesty the King increased, and I prayed day and night for the prolongation of his life and the perpetuation of his reign. I could imagine nothing better than this, and may God be praised at all times.

> The heart is a servant of love and has a guardian,
> The wandering soul and body does have a guide![215]

In order to transport the bier of my late mother,[216] may she rest in peace, and for a change of climate, and in response to the requests of my *murīd*s from different places, I left Bombay and began travelling for about a year. When I returned, I received the news of the downfall of Mīrzā Taqī Khān and the rise of Mīrzā Āqā Khān Nūrī[217] to the position of Chief Minister. Since I was acquainted with the aforementioned individual and had had good relations with him since the days of the late King, I considered this to be good omen. I sent a gift of an elephant and a giraffe to the royal court, along with other gifts for Mīrzā Āqā Khān and his son Niẓām al-Mulk, alongside my petition. My thoughts grew brighter because of the abundance of affection and royal favour, as several of my ancestral properties were restored to my agents as a sign of goodwill. I was overjoyed and began preparing my relatives and dependents to move to that land. The commands issued from the sphere of Mīrzā Āqā Khān revealed his good nature, so much so that the phrase 'May God's mercy be first upon the grave robbers' was constantly on one's tongue.

---

214 Verse by Ḥazīn Lāhījī.

215 Verse by Ḥazīn Lāhījī.

216 The Aga Khan's mother, Bībī Sarkāra, died in the city of Cutch in 1267/1851.

217 Mīrzā Āqā Khān Nūrī (d. 1281/1865), known as I'timād al-Dawla, served as chief minister under Nāṣir al-Dīn Shāh Qājār from 1851 to 1858.

In summary, in the time of His Excellency's ministry this verse was constantly on one's tongue:

This is a time when, due to great injustice
It is impossible for anyone to have any peace.
Who can we expect goodness from at such time?
When if people do not do anything evil, it is considered the
utmost of benevolence!

In the end, the properties granted by the King were reverted, although I had no notion of profiting from those properties other than that the sayyids might be supported and that they might offer prayers in support of the King and his reign. Now, it is evident to all the people concerned with justice how evil-natured this confidant of the royal court was, while his piety in attending to the obligations of the realm and its people have become clear. Hence, it is no wonder if one resorts to the dictum, 'May God bless the soul of all the predecessors!' Alas! 'Where is a man at the time of greed and lust?!'[218]

When I look at those raised and nurtured by the government and the royal court at the time of the late King or in this government until today, which is the year 1278/1861–1862, from whatever I have seen and assessed, I testify to God that I have seen nothing except vile nature, evil intentions and treason against their master, destroying the land and the common people. They seek nothing but the accumulation of wealth by coercion and bribery, which is more licit to them than their mother's milk. However, it is apparent that today there are those who are well-trained and good-natured who are presently engaged in the service of the government and in caring for the army and the common people, and who are agreeable in the eyes of the people. May they, God willing, all have long lives and good health in the service of the realm, for it is said:

Everyone will reap what they sow![219]
For me, even though
For some time my heart pursued desires
My soul became a target for the offences of the enemies

---

218 Verse by Jalāl al-Dīn Rūmī.
219 Verse by Ḥāfiẓ Shīrāzī.

Since my path was blocked on all sides
The path to the beloved's abode emerged![220]
O pain! You are the cure of the injured heart!
You are the lover, the love and the beloved!
You are the compass! You are the centre! You are the circle!
This means you are manifest through every veil![221]

Finally, I relinquished all desires and whims. I lost the lordship which was in my heart through the tumultuous events that transpired after the damage to my leg. I told myself:

You travelled all the universe!
You saw everything that deserved to be seen by your eyes!
Now, let go of these colours and perfumes!
How long will you remain trapped by fears and hopes?[222]

In these recent years I have passed the time in relaxation and horse-racing, sometimes inclining towards hunting, at other times conversing with the people of the age, while at other times taking the hand of the exhausted or sitting with the indigent, or observing the world with the people of knowledge.

In the quarter of the tavern, there are many men
Who can decipher secrets from the tablet of existence,
Outside the wonders of the conditions of the world
They are aware of secrets but they lead their normal lives.[223]

My purpose in writing about these events was to give some signs to the people who observe the events of the world and its inhabitants, so that, in every situation, with a knowledge of what has passed and what will come, they may find a solution, and so that they may consider the Almighty creator to be the Originator of the World and all the contingencies in the universe. He is the One who has no partners or opponents.

---

220 Verse by Ḥazīn Lāhījī.
221 Verse by Ḥazīn Lāhījī.
222 Verse by Ḥazīn Lāhījī.
223 Verse by Shihāb al-Dīn Yaḥyā Suhravardī (d. 587/1191).

His sanctified essence is not conjoined, but rather is elementary, and He governs things.

He is neither matter nor material. He has neither any direction nor any place. Seeing Him is not possible, other than through spiritual eyes. Observing Him is not possible other than through the sight of the speaking soul, which is purified of material pollution. His sanctified essence has no association with any origin or station. Existence and annihilation cannot penetrate the courtyard of His majesty. He is the One who bestows life and the One who takes away life, and the One who provides daily sustenance for all created things. His worthiness of worship is His station, His glory, and His greatness.

> Not a thorn would cut anything without his will.
> Not a hair would be ruptured without his will.[224]

Thus concludes the exalted book of *ʿIbrat-afzā*, in accordance with the order of the chief of glory, majesty and dignity, to whom is conjoined greatness and magnificence, partnered with sayyid-hood, generosity and bravery. He laid out the foundation of peace and security, and destroyed the foundations of injustice and rebellion. He is the one who increases the allotment of the pensioners of the family of Muṣṭafā, the blossoms of the meadow of Murtaḍā, and the buds of the garden of the Ḥusaynī sayyids. He is the ocean of kindness and munificence, the one who mends hearts broken by poverty and destitution: Muḥammad Ḥasan al-Ḥusaynī, known as the Āqā Khān, may God prolong his glory and majesty. This was transcribed by the most humble of the pilgrims and servants of God, Muḥammad Ibrāhīm, known as Āqā, with the penname Ṣafā, son of the late Muḥammad Ḥusayn Khān Awliyā Samīʿ Shīrāzī, may his soul be sanctified in the ocean of God's mercy.[225] It was completed at the port of Bombay and printed in the factory of Dādū Mīyān[226] in the month of Ramaḍān 1278 (March–April 1862).

---

224 Verse by Nūr al-Dīn ʿAbd al-Raḥmān Jāmī (d. 898/1492).

225 Muḥammad Ibrāhīm Awliyāʾ samīʿ Shīrāzī was a well-known poet and calligrapher from Shīrāz who travelled to India and worked for a number of years in Bombay and Hyderabad as a scribe, bookseller and teacher. He later returned to Iran and died in Shīrāz in 1301/1884.

226 According to Garmārūdī (p. 163, n. 505), this was the printing house of ʿAbd al-Ghafūr b. Muḥammad b. ʿAbdullāh Dihāʾilī, known as Dādū Miyān.

Bibliography

Abbreviations

EI2 *The Encyclopaedia of Islam*. New ed., Leiden and London, 1960–2004.
EIr *Encyclopaedia Iranica*. London and New York, 1982–.

Abisaab, Rula Jurdi. *Converting Persia: Religion and Power in the Safavid Empire*. London, 2004.
Ādamīyat, Farīdūn. *Amīr Kabīr va Īrān*. Tehran, 1362 Sh./1983.
'Aḍud al-Dawla, Aḥmad Mīrzā. *Tārīkh-i 'Aḍudī*, ed. Kāẓim 'Ābidīnī Muṭlaq. Qumm, 1388 Sh./2009.
Aga Khan, Muḥammad Ḥasan al-Ḥusaynī. *'Ibrat-afzā*, ed. Ḥusayn Kūhī Kirmānī. Tehran, 1325 Sh./1946.
———. *'Ibrat-afzā: khāṭirāt-i Āqā Khān Maḥallātī*, ed. Muḥsin Mūsavī Garmārūdī. Mashhad, 1393 Sh./2015.
Aga Khan III, Sultan Muhammad Shah. *The Memoirs of Aga Khan: World Enough and Time*. London, 1954.
———. *Selected Speeches and Writings of Sir Sultan Muhammad Shah*, ed. K. K. Aziz. 2 vols. London, 1998.
Akhtar, Iqbal. *The Khōjā of Tanzania: Discontinuities of a Postcolonial Religious Identity*. Leiden, 2016.
Āl-i Dāvūd, Sayyid 'Alī. 'Abu'l-Ḥasan Khān Bīglarbigī Maḥallātī', in *Dā'irat al-Ma'ārif-i Buzurg-i Islāmī*, vol. 5, ed. Kāẓim Musavī Bujnurdī (Tehran, 1382 Sh./1993), pp. 339–341.
Alder, G. J. 'The Key to India? Britain and the Herat Problem 1830–1863: Part I', *Middle Eastern Studies*, 10 (1974), pp. 186–209.
———. 'The Key to India? Britain and the Herat Problem 1830–1863: Part II', *Middle Eastern Studies*, 10 (1974), pp. 287–311.
Algar, Hamid. *Religion and State in Iran, 1785–1906: The Role of the Ulama of the Qajar Period*. Berkeley, 1969.
———. 'Religious Forces in Eighteenth and Nineteenth-Century Iran', in Peter Avery, Gavin Hambly and Charles Melville, ed., *The Cambridge History of Iran*, Volume 7: *From Nadir Shah to the Islamic Republic*. Cambridge, 1991, pp. 705–731.

———. 'Shi'ism and Iran in the Eighteenth Century', in T. Naff and R. Owens, ed., *Studies in Eighteenth Century Islamic History*. Carbondale, 1977, pp. 288–302.

———. 'The Revolt of Āghā Khān Maḥallātī and the Transference of the Ismā'īlī Imāmate to India', *Studia Islamica*, 29 (1969), pp. 55–81.

———. 'Āqā Khan', *EIr*.

———. 'Amīr-e Kabīr, Mīrzā Taqī Khan', *EIr*.

———. 'Maḥallātī, Āg͟hā K͟hān', *EI2*.

Algar, Hamid, and J. Burton-Page. 'Ni'mat-allāhiyya', *EI2*.

Ali, Syed Mujtaba. *The Origin of the Khojāhs and Their Religious Life Today*. Bonn, 1936.

Allen, Isaac Nicholson. *Diary of a March through Sinde and Affghanistan with the Troops*. London, 1843.

Amanat, Abbas. *Pivot of the Universe: Nasir al-Din Shah Qajar and the Iranian Monarchy, 1831–1896*. Berkeley, 1997.

———. 'The Downfall of Mirza Taqi Khan Amir Kabir and the Problem of Ministerial Authority in Qajar Iran', *International Journal of Middle East Studies*, 23 (1991), pp. 577–599.

———. 'Āqāsī, Ḥājjī Mīrzā Abbās Īravānī', *EIr*.

———. 'Herat vi: The Herat Problem', *EIr*.

Ansari, Sarah F. D. *Sufi Saints and State Power: The Pirs of Sind, 1843–1947*. Cambridge, 1992.

Arberry, Arthur J. *Sufism: An Account of the Mystics of Islam*. London, 1950.

Arjomand, Said Amir. *The Shadow of God and the Hidden Imam: Religion, Political Order and Societal Change in Shi'ite Iran from the Beginning to 1890*. Chicago, 1984.

Asani, Ali S. 'From Satpanthi to Ismaili Muslim: The Articulation of Ismaili Khoja Identity in South Asia', in Farhad Daftary, ed., *A Modern History of the Ismailis: Continuity and Change in a Muslim Community*. London, 2011, pp. 95–128.

———. 'The Khojahs of Indo-Pakistan: The Quest for an Islamic Identity', *Journal of the Institute of Muslim Minority Affairs*, 8 (1987), pp. 31–41.

Ashraf, Muhammad. *A Catalogue of Persian Manuscripts in the Salar Jung Museum & Library*, Vol. 2. Hyderabad, 1965.

Ashrafī, Majīd. *Ḥājj Mīrzā Āqāsī: Ṣadr-i a'ẓam-i Muḥammad Shāh Qājār*. Tehran, 1386 Sh./2008.

Aubin, Jean. 'De Kûhbanân à Bidar: La Famille Nimatullahī', *Studia Islamica*, 20 (1991), pp. 233–261.

Avery, Peter. 'Nādir Shāh and the Afsharid Legacy', in Peter Avery, Gavin Hambly and Charles P. Melville, ed., *The Cambridge History of Iran*, Volume 7: *From Nadir Shah to the Islamic Republic*. Cambridge, 1991, pp. 3–62.

Axworthy, Michael. *The Sword of Persia: Nader Shah, from Tribal Warrior to Conquering Tyrant*. London, 2006.

Babayan, Kathryn. *Mystics, Monarchs and Messiahs: Cultural Landscapes of Early Modern Iran*. Cambridge, MA, 2002.

———. 'The Safavid Synthesis: From Qizilbash Islam to Imamite Shi'ism', *Iranian Studies*, 27 (1994), pp. 135–161.

Baker, Robert L. 'The Aga Khan: Moslem Pontiff', *Current History*, 42 (1935), pp. 591–597.

Bāmdād, Mahdī. *Sharḥ-i ḥāl-i rijāl-i Īrān dar qarn-i 12, 13, 14 hijrī*. Tehran, 1347 Sh./1968.

Bāstānī Pārīzī, Muḥammad Ibrāhīm. *Farmānfarmā-yi ʿālam*. Tehran, 1364 Sh./1985.

Beben, Daniel. 'The Legendary Biographies of Nāṣir-i Khusraw: Memory and Textualization in Early Modern Persian Ismāʿīlism'. PhD dissertation, Indiana University, 2015.

———. 'The Fatimid Legacy and the Foundation of the Modern Nizārī Ismaili Imamate', in Farhad Daftary and Shainool Jiwa, ed., *The Fatimid Caliphate: Diversity of Traditions*. London, 2018, pp. 192–216.

———. 'Remembering Saladin: The Politics of Heresy and the Legacy of the Crusades in Persian Historiography', *Journal of the Royal Asiatic Society*, 28 (2018), pp. 231–253.

———. 'Re-imagining *Taqiyya*: Strategies of Secrecy among the Ismāʿīlīs of Central Asia', in A. Akasoy, L. Di Giacinto, et al., ed., *Religious Secrecy as Contact: Secrets as Promoters of Religious Dynamics*. Leiden, forthcoming.

Bliss, Frank. *Social and Economic Change in the Pamirs, Tajikistan*. London, 2005.

Boivin, Michel. *La rénovation du Shīʿisme Ismaélien en Inde et au Pakistan*. London, 2003.

———. 'New Problems Related to the History and to the Tradition of the Āghākhānī Khojahs in Karachi and Sindh', *Journal of the Pakistan Historical Society*, 46 (1998), pp. 5–33.

———. 'Contestation et identité chez les Khojas Indo-Pakistanais (1866–1986)', *Lettre d'information – La transmission du savoir dans le monde musulman peripherique*, 17 (1997), pp. 4–23.

Bos, Matthijs van den. *Mystic Regimes: Sufism and the State in Iran, from the late Qajar Era to the Islamic Republic*. Leiden, 2002.

Brown, Peter. *The Cult of the Saints: Its Rise and Function in Latin Christianity*. Chicago, 1981.

———. 'The Rise and Function of the Holy Man in Late Antiquity', *Journal of Roman Studies*, 61 (1971), pp. 80–101.

Busse, Heribert. 'Kermān im 19. Jahrhundert nach der Geographie des Wazīrī', *Der Islam*, 50 (1973), pp. 284–312.

———. 'Abu'l-Ḥasan Khan Maḥallātī', *EIr*.

Cavenagh, Orfeur. *Reminiscences of an Indian Official*. London, 1884.

Daftary, Farhad. *The Ismāʿīlīs: Their History and Doctrines*. Cambridge, 2nd ed. Cambridge, 2007.

———. *Ismaili Literature: A Bibliography of Sources and Studies*. London, 2004.

———. *The Assassin Legends: Myths of the Ismaʿilis*. London, 1994.

———. 'Ismaili–Sufi Relations in Post-Alamut Persia', in F. Daftary, *Ismailis in Medieval Muslim Societies*. London, 2005, pp. 183–203.

———. 'Shāh Ṭāhir and the Nizārī Ismaili Disguises', in Todd Lawson, ed., *Reason and Inspiration in Islam: Theology, Philosophy and Mysticism in Muslim Thought: Essays in Honour of Hermann Landolt*. London, 2005, pp. 395–406.

———. 'The Isma'ilis and the Crusaders: History and Myth', in Zsolt Hunyadi and József Laszlovszky, ed., *The Crusades and the Military Orders: Expanding the Frontiers of Medieval Latin Christianity*. Budapest, 2001, pp. 21–41.

———. 'The "Order of the Assassins": J. von Hammer and the Orientalist Misrepresentations of the Nizari Ismailis', *Iranian Studies*, 39 (2006), pp. 71–81.

———. 'Kitābī na-chandān muhim dar tārīkh-i Ismā'īliyya', *Nashr-i Dānish*, 4 (1984), pp. 32–37.

———. 'Isma'ilism i: Isma'ili Studies', *EIr.*

———. 'Fedā'ī Khorāsānī', *EIr.*

Dalrymple, William. *Return of a King: The Battle for Afghanistan, 1839–42*. New York, 2013.

DeWeese, Devin. 'The Politics of Sacred Lineages in 19th-Century Central Asia: Descent Groups Linked to Khwaja Ahmad Yasavi in Shrine Documents and Genealogical Charters', *International Journal of Middle East Studies*, 31 (1999), pp. 507–530.

Digby, Simon. 'The Sufi Shaikh as a Source of Authority in Medieval India', in Richard M. Eaton, ed., *India's Islamic Traditions, 711–1750*. Delhi, 2003, pp. 234–262.

———. 'The Sufi Shaykh and the Sultan: A Conflict of Claims to Authority in Medieval India', *Iran: Journal of the British Institute of Persian Studies*, 28 (1990), pp. 71–81.

Dumasia, Naoroji M. *The Aga Khan and His Ancestors: A Biographical and Historical Sketch*. Bombay, 1939.

———. *A Brief History of the Aga Khan*. Bombay, 1903.

Eaton, Richard M. *The Sufis of Bijapur, 1300–1700: Social Roles of Sufis in Medieval India*. Princeton, 1978.

Eboo Jamal, Nadia. *Surviving the Mongols: Nizārī Quhistānī and the Continuity of Ismaili Tradition in Persia*. London, 2002.

Ekhtiar, Maryam. 'Innovation and Revivalism in Later Persian Calligraphy: The Visal Family of Shiraz', in Doris Behrens-Abouseif and Stephen Vernoit, ed., *Islamic Art in the 19th Century: Tradition, Innovation, and Eclecticism*. Leiden, 2006, pp. 257–280.

Fasā'ī, Mīrzā Ḥasan Ḥusaynī. *Fārs-nāma-yi Nāṣirī*, tr. Heribert Busse as *History of Persia under Qājār Rule*. New York, 1972.

Fidā'ī Khurāsānī, Muḥammad b. Zayn al-'Ābidīn. *Hidāyat al-mu'minīn al-ṭālibīn*, ed. A. A. Semenov. Moscow, 1959; reprinted, Tehran, 1362 Sh./1983.

Forsyth, Douglas. *Report of a Mission to Yarkund in 1873*. Calcutta, 1875.

Fraser, James Baillie. *Narrative of a Journey into Khorasan in the Years 1821 and 1822*. London, 1825.

Frere, Bartle. 'The Khojas: The Disciples of the Old Man of the Mountain', *Macmillan's Magazine*, 34 (1876), pp. 342–350, 430–438.

Gellner, Ernest. *Saints of the Atlas*. London, 1969.

Gordon, T. E. *The Roof of the World; being the narrative of a journey over the high plateau of Tibet to the Russian frontier and the Oxus sources on Pamir*. Edinburgh, 1876.

Graham, Terry. 'The Niʿmatu'llāhī Order Under Safavid Suppression and in Indian Exile', in Leonard Lewisohn and David Morgan, ed., *The Heritage of Sufism*, Volume 3: *Late Classical Persianate Sufism (1501–1750)*. Oxford, 2000, pp. 165–200.

———. 'Shāh Niʿmatullāh Walī: Founder of the Niʿmatullāhī Order', in Leonard Lewisohn, ed., *The Legacy of Mediaeval Persian Sufism*. London, 1992, pp. 173–190.

Green, Nile. *Sufism: A Global History*. Malden, 2012.

———. *Bombay Islam: The Religious Economy of the Western Indian Ocean, 1840–1915*. Cambridge, 2011.

———. *Islam and the Army in Colonial India: Sepoy Religion in the Service of Empire*. Cambridge, 2009.

———. *Indian Sufism since the Seventeenth Century: Saints, Books and Empires in the Muslim Deccan*. London, 2006.

———. 'Making Sense of "Sufism" in the Indian Subcontinent: A Survey of Trends', *Religion Compass*, 2 (2008), pp. 1044–1061.

———. 'The *Faqir* and the Subalterns: Mapping the Holy Man in Colonial South Asia', *Journal of Asian History*, 41 (2007), pp. 57–84.

———. 'Blessed Men and Tribal Politics: Notes on Political Culture in the Indo-Afghan World', *Journal of the Economic and Social History of the Orient*, 49 (2006), pp. 344–360.

———. 'A Persian Sufi in British India: The Travels of Mīrzā Ḥasan Ṣafī ʿAlī Shāh (1251/1835–1316/1899)', *Iran: Journal of the British Institute of Persian Studies*, 42 (2004), pp. 201–218.

Grondelle, Marc van. *The Ismailis in the Colonial Era: Modernity, Empire and Islam*. New York, 2009.

Gross, Jo-Ann. 'Multiple Roles and Perceptions of a Sufi Shaykh: Symbolic Statements of Political and Religious Authority', in Marc Gaborieau, Alexandre Popovic and Thierry Zarcone, ed., *Naqshbandis: Cheminements et situation actuelle d'un ordre mystique musulman*. Istanbul, 1990, pp. 109–121.

———. 'The Economic Status of a Timurid Sufi Shaykh: A Matter of Conflict or Perception?', *Iranian Studies*, 21 (1988), pp. 84–104.

Gustafson, James M. *Kirman and the Qajar Empire: Local Dimensions of Modernity in Iran, 1794–1914*. New York, 2016.

———. 'Geographical Literature in Nineteenth-Century Iran: Regional Identities and the Construction of Space', *Journal of the Economic and Social History of the Orient*, 59 (2016), pp. 793–827.

———. 'Kerman viii: Afsharid and Zand Period', *EIr*.

———. 'Kerman ix: Qajar Period', *EIr*.

Hammer-Purgstall, Joseph von. *Die Geschichte der Assassinen aus morgenländischen Quellen*. Stuttgart und Tübingen, 1818, English trans. *The History of the Assassins*, tr. Oswald Charles Woods. London, 1835.

Hans, Raj Kumar. 'The Legitimation of the Agha Khan's Authority over the Khojas of Western India under Colonial Dispensation in the Nineteenth Century', *Islamic Culture*, 71 (1997), pp. 19–35.

Hidāyat, Riḍā Qulī Khān. *Majmaʿ al-fuṣahā*, ed. Maẓāhir Muṣaffā, 6 vols. Tehran, 1336–1340 Sh./1957–1961.

———. *Rawḍat al-ṣafā-yi Nāṣirī*. Tehran, 1339 Sh./1960.

Hollister, John Norman. *The Shiʿa of India*. London, 1953.

Hopkins, B. D. *The Making of Modern Afghanistan*. New York, 2008.

———. 'The Bounds of Identity: The Goldsmid Mission and the Delineation of the Perso-Afghan Border in the Nineteenth Century', *Journal of Global History*, 2 (2007), pp. 233–254.

Hughes, A. W. *A Gazetteer of the Province of Sindh*. London, 1874.

Huttenback, Robert A. *British Relations with Sind, 1799–1843: An Anatomy of Imperialism*. Berkeley, 1962.

Iloliev, Abdulmamad. '*Pirship* in Badakhshan: The Role and Significance of the Institute of the Religious Masters (*Pirs*) in Nineteenth and Twentieth Century Wakhan and Shughnan', *Journal of Shiʿa Islamic Studies*, 6 (2013), pp. 155–176.

Iʿtimād al-Salṭana, Muḥammad Ḥasan Khān. *Mirʾāt al-buldān*, ed. ʿAbd al-Ḥusayn Navāʾī, 4 vols. Tehran, 1368 Sh./1989.

———. *Tārīkh-i muntaẓam-i Nāṣirī*, ed. Muḥammad Ismāʿīl Riḍvānī, 3 vols. Tehran, 1367 Sh./1988.

Ivanow, Wladimir. *Ismaili Literature: A Bibliographical Survey*. Tehran, 1963.

———. *Brief Survey of the Evolution of Ismailism*. Leiden, 1952.

———. 'Tombs of Some Persian Ismaili Imams', *Journal of the Bombay Branch of the Royal Asiatic Society*, New Series, 14 (1938), pp. 49–62.

Kashani-Sabet, Firoozeh. *Frontier Fictions: Shaping the Iranian Nation, 1804–1946*. Princeton, 1999.

Khayrkhwāh-i Harātī, Muḥammad Riḍā b. Khwāja Sulṭān Ḥusayn. *Taṣnīfāt*, ed. Wladimir Ivanow. Tehran, 1961.

Khodzhibekov, Ėl'bon. *Ismailitskie dukhovnye nastavniki (piry) i ikh rol' v obshchestvenno-politicheskoĭ i kul'turnoĭ zhizni Shugnana (vtoraia polovina XIX–30-e gody XX vv.)*. Dushanbe, 2015.

Khūrmūjī, Muḥammad Jaʿfar. *Ḥaqāʾiq al-akhbār-i Nāṣirī*, ed. Ḥusayn Khadīv-Jam. Tehran, 1363 Sh./1984.

Kinneir, John Macdonald. *A Geographical Memoir of the Persian Empire*. London, 1813.

Levi, Scott C. *The Indian Diaspora in Central Asia and Its Trade, 1550–1900*. Leiden, 2002.

———. 'India, Russia and the Eighteenth-Century Transformation of the Central Asian Caravan Trade', *Journal of the Economic and Social History of the Orient*, 42 (1999), pp. 519–548.

Lewisohn, Leonard. 'An Introduction to the History of Modern Persian Sufism, Part I: The Niʿmatullāhī Order: Persecution, Revival and Schism', *Bulletin of the School of Oriental and African Studies*, 61 (1998), pp. 437–464.

Lisān al-Mulk Sipihr, Muḥammad Taqī. *Nāsikh al-tavārīkh: Tārīkh-i Qājāriyya*, ed. Jamshīd Kiyān-far, 4 vols. Tehran, 1390 Sh./2011.

Losensky, Paul E. 'Hedāyat, Rezāqoli Khan', *EIr*.

———. 'Waḳār, Mīrzā Aḥmad Shīrāzī', *EI2*.

MacLean, Derryl N. *Religion and Society in Arab Sind*. Leiden, 1989.

Macmurdo, James. 'An account of the province of Cutch, and of the countries lying between Guzerat and the river Indus', *Transactions of the Literary Society of Bombay*, 2 (1820), pp. 217–255.

Madelung, Wilferd. 'Aspects of Ismāʿīlī Theology: The Prophetic Chain and the God beyond Being', in Seyyed Hossein Nasr, ed., *Ismāʿīlī Contributions to Islamic Culture*. Tehran, 1977, pp. 53–65.

Maḥallātī, Muḥammad Taqī b. ʿAlī Riḍā. *Āthār-i Muḥammadī*. MS 919, Institute of Ismaili Studies, London.

Markovits, Claude. *The Global World of Indian Merchants, 1750–1947*. Cambridge, 2000.

Marvī, Muḥammad Kāẓim. *ʿĀlamārā-yi Nādirī*, ed. Muḥammad Amīn Riyāḥī, 3 vols. Tehran, 1364 Sh./1985.

Masselos, James C. 'Change and Custom in the Format of the Bombay Mohurrum during the Nineteenth and Twentieth Centuries', *South Asia: Journal of South Asian Studies*, 5 (1982), pp. 47–67.

———. 'The Khojas of Bombay: The Defining of Formal Membership Criteria During the Nineteenth Century', in Imtiaz Ahmad, ed., *Caste and Social Stratification among Muslims in India*. New Delhi, 1978, pp. 97–116.

Mastibekov, Otambek. *Leadership and Authority in Central Asia: An Ismaili Community in Tajikistan*. London, 2014.

Maʿṣūm ʿAlī Shāh, Muḥammad Maʿṣūm Shīrāzī. *Ṭarāʾiq al-ḥaqāʾiq*, ed. Muḥammad Jaʿfar Maḥjūb, 3 vols. Tehran, 1339–1345 Sh./1960–1966.

Matthee, Rudolph P. *Persia in Crisis: Safavid Decline and the Fall of Isfahan*. London, 2012.

Maẓharī, ʿAlī Aṣghar. 'Rābiṭa-yi Ismāʿīliyān bā ṣūfiyān-i ṭarīqat-i Niʿmatullāhī', *Ṣūfī*, 27 (1374 Sh./1995), pp. 6–18.

Mohammad Poor, Daryoush. *Authority without Territory: The Aga Khan Development Network and the Ismaili Imamate*. New York, 2014.

Moir, Zawahir. 'Historical and Religious Debates amongst Indian Ismailis 1840–1920', in Mariola Offredi, ed., *The Banyan Tree: Essays on Early Literature in New Indo-Aryan Languages*. New Delhi, 2000, vol. 1, pp. 131–153.

Mojtahed-Zadeh, Pirouz. *Small Players of the Great Game: The Settlement of Iran's Eastern Borderlands and the Creation of Afghanistan*. London, 2004.

Morikawa, Tomoko. 'Pilgrimages to the Iraqi ʿAtabat from Qajar Era Iran', in Pedram Khosronejad, ed., *Saints and Their Pilgrims in Iran and Neighbouring Countries*. Wantage, 2012, pp. 41–60.

Morimoto, Kazuo, ed. *Sayyids and Sharifs in Muslim Societies: The Living Links to the Prophet*. Abingdon, 2012.

Mukherjee, Soumen. *Ismailism and Islam in Modern South Asia: Community and Identity in the Age of Religious Internationals*. Cambridge, 2017.

Nanji, Azim. *The Nizārī Ismāʿīlī Tradition in the Indo-Pakistan Subcontinent*. Delmar, NY, 1978.

Napier, William F. P. *The History of General Sir Charles Napier's Conquest of Scinde*. 2nd ed., London, 1857.

———. *The Life and Opinions of General Sir Charles James Napier*, 4 vols. London, 1857.

———. *History of General Sir Charles Napier's Administration of Scinde*. London, 1851.

Navvābī, Māhyār. *Khāndān-i Viṣāl-i Shīrāzī*. Tehran, 1335 Sh./1956.

Noelle, Christine. *State and Tribe in Nineteenth-Century Afghanistan: The Reign of Amir Dost Muhammad Khan (1826–1863)*. Richmond, 1997.

Noelle-Karimi, Christine. *The Pearl in its Midst: Herat and the Mapping of Khurasan (15th–19th Centuries)*. Vienna, 2014.

Noorally, Zawahir. 'The First Agha Khan and the British, 1838–1868: A Study in British Indian Diplomacy and Legal History'. MA thesis, School of Oriental and African Studies, University of London, 1964.

Outram, James. *The Conquest of Scinde: A Commentary*, 2 vols. Edinburgh, 1846.

Pagès, Meriem. *From Martyr to Murderer: Representations of the Assassins in Twelfth- and Thirteenth-Century Europe*. Syracuse, 2014.

Perry, John R. *Karin Khan Zand: A History of Iran, 1747–1779*. Chicago, 1979.

Picklay, A. S. *History of the Ismailis*. Bombay, 1940.

Pirumshoev, Munir. *Pamir v russkoĭ istoriografii vtoroĭ poloviny XIX–nachala XX vv*. Dushanbe, 2012.

Pīrzāda Nā'īnī, Ḥājjī Muḥammad 'Alī. *Safar-nāma-yi Ḥājjī Pīrzāda*, ed. Ḥāfiẓ Farmānfarmā'iyān, 2 vols. Tehran, 1342 Sh./1963.

Poonawala, Ismail K. *Biobibliography of Ismā'īlī Literature*. Malibu, CA, 1977.

Porter, Robert Ker. *Travels in Georgia, Persia, Armenia, Ancient Babylonia, etc., during the years 1817, 1818, 1819, and 1820*. 2 vols. London, 1821–1822.

Pourjavady, Nasrollah. 'Opposition to Sufism in Twelver Shiism', in Frederick de Jong and Bernd Radtke, ed., *Islamic Mysticism Contested: Thirteen Centuries of Controversies and Polemics*. Leiden, 1999, pp. 614–623.

Pourjavady, Nasrollah, and Peter Lamborn Wilson. *Kings of Love: The Poetry and History of the Ni'matullāhī Sufi Order*. Tehran, 1978.

———. 'Ismā'īlīs and Ni'matullāhīs', *Studia Islamica*, 41 (1975), pp. 113–135.

———. 'The Descendants of Shāh Ni'matullāh Walī', *Islamic Culture*, 48 (1974), pp. 49–57.

Purohit, Teena. *The Aga Khan Case: Religion and Identity in Colonial India*. Cambridge, 2012.

al-Qummī, Qāḍī Aḥmad. *Khulāṣat al-tavārīkh*, ed. Iḥsān Ishrāqī, 2 vols. Tehran, 1383 Sh./2004.

Rawlinson, Henry C. *England and Russia in the East: A Series of Papers on the Political and Geographical Condition of Central Asia*. London, 1875.

Rousseau, Jean Baptiste. 'Mémoire sur les Ismaélis et les Nosaïris de Syrie', *Annales des Voyages*, 14 (1811), pp. 271–303.

Sā'ī, Muḥsin. *Āqā Khān Maḥallātī va firqa-yi Ismā'īliyya*. Tehran, 1329 Sh./1950.

Sārū'ī, Muḥammad Fatḥullāh b. Muḥammad Taqī. *Tārīkh-i Muḥammadī (Aḥsan al-tavārīkh)*, ed. Ghulām Riḍā Ṭabāṭabā'ī Majd. Tehran, 1371 Sh./1992.

Scharbodt, Oliver. 'The *Quṭb* as Special Representative of the Hidden Imam: The Conflation of Shi'i and Sufi *Vilāyat* in the Ni'matullāhī Order', in Denis

Hermann and Sabrina Mervin, ed., *Shi'i Trends and Dynamics in Modern Times (XVIIIth–XXth Centuries)*. Beirut, 2010, pp. 33–49.

Sefatgol, Mansur. 'From *Dār al-Salṭana-yi Iṣfahān* to *Dār al-Khilāfa-yi Ṭihrān*: Continuity and Change in the Safavid Model of State-Religious Administration during the Qajars (1795–1895/1209–1313)', in Robert Gleave, ed., *Religion and Society in Qajar Iran*. London, 2005, pp. 71–83.

Shahvar, Soli. 'Communications, Qajar Irredentism, and the Strategies of British India: The Makran Coast Telegraph and British Policy of Containing Persia in the East (Baluchistan), Part I', *Iranian Studies*, 39 (2006), pp. 329–351.

Shihāb al-Dīn Shāh al-Ḥusaynī. *Khiṭābāt-i 'āliya*, ed. Hūshang Ujāqī. Bombay, 1963.

Shirvānī, Zayn al-'Ābidīn. *Ḥadā'iq al-sīyāḥa*, ed. Sulṭān Ḥusayn Tābanda, Riḍā 'Alī Shāh. Tehran, 1348 Sh./1969.

———. *Riyāḍ al-siyāḥa*, vol. 1, ed. Aṣghar Ḥāmid Rabbānī. Tehran, 1339 Sh./1960.

———. *Būstān al-siyāḥa*, ed. Āghā Mīrzā Ḥabibullāh. Tehran, 1315/1897.

Shodhan, Amrita. *A Question of Community: Religious Groups and Colonial Law*. Calcutta, 2001.

———. 'Legal Formulation of the Question of Community: Defining the Khoja Collective', *Indian Social Science Review*, 1 (1999), pp. 137–151.

Silvestre de Sacy, Antoine Isaac. 'Mémoire sur la dynastie des Assassins, et sur l'étymologie de leur nom', *Mémoires de l'Institut Royal de France*, 4 (1818), pp. 1–84; English trans. in F. Daftary, *The Assassin Legends*, pp. 129–188.

Smarandache, Bogdan. 'The Franks and the Nizārī Ismā'īlīs in the Early Crusade Period', *Al-Masāq*, 24 (2012), pp. 221–239.

Speziale, Fabrizio. 'A propos du renouveau *Ni'matullāhī*: Le centre de Hyderabad au course de la première modernité', *Studia Iranica*, 42 (2013), pp. 91–118.

Spooner, Brian. 'Who are the Baluch? A Preliminary Investigation into the Dynamics of an Ethnic Identity from Qajar Iran', in C. E. Bosworth and Carole Hillenbrand, ed., *Qajar Iran: Political, Social, and Cultural Change, 1800–1925*. Costa Mesa, 1992, pp. 93–110.

———. 'Baluchistan i. Geography, History and Ethnography', *EIr*.

Sykes, Percy Molesworth. *Ten Thousand Miles in Persia or Eight Years in Irán*. London, 1902.

Thornton, Edward. *A Gazetteer of the Countries Adjacent to India on the North-West; including Sinde, Afghanistan, Beloochistan, the Punjab, and the Neighbouring States*, 2 vols. London, 1844.

Tucker, Ernest. *Nadir Shah's Quest for Legitimacy in Post-Safavid Iran*. Gainesville, FL, 2006.

———. 'Nadir Shah and the Ja'fari *Madhhab* Reconsidered', *Iranian Studies*, 27 (1994), pp. 163–179.

Vazīrī, Aḥmad 'Alī Khān. *Tārīkh-i Kirmān*, ed. Muḥammad Ibrāhīm Bāstānī Pārīzī. Tehran, 1393 Sh./2014.

———. *Jughrāfiyā-yi Kirmān*, ed. Muḥammad Ibrāhīm Bāstānī Pārīzī. Tehran, 1376 Sh./1997.

Virani, Shafique N. *The Ismailis in the Middle Ages: a History of Survival, a Search for Salvation*. Oxford, 2007.

Watson, Robert G. *A History of Persia from the Beginning of the Nineteenth Century to the Year 1858*. London, 1866.

Willey, Peter. *Eagle's Nest: Ismaili Castles in Iran and Syria*. London, 2005.

Yapp, Malcom E. 'The Revolutions of 1841–2 in Afghanistan', *Bulletin of the School of Oriental and African Studies*, 27 (1964), pp. 333–381.

Index

ʿAbbās, Shāh, 21
Abu'l-Ḥasan ʿAlī, Sayyid, 27–28
Abu'l-Ḥasan Khān, Sardār (brother of Aga Khan I), 53, 83, 92, 109–110, 115, 125
  defeat of, 54
Abu'l-Qāsim, Mīrzā, 82
Afghanistan
  Aga Khan I's arrival in, 47
  British occupation of, 39, 45, 47
    end of, 48
    revolt against, 48–49
  Russian influence in, 39
  Twelver Shiʿi Qizilbāsh forces, 49
  withdrawal of British forces from, 48
Afshārid dynasty, 23
Aga Khan Case of 1866, xxii, 7, 59
Aga Khan I (Imam Ḥasan ʿAlī Shāh), xv, 1, 28, 29, 60, 61
  activities in Persia, 12
  annual pension, xxi, 51
  arrival in
    Afghanistan, 6, 47–48
    India, xviii, 2, 54–60
  assistance to the British, *See* British–Aga Khan I relationship
  battles against Faḍl ʿAlī Khān, 45, 54, 98, 100–101, 105, 109, 125–126
  British protection, xxi
  chronology of career of, 2
  conflict with the Qājār government, 1, 31, 46, 53
  contacts with followers in India, xxi
  departure from
    Maḥallāt, 42
    Persia, xviii, 37, 38–47
  relationship with Zayn al-ʿĀbidīn Shirvānī, 37
  governorship of Kirmān, xviii, 29, 39
    dismissal from, xix, 30–31
    tribal uprisings, 30
  imprisonment of, 39–40
  as military commander, 46
  patronage of pan-Shiʿi activities in India, 59
  residence in Maḥallāt, 40–41
  return to Persia, xxi
  reverses in fight with Balūchī chiefs, 51–52
  revolt against government of Persia, 6, 38–47
  settlement in Bombay, xxii, 1, 56–57
  as spiritual head of a Muslim community, xxii
Aga Khan II (Āqā ʿAlī Shāh), 38, 59–60
Aga Khan III (Imam Sultan Muhammad Shah), 57, 59
  memoirs of, 68
  visit to Iran, 68
Aga Khan IV (Shāh Karīm al-Ḥusaynī), 68
Āghā Muḥammad Khān Qājār, 34
Aḥmad Khān, Sayyid, 59
Aḥmad, Mīrzā, 119
Algar, Hamid, 31, 36, 62
ʿAlī Khan, Muḥammad, 53, 120
ʿAlī Shāh Mushtāq, 33
al-Kuttāb, Mīrzā Bāqir Malik, 82
Allen, Isaac, 6

All-India Muslim League, 59
Amīr Kabīr, Mīrzā Taqī Khān, 10, 55–56, 129, 131
Anglo-Indian army, xxi
Anglo-Persian treaty of 1229/1814, xxi
Anglo-Sikh War, 58
Āqāsī, Ḥājji Mīrzā, xx–xxi, 31, 34, 38, 85
  demand for Aga Khan's extradition from British India, xxi
Army of the Indus, 47
'Assassins' legends, legacy of, 3–9
  Western perceptions of, 3
'Aṭā'ullāhīs (Khurāsānī tribesmen), 24
'August Master' (*makhdūm-i mukarram*), 129

Bābī uprising in Māzandarān, 129
Bāgh-i Nargis, 100–101
Bahmanid dynasty of the Deccan, 32
Bahman Mīrzā, 42–43, 45, 96
Bahrām ū Bihrūz, 62, 63, 65
Bakhtiyārī tribes, 27
Baldwin II (King of the Latin Kingdom of Jerusalem), 8
Balūch of Sindh, 118
Bamfahl (Bampūr) fortress, 53, 120, 124
Bam fortress, 30, 83, 87
  general view of, 40
  siege of, 39
Bandar 'Abbās, 27, 47, 100, 108
Bombay Legislative Council, 59
British–Aga Khan I relationship, xxi, xvii, xxi
  in Afghanistan and Sindh, 47–54
  on campaigns against the chiefs of Sindh, 50–51
  first documented contacts, 6
  on issue of extradition, 55
  on pension of 1,000 rupees per month, 51
  on recognition as spiritual leader of the Ismailis, xxii
  on subduing of Balūch chiefs, 51
British East India Company, 47, 113
British empire, *See* British Raj
British India, *See* British Raj
British judiciary system, xxii
  Aga Khan Case of 1866, xxii, 7, 59
British Raj, xxi, 57
  annexation of
    Afghanistan, 47
    Karachi, 50
    Sindh, 51
  contest with Russian empire over Central Asia, 47
  Great Game, 47
  Miani, Battle of (1843), 51
  Nāṣir Khān revolt against, 50
  support for Aga Khan I, xxii

career of Aga Khan, interpretation of, 13–18
  chronology of, 2
Cavenagh, Captain, 127
Christian saints, social and political roles of, 16
Crusades
  Ismaili–European relations during, 4, 6, 8

da'wa, xviii
Desalji, Maharaj Rao, 120–121
discipleship, claim of, 36–37
Dūst Muḥammad, 47–48

educational schemes for Indian Muslims, 59
Elphinstone, William, 48
England, Richard, 49
European colonial powers, 5, 39
European naval powers, 26

Faḍl 'Alī Khān, 45, 54, 98, 100, 101, 105, 109, 125, 126
Faqīr Muḥammad, 119
Farāhānī, Muḥammad 'Alī Beg, 104–105
Farīdūn Mīrza, 39, 92
Fatḥ 'Alī Shāh Qājār, xvi, xvii, 29, 30, 34

Frere, Henry Bartle, 8

Ghilzāʾī Afghans, 48
Grand Master of the Templars, 8
Great Game, 47
Green, Nile, 15, 59
Gross, Jo-Ann, 17
Gustafson, James, 12

Ḥasan ʿAlī, Imam, 22, 23, 27
Ḥasan-i Ṣabbāḥ, xvii
Ḥaydarābādīs, 25
Hidāyat, Riḍā Qulī Khān, 42
Hidāyat al-muʾminīn al-ṭālibīn, 67
Howard, Edward Irving, 7–8
Ḥusayn Khān, Mīrzā, 27, 56, 103, 104, 130
Ḥusayn Yazdī, Mullā, 28–29

Ibrāhīm Khān Qājār, 91
ʿIbrat-afzā, xv, xvii–xviii, xix, xxii, 1–3, 11, 36, 42–43, 56, 134
  authorship of, 61–64
  composition of, 64, 69
    in classical Persian style, 69
    poetic quality of, 69
  contents of, 68
  fall into obscurity, 67
  fate and significance of, 66–69
  handwritten copy of, 65
  manuscripts and editions of, 64–66
  note on the text and translation, 69–70
  printed editions of, 66
  publication of, 68
  purpose for production of, 68
  as source of Ismaili historiography, 66
imām–murīd bond, xix
Imam's exile from Persia, 1
India, Aga Khan in, xviii, 2, 54–60
  patronage of pan-Shiʿi activities, 59
  sponsoring of *taʿziya* commemorations, 54, 121, 127, 129
Indian Ocean trade, 26
Isfandīyār Khān, 101–102
Islamic school of jurisprudence, 22
Ismaili Imamate of the Fatimid period, rival branches of
  Mustaʿlian, xvii
  Nizārī, xvii
Ismaili Imams, xv, xvi, 60
  Aga Khan's role as, 3
  autobiographical writing by, 69
  claim as living successors to Imam ʿAli, 19
  end of, 47
  European experience with, 3–4
  global profile of, 2
  medieval history of, 10
  as notables and landholders in the Anjudān region, 21
  official status of, 14
  in post-Mongol period, 2
  relation with
    Europeans, 8
    Khoja communities, 7
  relation with Persia, 68
  sayyid lineage of, 18
  story of the transition of, 2
  Western perceptions of, 3
Ismaili *pīrs*, role and functions of, 17
Ismailism
  18th-century transformation in, 21–24
  modern history of, 56
  in post-Mongol Persia, 18–21
  study of, 10
Ivanow, Wladimir, 7, 19, 62

Jaʿfar al-Ṣādiq, Imam, 25, 26
Jaʿfarī *madhhab,* 22
jamāʿats, 119–121
Jung, Ṣafdar, 49, 114–115

Kalātī, Amīr Nāṣir Khān, 50
revolt against the British, 50
Kālmand, 96, 101
Karachi, British annexation of, 50
Karāmat ʿAlī, Mīr, 128
Khān, ʿAbdullāh, 104
Khiṭābāt-i ʿāliya, 66
Khojas (Ismailis of India), xviii, xxii, 7, 26
relationship with Ismaili imamate, 7
religious identity of, xxii
Kirmān, 87
Afghan invasion of, 27, 82
Balūch invasion of, 82
history of, 24–28
Qājār capture of, 28
taxes of, 79
Kīshkūī, Ḥājjī Faḍlullāh, 99

Lārī, ʿAlī Khān, 104
Lārījānī, ʿAbbās Qulī Khān, 92
Latin Crusader kingdoms, 4
Lavāsānī, Ḥājjī ʿAlī, 128
League of Nations, 59
Luṭf ʿAlī Khān Zand, 27, 82

Macnaghten, William Hay, 48
Maddock, Sir, 127
Maḥallāt, 83, 94
Majdhūb ʿAlī Shāh, xvi
master–disciple relationship, 37
Masʿūd, Mīrzā, 86
Maʿṣūm ʿAlī Shāh, xv, 34
mausoleum of Aga Khan I, in Hasanabad, Bombay, 61
Miani, Battle of (1843), 51
Mīr Naṣīr Khān, 116, 127
Mīrzā Taqī Khān, 10, 55–56, 129, 131
modern scholarship, on Aga Khan I, 9–12
Mongol conquests, in Middle East, 5, 18
destruction of Nizārī Ismaili headquarters at Alamūt, 18
murder of Imam Rukn al-Dīn Khūrshāh, 18
Muḥammad Akbar Khān, 48, 128
Muhammadan Anglo-Oriental College, 59
Muhammadan National Association, 59
Muḥammad Bāqir Khān (brother of Aga Khan I), 30, 39, 45, 51, 53, 91, 96, 98–99, 105, 117, 119–120, 124–125
Muḥammad Jaʿfar Khān , 119
Muḥammad Ṣādiq Khān, 39, 92
Muḥammad Shāh Qājār, xvii, xix, xx, 40, 42, 53
campaign to retake Herat, 39
death of, xxi, 55
Muḥammad, the Prophet, 14
Muḥammad Tīmūr, 48, 113
Muḥarram, 45, 54, 55, 101, 121, 129
Murād Mīrzā, 19, 21
Mushtāqiyya, 33
Mustaʿlian Ismailis, xvii
Mustawfī, Mīrzā ʿAlī Riḍā, 87, 93

Nādir Qulī-Beg (Nādir Shāh)
death of, 27, 38
invasion of India, 23
Jaʿfarī *madhhab,* 22
public emergence of Nizārī imamate under, 24
reforms to consolidate his power, 22
relationship with
Imam Ḥasan ʿAlī, 22–23
Nizārī imamate, 23, 24
religious policy, 22
as shah of Persia, 21–22
Nakhaʿī tribe, 111
Napier, Charles, xxi, 6, 50, 52, 116–117, 119
campaigns against chiefs of
Balūch, 51
Sindh, 51
Miani, Battle of (1843), 51
Nāṣir al-Dīn Shāh Qājār, xxii, 42, 54, 55, 68, 129

Narmāshīr, 83, 87, 89, 106, 126
Niʿmatullāhī shaykhs, 36
Niʿmatullāhī Sufi order, xv, xviii, 31
  claim to *vilāyat,* 33
  late 18th-century revival of, 33
  master of, 34
  Nizārīs and, 31–38
  revival of, 34
  rivalries for the leadership of, xix
  and Twelver *ʿulamāʾ,* 33
Niʿmatullāh Valī, Shāh, xv, 32
Nizārī Ismailis, xv, xvii, xviii, 13–14
  Anjudān revival of, 19
  destruction by Mongols, 18
  ethos and identity, xix
  following in India, 25
  Khoja followers, xxii, 26
  and Kirmān, 24–28
  military actions against Saljūq Turks, 8
  modern phase in history of, xxii
  in Persia, 20–21, 29
  public emergence under Nādir Shāh, 24
  re-emergence of, 19
  relation with
    Afshārid dynasty, 23
    Niʿmatullāhiyya, 31–38
    Qājārs, 28
  status of, 21
Nott, William, 49
Nūmlī, Shīr Muḥammad Khān, 118
Nūr ʿAlī Shāh, xv
Nūrī, Darvīsh, 108
Nūrī, Mīrzā Āqā Khān, 131

Old Man of the Mountain, 4–6, 8
Outram, Sir, 50, 116–117

Pahlavi dynasty, 68
pension, of Aga Khan I, xxi, 51
People of God (*khalq Allāh*), 95, 114, 117
Persia (Iran)
  Aga Khan's departure from, xviii, 37, 68
  British occupation of Khārg island, 39
  defeat by Russia, 39
  establishment of the Nizārī Ismaili imamate, 20
  Nādir Shāh (shah of Persia), 22
  Pahlavi dynasty, 68
  relation with Ismaili imamate, 68
  religious conversion to Twelver Shiʿism, 20
  Safavid conquest of, 19–20, 32
  Turkmanchay, Treaty of (1827), 39
  Twelver clergy in, 34
  visit by Aga Khan III, 68
Polo, Marco, 5

Qāʾim-maqām-i Farāhānī, xix
Qājār monarch, 36
  political crises faced by, 68
  Russian influence on, 39
  Shadow of God, 36
Qandahār, 48–49, 113
  Aga Khan stay at, 49
  retreat of British garrison from, 49
Qaryat al-ʿArab, 106
Quetta, 49
  Aga Khan arrival in, 49–50
Qumm, xv–xvii, 21, 24, 29, 80, 93
Qurʾan, 90, 104

Raḥmat Alī Shāh, 38
Rawlinson, Henry, xxi, 48–49, 113
religious identity
  of Khoja community, xxii
  of Shiʿi community, xix
revolt of Aga Khan, against government of Persia, 1, 6, 9–11, 31, 37, 38–47
Riḍā ʿAlī Shāh Dakkanī, 32
Rousseau, Jean Baptiste, 5, 28
Rukn al-Dīn Khurshāh, xvii, 18

Ṣadr al-Mamālik Mīrzā Naṣrullāh, 86
Safavid empire
  adoption of Shiʿism as the religion, 19
  conquest of Persia, 19–20
  fall of, 21, 26
  religious policies of, 19
  state of Ismaili communities in, 19–20
Sālār insurrection in Khurāsān, 129
Saljūq Turks, 8
Sawghān fort, 100
Sayyid ʿAlī Mūsā pass, 102
Sevener Shiʿas, 25
Shahr-i Bābak, in Kirmān, 27, 42, 45, 97
Shāh Khalīlullāh, xv–xvi, 5, 21, 28–31
Shāh Nizār ʿAlī (Nizār II), 24
Shāhrukh Khān, 85, 91
Shāh Shujāʿ, 47–48
  assassination of, 49
Sheil, Justin, xxi
Shia Imami Ismailis, xxii
Shiʿi community, religious identity of, xix
Shīr Muḥammad Khān, 51, 81, 117–118
Shujāʿ al-Salṭana, 82
silsila, 25
Sindh
  Aga Khan I arrival in, xvii, xxi, 50
  British conquest of, 51
  as major centre of Ismaili communities, 50
  revolt of Sindhī *amīr*s against British, 50–51
Sindhī *amīr*s, defeat of, 51
Sipahdār, Ghulām Ḥusayn Khān, 82
Sipihr, Muḥammad Taqī, 43
succession dispute, xvii
Sufi orders, 11, 20, 31, 36, 38
Sufi saints, 16
Sufi shaykhs, 17
Sufism, xvi, 15, 16

taqiyya, 18
Tīmūr, Amīr, 32
trade, patterns of
  European naval powers, 26
  Indian Ocean trade, 26
  overland trade routes of Asia, 26
  sea-based, 26
Turkmanchay, Treaty of (1827), 39
Twelfth Imam, 19, 33
Twelver Shiʿism
  interpretation of, 20
  official patronage of, 22
  religious conversion to, 20
Twelver *ʿulamāʾ*, 33–34

ʿulamāʾ, 23, 28, 33–35, 129
ʿulamāʾ-i millat, 94

Vazīrī, Aḥmad ʿAlī Khān, 24–27, 83
vilāyat (spiritual authority), 33
Viqār-i Shīrāzī, Aḥmad, xvii, 61–64
Viṣāl-i Shīrāzī, 61, 62
von Hammer-Purgstall, Joseph 4, 8

Western scholarship, Aga Khan I in, 3–18
  'Assassins', legend of, 3–9
  career of the Aga Khan, 13–18
  modern scholarship on, 9–12

Yazd, xx, 28, 42, 79, 80, 95, 96, 109, 110

Zayn al-ʿAbidīn Shirvānī, Ḥājjī, xvi, xix, 31, 34, 82, 85, 89
  Aga Khan's relationship with, 37
Zayn al-ʿAbidīn, Ḥājjī, 82, 89

ʿIbrat-afzā

of

Muḥammad Ḥasan al-Ḥusaynī,
also known as Ḥasan ʿAlī Shāh

Edited by

Daniel Beben
and
Daryoush Mohammad Poor

عبرت افزا

تألیف محمّد حسن الحسینی

تصحیح و ترجمه

از

دنیل بیبن و داریوش محمّدپور

بسم الله الرّحمن الرّحیم

حمد و ثنا یگانه خالقی را رواست که جملهٔ جهان و جهانیان صورت یکتائی اوست، ولی

یارای زبان کو که ثنایش گویم
یا وصف کمال کبریایش گویم

لا اثنی ثناء علیک کما اثنیت علی نفسک و نعت رسولش را سزاست که لولاک لما خلقت الافلاک شمّهٔ از اوصاف بیهمتائی اوست.

از عکس رخش گلشن جان پیدا شد
و ز سایهٔ او سرو روان پیدا شد
بلغ العلی بکماله کشف الدّجی بجماله
هم نقطه و هم دایره و هم پرگار

و درود بر اوصیای بحقّ و اولیای مطلقی زیباست خلفاً عن سلف که در هر ازمنه و ادوار بمدلول آیهٔ[1] شریفه **یَا أَیُّهَا الَّذِینَ آمَنُوا أَطِیعُوا اللَّـهَ وَأَطِیعُوا الرَّسُولَ وَأُولِي الْأَمْرِ مِنكُمْ** و مضمون حدیث «انّی تارک فیکم الثّقلین ما ان تمسّکتم بهما لن تضلّوا بعدی کتاب الله وعترتی حبلان

[1] ب ٣.

ممدودان لا ینقطعان و لاینقصمان الی یوم القیمة حتّی یردا[۲] علیّ الحوض» خاصهٔ وجود فیض‌آمود ایشان است.

و بعد چون در کارخانهٔ آفرینش نوع انسانرا شایسته‌ترین منش و بینش تحصیل عبرت است لهذا این سرگشتهٔ دایرهٔ امکان و پا شکستهٔ دور زمان بنظر عبرت ملاحظهٔ احوال گذشتهٔ خود را نموده مجملی از تفصیل سرنوشت سرشت و سرگذشت تقلیب حالات و تقریب رویدادات واردهٔ دوری نسبت بخود را بجهة فائدهٔ بینندگان برشتهٔ تحریر کشیده تا سررشتهٔ نقل احوالات دیگران گردیده میزان تجربه حاصل نمایند چه شخص را در بیان شرح احوال خود مجال[۳] اشتباه و تخلیط محال است.

فما ثمّ الّا الصّمت و الحقّ ناطق
و ما ثمّ الّا الله لاغیر خالق
فیشهدنا تکوینه فی شهودنا
یدلّ علیه فی الوجود حقائق
فمن شاء فلیؤمن و من شاء فلیقل
خلاف الذّی قلناه و الله صادق

وَمَا تَشَاءُونَ إِلَّا أَن يَشَاءَ اللَّـهُ

---

[۲] درنسخه‌ها بدین صورت ضبط شده است: یردّ.

[۳] در هر دو نسخه این کلمه «جمال» آمده است که تصحیف می‌نماید.

و ضمناً رعایت اختصار می‌نماید[۴] که طول مقال موجب ملال نگرندگان نگردد.

این کوچهٔ عمر وحشت‌افزا راهی است
حیرت‌زده است هر کجا آگاهی است
بازیگر روزگار را معرکه‌ها است
میدان جهان عجب تماشاگاهی است

و این مسمّی به محمّد حسن الحسینی الشّهیر بآقاخان ابن شاه خلیل‌الله را احوالات از زمان تولّد تا پنجم مرحله که از عمر سپری شد چنانچه اقتضای حرکات صبیان است مقتضی شرح و بیان نیست در سال ششم بمکتبم بردند و بملّا علی محمّد ادیبم سپردند و سواد مشار الیه بمثابهٔ بود که فرق سواد از بیاض بآسانی مشکل می‌نمود چنانچه در افادهٔ گلستان سعدی، «اسب تازی که تک[۵] رود بشتاب» توجیه بسگ شکاری می‌کرد و در استفاده از درس نصاب در معنی حُسِد حافده متغیّرانه می‌سرود که اطفال را بپرسیدن مزخرفات صوفیّه چه خیال؟ بگذارید و بگذرید که بیان این معانی موجب اختلال دین و اضلال آئین است. خدایش رحمت کناد.

---

۴ ب ۴.

۵ صورت اصلی عبارت در شعر سعدی بدین شکل است: دو تک.

بالجمله در هفت سالگی مرحوم والد شهید را به یزد بردند و ایمانی خان فراهانی مأمور به نیابت دهات متعلّق بما، که مرحوم آقا محمّد خان پس از حرکت دادن والد و وابستگان را از کرمان در عوض بعضی از املاکات آنملک واگذار کرده بودند، شد و چون محمّد علی نام[۶] که کدخدای قصبهٔ ریوگان محلّات بود تمکین حکومت او را نمی‌نمود بجههٔ اطمینان او کاغذی مؤکّد به پیمان و ایمان غلاظ و شداد نزد مرحومهٔ والده فرستاد و آن مرحومه بعد از مطمئن ساختن او را روانهٔ فراهان نمود و خان موصوف خلاف عهد و سوگند کرده او را مقیّد و محبوس و محصّلان فرستاده خانه و اساس البیت او را حتّی ملبوس زنانهٔ او را غارت نموده بردند و والده بجههٔ وساطت و شفاعت او روانهٔ فراهان شد و خان مزبور از مشک آباد که مسکن او بود بدهات دیگر رفته روی پنهان نمود. از این سببها ناچار ترک خانه و مسکن محلّات را نموده، در هشت سالگی مستأصلاً در قم مأمن قسمت افتاد و در آنجا از وجدان ارباب نفاق و فقدان اصحاب وفاق چندان اضطرار و دست تنگی در وسعت مکنت اتّفاق افتاد که راستی نان و ماست در قوت لایموت بسختی دست می‌داد و بهیچوجه تفقّدی از اقارب و اجانب متصوّر نبود تا طیّ سیزده مرحله از عمر شد هم در این سال مرحوم والد را در یزد شهید کردند.

---

۶ ب ۵.

و پس از وقوع این واقعه خویش و بیگانه یگانه‌وار بمخالفتم موافقت نمودند و تقویت امنای دولت سلطانی بمعاونت اضداد مزید بر علّتها گشته تا آن که والدهٔ مرحومه ملجاء شده روانهٔ دارالخلافهٔ طهران گشت[۷] و در حریم محترم خاقانی بدادخواهی نشست تا:

از خاک صفا صفا پذیرد
مروا ز جمال مروه گیرد

و در مشکوی خاص سلطنت بمزید عزّت اختصاص یافته بمعرض تظلّم شتافت.

چنانکه گفته‌اند:

آتشکدهٔ سینهٔ ما خالی نیست
بتخانهٔ آذری خلیلی دارد

سوز دادخواهی آن مرحومه بعروق شخص سلطنت تافته کارد از کمر کشیده بقصد مرحوم ظلّ السّلطان از جا حرکت و بشنعت تمام او را مخاطب ساخته فرمایش فرموده بود که این چهار پنج ده خراب را که مرحوم آقا محمّد خان عوض املاک کرمان بایشان واگذار نموده بود تو

---

۷ ب ۶.

بکدام حکم و جرأت مدخلیّت نمودی و فی‌الواقع اگر مرحومهٔ والده شفاعت نکرده بود صدمات کلّی البتّه بظلّ السّلطان وارد می‌آمد.

پس نصفت شهریاری در صدد تدارک مافات و اصلاح مفاسدی که بمرور شهور سنوات و ایّام و اوقات گذشته بما وارد شده بود بر آمدند و از مکارم اخلاق و لوازم اشفاق، بطیب خاطر محرّک سلسلهٔ وصلت و وداد گشته بازدواج صبیّهٔ جلیلهٔ خود باین درویش ضعیف والده را تکلیف فرمودند و والده بعبارتی خاص معذرت خواستند که خیمهٔ سلطنت را با فضای درویشی چه مناسبت.

وانگهی با این پریشانی‌ها چون این خیال در ضمیر آفتاب تأثیر سلطانی[۸] مجال تمام یافته بود مطابق بیست و سه هزار تومان نقد از خزانهٔ عامره بجهة مخارج مرحمت فرمودند و این درویش را بمظاهرت تمام بین الانام بمصاهرت امتیاز دادند و مادام الحیات رعایت عزّت و احترام مرا زیاده از شاهزادگان عظام می‌نمودند و وساطت مرا دربارهٔ اکابر و اصاغر قبول می‌کردند بلکه در اکثر محافل از وصلت با من اظهار مفاخرت می‌فرمودند، اسکنه الله تعالی فی بحبوحة الجنان.

مرید ذرّهٔ ذرّات کائنات شود
دلی که جلوهٔ خورشید را طلبکار است

---

۸ ب ۷.

چون مقصود اظهار کلیّات احوال است از اطناب شرح جزئیات اجتناب می‌رود.

پس از رحلت آن مغفور و ظهور وحشت و فتور ما بین امیر و مأمور، نزدیک و دور و وصول موکب پادشاه مرحوم محمّد شاه - جعل الجنة مثواه - بدارالخلافهٔ طهران، از هر ملک شاهزادگان و حکّام و امرا و عمّال متوجه دارالخلافه گشتند و از حوادث یغما و تاراجی که در بین رحلت و جلوس آن دو پادشاه رحمت مأنوس واقع شده بود، اکثری بگیر و دار مؤاخذه گرفتار و من چنانچه رسم یاران است در صحبت غلام حسین خان سپهدار بجهة تهنیت جلوس وارد دربار سلطانی شدیم. چون در مدّت اغتشاش از دست انداز رنود و اوباش در بلاد عراق و سائرین[۹] در اموال مجاورین و مسافرین نهب و تاراج کلّی اتّفاق افتاد و مکاریان از هر سمت در حدود متعلّق بمن مأمن گزیده ایمن زیستند تا بسلامت بمقصد رسیدند.

انتشار این گونهٔ محافظت و خیرخواهی موجب خوشنودی خاطر پادشاهی گردید و نیز ملک کرمان که از کثرت تاخت‌وتاز بلوچ و افغان ویران و بتصرّف اولاد مرحوم شجاع السّلطنه بود، بملاحظهٔ رصانت قلاع و ارگ بم که باستحکام مشهور است و زیادتی جمعیّت مخالفین امنیتش بآسانی مشکل می‌نمود. لهذا پادشاه مرحوم بصوابدید میرزا ابوالقاسم قائم

---

۹ ب ۸.

مقام رحمه الله که از کماهی احوال و اعمال و اقوال این خاندان اباً عن جدّ بخوبی مطّلع بود مرا طلبیدند و فرمودند که چون حکومت کرمان متعلّق باجداد تو بود حال نیز تعلّق بتو دارد وجه تدارک مخارج لشکری را از خزانه دریافت نموده بزودی تدارک دیده روانه شو.

پس من بملاحظهٔ این گونهٔ رافت و اقتضای وقت عرض کردم که اگر چه حال ملک کرمان بتصرّف غیر است و در زمانی که لطفعلی خان در کرمان بود مرحوم آقا محمّد خان چند مدّت با لشکر بسیار و مخارج بی شمار بنفس نفیس زحمات کلّی کشید تا مفتوح گردید و حال چون این خدمت به عهدهٔ من مقرّر است به تأئید الهٰی و اقبال پادشاهی میروم و دیناری از خزانهٔ[۱۰] عامره نمیخواهم تا إنشاء الله ملک را از تصرّف بیگانه و اولاد شجاع السّلطنه انتزاع و امن نمایم. پس از انجام این خدمت بهر نوع موهبتی که سزاوارم دانند، سرافرازم فرمایند.

پس [از] رخصت و حکم همایون روانهٔ محلّات شده چند روزی جهة تدارک توقّف نموده، عزیمت سمت مقصود را مصمّم گشتم. و قبل از ورود بکرمان اولاد شجاع السّلطنه شهر را تخلیه و بشتاب بطرف بم و نرماشیر عنان تاب شده بودند و بعد از ورود شهر را تصرّف و یک چند جهة تمشیت توقّف و برادر خود سردار ابوالحسن خان را با خوانین و

---

[۱۰] ب ۹.

سرکردگان ایل صداقت دلیل[۱۱] عطاءاللّهی و خراسانی و سایر را مأمور بطرف بم و نرماشیر نمودیم و اولاد شجاع السّطنه قلاع نرماشیر و بم را بافغان و بلوچ سیستانی سپرده، خود با خدم و حشم فرار را بر قرار اختیار و جلوریز دشت گریز را پیش گرفته، پشت دادند و افغان و سیستانی بهوای این که مدّت یازده سال در عهد خاقان مغفور که هر ساله علاوه بر مالیات کرمان سالی چهل هزار تومان خرج لشکری می‌شد و دفع آنها صورت نگرفته بود جسور و جری شده بودند. و قلاع متصرّفی خود را بذخیرهٔ بسیار و مردان کار مضبوط ساخته و خود باستکمال صفوف و استعمال آتشخانه و سیوف بمقابله پرداخته نهایت استعداد خود را در دلاوری ظاهر می‌نمودند. تا این که من خود[۱۲] بعد از تنظیم و تنسیق امورات بلده، مقابله و مدافعه را مصمّم گشته بسمت نرماشیر ایوار و شبگیر نمودم. و مدّت یک سال و کسری آسایش و آرام بر خود حرام و غلّهٔ یک من تبریزی پنج هزار دینار از اطراف بنوکر رسانیدم و با وجود قحطی و استحکام قلاع و افزونی جمعیّت مخالفین بلوچ و افغان تا مجموع آنها را بعد از وضع آنچه در جنگها کشته شدند دستگیر و اسیر نکردم از پا ننشستم. و بعد از اطلاق و اخراج گرفتاران جرح و تعدیلی که از سرکشان

---

۱۱ بر اساس نسخه‌ی کتابخانه ملی.

۱۲ ب ۱۰.

و مفسدین ملک بجهة امنیّت و آسایش سپاه و رعیّت و افزایش منال دیوان سلطنت لازم بود نمودم.

پس از فراغ، میرزا علی رضای مستوفی را جهة پرداختن محاسبات مالیات پادشاهی و دریافت مفاصا با فرمان تحسین خدمات مفصّلهٔ فوق روانهٔ دارالخلافه کردم و خود بخیال فراغت آسودم و منتظر نتیجهٔ قول و قراری که ما بین پادشاه مرحوم و این درویش رفته بود بودم و با خود همواره این نکته را می‌سرودم:

ساقیا می بده و غم مخور از دشمن و دوست
که بکام دل ما آن بشد و این آمد

چه من بقول خود وفا کردم و خدمات خود را حسب الخواهش اولیای دولت بجا آوردم و بامید نتایج فرمایشات شهریاری هر دم تصوّرات نشاط‌افزا[۱۳] بخاطر می‌آوردم.

پس از چندی چاپاری از جانب یکی از محرمان بزم حضور سلطنت و درویشی وارد و مختصر مراسله باین مضمون نمود که چون قانون دولت ایران را چنان که میدانی که در تغییر و تبدیل وزرا لامحاله تغییر احکام و حکّام وزیر سابق در زمان وزیر لاحق میشود که استقلال وزارت ثابت

---

۱۳ ب ۱۱.

گردد و چون خدمات تو بزرگ و نمایان بود و حکومت کرمان را در حالتی که بتصرّف دشمنان قوی بود و دولت قوامی نگرفته بود بتو دادند و بدون سببی که مستلزم نقض قول پادشاهی گردد عزل نمودن تو ممکن نبود. لهذا بفراهم آمدن اسبابی که حواله بتقریر حامل است، تفصیل سبب و تحصیل مطلب را درک خواهید نمود و آن این است که چون مرحوم حاجی زین‌العابدین شیروانی که در حیات خاقان مغفور بگستردن بساط ارشاد انبساطی داشت و در خفیه بهر بوم و برزن در طریق نعمت‌اللّهی علم نشاط می‌افراشت و باکثری از شاهزادگان والا شأن، نوید سلطنت ایران را بپیمان و کتمان داده بود من جمله شاه مرحوم را اگر چه رشتهٔ ارادت و بیعت را سابق بعروهٔ ارشاد حاجی میرزا آقاسی رحمه الله محکم داشتند ولی از وفور صدق و یقین خاطر بذکر اورادی که از مرحوم حاجی شیروانی[۱۴] در سفر خراسان تلقین شده بود می‌گماشتند تا این که نوبت سلطنت بنام نامی آن پاک فطرت بلند آوا گردید. و حاجی مشارالیه از مرتبهٔ خلوت بمنصبهٔ جلوت قدم‌فرسا گشته، لوای جلالت را بنوای هل من مزید بلند گردانید و مورد اعتماد خدّام سلطنت و موجد اعتقاد بعضی از امنای دولت گردیده عزّت و احترام تمام یافت.

۱۴ ب ۱۲.

و در اوقاتی که موکب همایون شهریاری در هیجان حرکت بسمت جرجان بود مشارالیه بحقوق محبّت‌های سابق من که در عهد خاقان مغفور در زمانی که از فارس و عراق متواری و فراری شده پناه بمن آورده بود و من او را در دولت آباد که ملک محدثی من است پناه داده مدّتها نگاهداری نمودم تا از خطر جانی ایمن شده بمسکن امانی مأمن گزید این اوقات اظهار صداقت و محبّت بمن مینمود.

لهذا بعد از حرکت از کرمان و ملحق شدن بأُردوی همایون در مقام تلافی بر آمده در خدمت شاه مرحوم از باب فخریّه معلوم نموده بود که من مثل آقاخان مریدی که در اکثر بلاد عالم کرورها مرید دارد دارم. و ضمناً چون من مقرّر کرده بودم که از مال حلال خود ماهی پانصد تومان جهة خرج نهار و شام شهریار خُلد مقام و یکصد تومان جهة خرج سفرهٔ[۱۵] مرحوم حاجی میرزا آقاسی میدادم در حین روانگی حاجی مشارالیه از کرمان بطرف أُردوی همایون وجوه مزبور را شش ماهه مصحوب عالیجاه ارجمندی شاهرخ خان[۱۶] در صحبت ایشان بجرجان فرستادم.

چون در آن اوقات حاجی زین‌العابدین بخیال انتظام دادن مهام سلطنت افتاده و همگی حواس را آماده پیاده ساختن حاجی وزیر از رخش وزارت

---

۱۵ ب ۱۳.

۱۶ یکی از بزرگان طریقهٔ نعمت‌اللّهی در این زمان است.

نموده، بدستیاری امنا و مقرّبین بزم حضور سلطنت مثل میرزا نصرالله صدر الممالک و میرزا مسعود وزیر دول خارجه و میرزا باقر ملک الکتّاب و بعضی دیگر از اصحاب و احباب مشارالیه تقصیرات چند که تفصیلش موجب اطناب است بر حاجی وزیر وارد آورده و فهرست نموده باطمینان تمام در شاهرود و بسطام مجال اضمحلال او را یافته باستظهار کلّی انجاح مقصود خود را جزوی شمرده فهرست را بنظر پادشاه مرحوم رسانید و بغرور این خیالات نیاز شش ماهه که جهة شاه مرحوم و حاجی وزیر فرستاده بودم نرسانید. بالحاصل شاهنشاه جنّت آرامگاه همان ساعت حاجی وزیر را طلبیده و فهرست را باو سپرده بودند. و مشارالیه بعد از ملاحظهٔ همین قدر گفته بود که خطای بزرگ مرا که نوّاب ضیاء السّلطنه را بنکاح میرزا مسعود درآوردم ننوشته‌اند.

بالجمله[۱۷] در شب آن روز حاجی مرشد را که درکمال عظمت و اجلال بود بنهایت خفّت و اضمحلال از اُردو و ملک اخراج و با وجود معیّن بودن صد اسپ و قاطر بار و سواری جهة ایشان، بیک یابو محتاج و أین المفر گویان در وادی حیرت پویا و سرگردان و بعد از آن کسی از شخص حضرتش نشان نداد تا رخت به بیدای خاموشان گشاد. خدایش رحمت کناد.

[۱۷] ب ۱۴.

خورشید علم بکوهساران زد و رفت
دلدار درِ امید واران زد و رفت
بلبل دستان نو بهاران زد و رفت
گل خنده بوضع روزگاران زد و رفت

بلی

به پیشکاری عقل شریف و رای درست
توان کمند تصرّف در آسمان افکند

و حاجی وزیر بملاحظهٔ صدق همان فخریّه که حاجی مرشد خدمت شاه مرحوم نموده بود که آقاخان مرید من است، و نیز نیاز ماهوار را باو نرسانیده بودند در تدارک خراب کردن من مستعد گردیده، باقصی‌الغایت بنای کوشش را پایه بست. و چون در وقت حرکت موکب همایون بطرف جرجان من عریضه خدمت شاه مرحوم عرض کرده بودم که با وجود وجع و الم پای مبارک چه لازم که بنفس نفیس زحمت مسافرت قرار می‌دهند. پنج فوج لشکر بمن بدهید تا انشاء الله باندک زمانی تا هرات را مفتوح و بممالک محروسه منضم سازم و این کیفیّت علاوه بر فتوحات[۱۸] کرمان و بم و نرماشیر در ضمیر آفتاب تأثیر سلطانی مؤثّر افتاده، مزید خوشنودی

---

[۱۸] ب ۱۵.

خاطر مقدّس شهریاری شده و در سلام عام فرموده بودند که کاش مثل آقاخان برادری داشتم تا علم آسایش می‌افراشتم و روزگار بفراغت می‌گذاشتم.

بالجمله حاجی رحمه الله از همانجا کمر عداوت و خرابی مرا بر میان بسته منتهز فرصت بود مگر بسبب زیادتی التفات پادشاهی نسبت بمن بی‌مستمسک نمیتوانست کاری از پیش برد.

لهذا میرزا علی رضای مستوفی را فرستاده مرا بنویدهای گزاف فریفته و مرا در خدمت پادشاه متّهم ساخته، باتمام کارم پرداختند. و در وقتیکه من در بم بودم و برادر خود سردار ابوالحسن خان را مأمور فتح بمفهل و بلوچستان نموده بودم که خبر حرکت سهراب خان بطرف کرمان رسید و چون من خود فوراً بملاحظهٔ این که مبادا وهن و خرابی از بلوچ و غیره بملک برسد، نتوانستم مراجعت بسمت کرمان نمایم هر چند بواسطهٔ رسل و رسائل خواستم دفع تهمت از خود و مهلت مراجعت سردار را از بمفهل بخواهم صورت نبست تا اینکه شد آنچه شد. بلی،

نباشد پسندیدهٔ شرع و عقل
که بی بینه شاه فرمان دهد
که همچون مضای قضا حکم او
گهی جان ستاند گهی جان دهد

خلاصه معلوم گشت که ارادهٔ الهٰی[۱۹] بنوعی دیگر متعلق است. با خود گفتم:

دانم که بجز خدای قهّاری نیست
بر خاطرم از ظلم کسی باری نیست
ماهیّت مخلوق نباشد غالب
مغلوب خدا شدن مرا عاری نیست

و الحکم لله واحد القهّار

گر در طلبش رنجی مارا برسد شاید
چون عشق حرم باشد سهل است بیابانها

و در این مقدّمات بر ارباب دانش و اصحاب بینش روشن است که بجز عدم غور و حکم فور چیزی مانع اولیای دولت علیّه نبود. و اگر تابع اهوای نفسانی و اغوای شیطانی نبودند و فی الجمله خیر دولت و پاس ناموس سلطنت منظور می‌نمودند، نه مانند من دولتخواهی که از مال و جان در خدمات سلطانی مضایقه نکرده بودم خراب و روگردان می‌شدم و نه آن همه نقصان مالی و جانی و نامی به اعلیحضرت خاقانی می‌رسید. بلکه علاوه بر ملک بلوچستان و سیستان ممالک دیگر نیز بی غایله جزو ممالک

---

۱۹ ب ۱۶.

محروسه می‌شد. و چنانکه اولاد مرحوم شجاع السّلطنه را با افغان و بلوچ از کرمان و بم و نرماشیر گریزانیده به بلوچستان و افغانستان و هرات متواری ساختم تعاقب نموده بانتزاع ممالک دیگر نیز می‌پرداختم. ولی افسوس،

آن شنیدستی که یار بردبار
چون که با او ضدّ شوی گردد چو مار[۲۰]

فاعتبروا یا اولوا الابصار

آن پیر با تزویر و آن وزیر بی تدبیر و آن پروردگان دولت و نعمت و آن بروز قدر و شوکت و آن تسخیر نمودن ممالک که اعلیحضرت سلطانی را در تلو این مقدّمات با آن کوکبه و حشمت محرک بسمت هرات شدند و بهمین طریقها از وساوس شیطانی و هواجس نفسانی که بجز خودبینی و خودرأیی سر موی خیر دولت و نام ولی‌نعمت و ناموس سلطنت را منظور نکرده، چنانچه بعالمی معلوم است بعد از کرورها نقصان با آن احوالات پریشان بی نیل مقصود مطرود ادنی بنده‌ای از بندگان شهریاری شدند.

ببین تفاوت راه از کجاست تا بکجا

---

۲۰ ب ۱۷.

و نتیجهٔ نمک بحرامی چنانچه دیده شد عاید حال تمامی گشت. و الخیر فیما وقع.

جملهٔ عالم ز کهن تا بنو
چون گذرنده است نیرزد بجو

بالحاصل در عین اضطرار، خودداری و وقار را اختیار نموده پا بدامن اصطبار کشیده استوار نشستم، و از سر تعلّقات هوائی بر خواسته رشتهٔ امید نتایج گذشته را گسسته و بالطاف نامنتاهی الهٰی پیوستم و باین ترانه مترنّم گشتم.

به نام نکو گر بمیرم رواست
مرا نام باید که تن مرگ راست
گر نیست مرا طالع پیروز چه باک
ور طبع نگردد الفت‌آموز چه باک[۲۱]
باید چو ز همدمان بریدن پیوند
گر همنفسی نباشد امروز چه باک

چون بخدا و ظلّ او اعلیحضرت پادشاه معلوم بوده و هست که در سر من سودای حکومت کرمان بلکه هوای سلطنت ایران و توران نبوده و

---

۲۱ ب ۱۸.

نیست و محض امتثال امر سلطانی و انجام خواهش و فرمایش خاقانی قبول نمودم و خلقی می‌داند که از فضل الهٰی و برکت آباء و اجداد طاهرینم سلطنتها را در فضای وسعت و رفعت درویشی خود بغایت پست می‌بینم. والحمد خداوند را:

اورنگ زمین داغ نگین بی‌کُلهی تاج
جم رشک برد حشمت شاهانه ما را

و بر عالمی معلوم است که سلطنت صوری و معنوی از ازل متعلّق بآباء و اجداد من بود و تا ابد نیز همین است و همین خواهد بود ولی با وجود این که اجداد بزرگوارم عروة الوثقای دین و حبل الله المتین که لانفصام لها در کتاب مبین و لا ینفصمان و لا ینقطعان در حدیث مشهور جدّم سیّد المرسلین صلّی الله علیه و آله اجمعین بوده‌اند و سر موئی بدنیا و ما فیها مقید نیستم. بلی بقدر امکان در رواج دین و شریعت خاتم النّبیین باقتداء اجداد طاهرین کوشش می‌رود و چنانچه ثابت است که در مصر[۲۲] چند پشت از اجدادم سلطنت و خلافت را متصدّی بودند و رواج مذهب جعفری را بقانون اثنی‌عشری که حال نسبت بشاه اسمعیل صفوی

---

۲۲ ب ۱۹.

می‌دهند ایشان دادند،[۲۳] و من بقیّهٔ آن خاندانم و اگر نگرندگان از عدم تامل و تعمّق نظر نکنند خواهند دانست که:

عالی‌گهران بنده‌نژادان منند
خونین‌جگران باده‌گساران منند
در کشور خود سلطنت ماست قدیم
پیران مغانه خانه‌زادان منند

و الحمد الله المنعم المفضل که بساط درویشی مرا در اکثر ممالک سلاطین معمورهٔ عالم بسیط و گسترده است و اگر سلاطین بلاد بزجر و عنف مالیات از رعیّت می‌گیرند، مالیات مرا بدون طلب در غایت عجز و انکسار، خاکسارانه آستانم را می‌بوسند و می‌رسانند. و اگر در حلال و حرام بموجب احکام محکم مَلِک علّام و شریعت سیّد انام حساب و عقابی را معتقد باشند میزانِ حقّ و باطل است درویشی ما و سلطنتها.

بالجمله چون خبر وصول سهراب خان متواتر شد و فرصت تدبیر رفع تهمت کم، برادران خود سردار ابوالحسن خان را از طرف بلوچستان و سردار محمّد باقر خان را از سمت راور طلبیدم. چون عرصهٔ مجال تنگ بود و خصم آمادهٔ جنگ، لهذا سردار محمّد باقر خان را بزخم گلوله از پا

---

۲۳ این عبارت در چاپ ساعی (ص. ۳۵) بدین شکل تغییر یافته است: «رواج مذهب تشیع که تا آن زمان در بیچارگی بود رونق گرفت». و ارجاع به شاه اسماعیل صفوی در آن حذف شده است.

درآوردند و با خدم و حشم جملگی گرفتار کردند، و با محمّد جعفر خان برادرزادهٔ مرا که در کرمان[۲۴] نایب الحکومه مقرّر کرده بودم مقید ساختند، و با لشکری آراسته بسرداری شاهرخ خان ولد ابراهیم خان قاجار بمحاصرهٔ بم پرداختند و من ناچار بجهة محافظت جان و ناموس محصور شدم و امتداد زمان محاصره مدّت چهارده ماه شد.

و چون مقصود من دفع تهمت از خود بود مُکرّر نوشتم که مرا راه بدهید خود می‌روم خدمت پادشاه. و اگر آنرا مانع خواهید شد راه بدهید از ملک ایران با عیال پریشان بمملکت دیگر می‌روم و هر چند از این باب لجاجت تکرار رفت، جواب بجز صدای توپ و تفنگ نیامد، و روز بروز بجمعیّت و کوشش در سختی محاصره می‌افزودند اگر چه مکرّر آنها را شکست فاحش دادم و توپخانهٔ آنها را گرفتم و اگر می‌خواستم بکلّی آنها را مضمحل می‌ساختم، و لیکن بتصور این که رشتهٔ مودّت گسیخته نشود و تهمت مدّعیان راست نیاید خودداری نمودم.

و بعد از اضطرار برادر خود سردار ابوالحسن خان را با عریضهٔ نیاز خدمت نوّاب فریدون میرزا بشیراز فرستاده استعداد طلبیدم. و آن سرکار محمّد صادق خان برادرزادهٔ خاقان مغفور را بجهة حرکت دادن من بطرف فارس فرستاد. و خان معزّی الیه بعد از ورود باتفاق عبّاسقلی خان لاریجانی که

---

۲۴ ب ۲۰.

از جانب پادشاه مرحوم بمحاصرهٔ بم مشغول بود با کلام الله[۲۵] مجید داخل قلعه گردیده، قسم خوردند و عهد نمودند که سر موئی دست انداز بمال من و نوکر من و عزّت من نکنند، و من قلعه را خالی نموده با نوکر و عیال خود روانهٔ فارس شوم.

بعد از عهد و پیمان و قسم در تدارک تخلیهٔ قلعه و حرکت خود بر آمده آنها را بداخل آمدن و نوکر خود را ببیرون رفتن حکم دادم که بیکدفعه داد و فریاد نوکرهای من بلند شد بعد که مُشخّص گشت یک‌یک گرفته و برهنه و بسته شده بودند و کار از چاره گذشته بود. باقی از نقیر تا قطمیر حتّی ملبوس بدن کبیر و صغیر را گرفتند و مارا بطریق اُسرا روانهٔ کرمان نمودند. چون این نوع بلایا موروثی بود رضا بقضای الهٰی داده بشکرگزاری[۲۶] افزودم.

بس بو العجبی است زیر این چرخ اثیر
عبرتکده‌ایست در نظر عالم پیر
جان گشته بقید تن گرفتار ببین
سیمرغ بدام عنکبوتست اسیر

---

۲۵ ب ۲۱.

۲۶ در نسخه‌ها «بشکرگذاری» آمده است.

پس مژدهٔ این فتح را بهرات فرستادند. چون نوّاب محمّد رضا میرزا شاهزاده که با حاجی زین‌العابدین هم مشرب و در سلک مریدان او مرتّب بود و از ضبط نمودن و نرسانیدن حاجی مشارالیه وجه خرج شش ماهه سفرهٔ شاه مرحوم و حاجی را مُطّلع بود و در همان سفر تفصیل را بحاجی وانمود کرده بود آن مرحوم نیز از آنچه در حقّ من کرده پشیمان گشته بود.

الغرض مدّت هشت ماه[27] در کرمان بطریق محبوسان بسر بردم. ولی از آنجا که فضل الهٰی آن فآن شامل حال این درویش بوده و هست در روز ورود بکرمان چندان تنخواه نقد از طرف هندوستان و خراسان و ترکستان و بدخشان جهة من آوردند که جبران آنچه از من و نوکرهای من برده بودند بالمضاعف شد.

بعد از ورود موکب همایون پادشاهی از طرف هرات بدارالخلافهٔ طهران بجهة حرف محمّد رضا میرزا مرا بدارالخلافه خواستند و فرستادند. و چون بحاجی غفر[ه] الله بیگناهی من ثابت بود لهذا بطریق احترام با من حرکت نمودند. لکن در مدّت توقّف اصلاً از من جویا نشدند که تو چه کردی و ما با تو چه کردیم و سبب نقض قول ما چه بود و حقّ خدمات تو چه شد. پس از ظهور این گونه بی احتسابی رخصت حامل نموده یکچند

---

۲۷ ب ۲۲.

در وشناوهٔ[۲۸] قم بجهة تبدیل آب و هوا ماندم و بعد روانهٔ محلّات شدم که آسوده شوم.

بعد از چندی حاجی عبد المحمّد که از رعایای پست محلّات بود در زمان ابتذال حاجی وزیر باسم من و رسم درویشی‌های متعارف مصاحب او شده بود، در عهد وزارت او رفته‌رفته محرم خاص‌الخاص گشته و بواسطهٔ او محرم و صدیق اعلیحضرت سلطانی گردیده بمزید اعتبار اختصاص[۲۹] داشت، از دارالخلافه وارد محلّات شد و بغرور عزّت چهار روزهٔ عاریتی داعیهٔ وصلت با من نمود. و چون هم کفو نبود از طرف من دعوتش باجابت مقرون نیامد و او را پس از ابراز این داعیه نزد خود راه ندادم.

بعد از مأیوسی در ثانی روانهٔ دارالخلافه و در آنجا مروراً باوقات خاص خاطر نشان پادشاه و حاجی نمود که آقاخان در تدارک جمع‌آوری لشکر و هوای مخالفت در سر دارد، بلی:

هر که در اصل بد نهاد افتاد
هیچ نیکی ازو مدار امید
ز آنکه هرگز بجهد نتوان ساخت
از کلاغ سیاه باز سفید

---

۲۸ ب و ت: وشنابهه.

۲۹ ب ۲۳.

رفته رفته این تهمت شهرت گرفت. و نیز از جانب بعضی از امنای دولت و امرای عراق و خراسان و علمای ملّت همه روزه رسل و رسائل پی در پی می‌رسید که حرکت کن که ما از مال و جان در راه تو دریغ نخواهیم کرد. و من تحاشی نموده عذرها بجواب زبانی می‌آوردم، تا وقتی که عرصه بر من از هر جهة تنگ شد و در آن هنگام موکب شاهی از دارالخلافه حرکت نموده در دلیجان که پنج فرسنگی محلّات است نهضت فرمود.

پس از آن بآب گرم که یک فرسنگی محلّات است تشریف آوردند و من در آن چند روز بشکار رفته بودم. سه روز در آب گرم توقّف فرموده بعد مراجعت و موکب همایون[۳۰] از دلیجان حرکت کرد.

پس من کاغذی بحاجی نوشتم که اگر مقصود نبودن من در این ملک است رخصت بدهید تا عیال خود را روانهٔ عتبات نمایم و خود بطرف مکّهٔ معظّمه بروم تا خود و خلق الله آسوده شویم. جواب نوشتند که می‌دانم چه قدر جمعیّت داری و چه خیال بخاطر می‌گماری لیکن بهر جا که اراده داری برو.

پس بطریق اضطرار مهاجرت و مفارقت وطن و عیال را اختیار نموده سرکار والدهٔ مغفوره و نوّاب شاهزادهٔ آزاده و اطفال را وداع و با خدمه و اتباع روانهٔ عتبات عالیات ساختم، و خود با برادران و برادرزادگان و وابستگان

---

۳۰ ب ۲۴.

و بعضی از عیال بتدارک سفر مکّهٔ مشرّفه پرداختم. و در چهارم شهر رجب هزار و دویست پنجاه و شش هجری از محلّات حرکت کردم، بی خبر از این که بحکّام و عمّال و ضبّاط بلده و بلوکات بین راه احکام محکم شهریاری جاری شده بود که غلّه و مایحتاج بما نفروشند و هر جا و هر کس بهر طریق که توانند در اسر و قتل ما بکوشند.

از این سبب در میبُد یزد بر سر ما شبیخون آوردند و بقدر امکان کوشش در یورش و شلیک تفنگ در جنگ کردند. مگر چون مدد الهٰی معین بیگناهی من بود بر آنها غالب گشتیم و بسلامت رفتیم. و نیز در مهریز یزد در حالتی که خسته و مانده وارد شدیم و نوکرها و متعلّقان[۳۱] هر چند نفر بخانه بجهة آسایش مقرّ گرفتند هنگام ظهر من جانب الله بخاطرم گذشت که باید از آبادی خارج گشت، چه گفته‌اند:

ز راه حرص بتعجیل سوی دانه مرو
به هوش باش که دامی است زیر هر دانه

همان ساعت حکم دادم که همگی رخت از قصبهٔ مزبوره بیرون کشیدند و در خارج آبادی آرمیدند. بعد که مُشخّص شد همان وقت نوّاب بهمن میرزای حاکم یزد با دو فوج سرباز و دو هزار سوار و پیاده از طرف دیگر

---

[۳۱] ب ۲۵.

وارد مهریز و بخیال دستگیر نمودن ما جلوریز شده بود. چون خداوند یار ما بود مجال انجام دادن خیال نیافتند.

پس از آنجا بعد از ادای نماز مغرب و عشا سوار شدیم. چون دهات مهریز متّصل بکنار راه بود همه جا شبانه تفنگ بما می‌انداختند تا نصف شب در یکی از دهات بسیار شدّت در بی‌حیائی تفنگ انداختن نمودند. من حکم دادم که نوکرها بزنند. و بفاصلهٔ نیم ساعت ده و قلعه را گرفتند و آنها را شکست دادند و چند نفر از آنها را دستگیر نموده نزد من آوردند و من آنها را رها کرده روانه شدیم.

و بوقت طلوع فجر وارد کالمند گشتیم و آذوقه و سیورسات هیچ نداشتیم و کالمند قلعه‌چهٔ کوچک بود در زمین پستی واقع و دو خانه‌وار در آنجا ساکن[۳۲] و دو باغ مخروبه داشت علی الصّباح قافله‌ای وارد و مایحتاج سیورسات را بقیمت اعلی رواج دادند و در وسط ظهر بخاطرم گذشت که باید از این گود کالمند خارج گشت. پس حکم دادم بنه بار و نوکر سوار شود. برادرها و بعضی از نوکرها عذر آوردند که چون نوکر و اسب همگی خسته و مانده‌اند، بهتر این است که اوّل مغرب اسبها دانه بخورند و سوار شویم من قبول نکردم و حکم دادم که همین ساعت باید سوار شد و خود

---

۳۲ ب ۲۶.

اسب خواستم و سوار شدم. پس بنه بار و سوار سوار شد و از گود کالمند بالا آمدیم.

ناگاه دیدیم دشت مالامال لشکر است و رسیدند. پس من بسردار محمّد باقر خان گفتم برو مشخّص کن که کیستند و چه مقصود دارند او با چند سوار روانه شد و قبل از آن که بهم برسند از طرف آنها شلیک توپ و تفنگ شد. پس سردار ابوالحسن خان و جمعی از سواران نیز تاختند و بکار مقابله پرداختند. و اگرچه آنها زیاده از چهار هزار سرباز و تفنگچی و سوار بودند لکن چون اکثری چریک و جنگ ندیده بودند فرصت دو شلیک زیاد نیافتند. و از مدد الهٰی مغلوب شدند و بقدر پانصد نفر دستگیر و مساوی دویست شتر و اسب و قاطر و بنهٔ آنها را بتصرّف آوردند. و سوار محیط‌وار دور آنها را احاطه کرده[۳۳] تا یکساعت بغروب مانده زد و خورد کردند یک نفر از غلامان من کشته و نصرالله خان عطاءاللٰهی و چهار نفر دیگر زخمی شدند پس فریاد الامان آنها بلند و از غایت تشنگی از پا افتادند پس من حکم دادم اسرا و بنهٔ آنها را رها کردند.

هم در آن وقت علی محمّد خان برادرزادهٔ میرزا حسین وزیر که حاکم و مالک بلوک دشتاب بود وارد شد. بعد از اطلاق لشکری خصم روانه شدیم و قریب بصبح در جائی سر چاهی پیاده شدیم. و میرزا عبدالغنی را با

---

۳۳ ب ۲۷.

چند سوار مأمور کردیم که بروند در انار سیورسات بخرند و حاضر نمایند که بعد از ورود بآنجا معطّلی بهم نرسد و خود بقاعدهٔ منزل بمنزل روانه شدیم. چهار روز بعد یکی از سواران مأموری به انار در بین راه رسید و مذکور ساخت که رفتیم و سیورسات مایحتاج خریدیم و انبار کردیم شب دوّم جمعی بر سرما ریختند و بما آویختند. من فرار کردم و باقی را کشتند.

پس از شنیدن این مقدّمه یقین کردم که نخواهند گذاشت که ما بسلامت بصوب مقصود روانه شویم. ناچار راه را تغییر و توکّل بعنایت خداوند قدیر نموده از طرف شهر بابک روانه شدیم. بعد از ورود بشهر بابک سردارهای قندهار کهن دل خان و خدارحم خان و مهردل خان که در قلعهٔ شهر بابک[۳۴] که ملک و خانهٔ موروثی من بود منزل داشتند. دروازهٔ قلعه را بروی ما بستند و از برج و باره بنای تفنگ انداختن را گذاشتند. من هم اضطراراً حکم دادم قلعه را محاصره کردند.

چون در قلعه آذوقه نداشتند بعد از سه روز که آنها را محاصره نمودم پیر خود را بامان نزد من فرستادند و اظهار عجز نموده مذکور ساخت که سردار کهن دل خان می‌گوید که چون پسر من محمّد عمر خان در طهران است و من از جانب امنای دولت پادشاهی مأمور بودم که راه عبور را بر شما به بندم. از این سبب باین حرکت نالایق اقدام کردم. و حال بهمین عذر

---

۳۴ ب ۲۸.

نمی‌توانم نزد شما بیایم و نه جرات دارم که قلعه را بشما بگذارم و نه طاقت جنگ دارم و می‌دانم که ملک و خانه مال شماست من هم مهمان شما هستم، لکن چون از ملک و خانهٔ خود آواره و پناه بخانهٔ شما آورده‌ام توقّع دارم که دست از محاصرهٔ من بکشید و مرا مخلص خود بشمارید و بحال خود بگذارید و گذرید.

پس من عذر آنها را پذیرفتم و حکم دادم نوکر از دور قلعه بر خواست و برادر خود محمّد باقر خان را با میرزا اسحق و آقا محمّد باقر اناری و خان بابا خان و عبّاسقلیخان را با چند سوار روانهٔ سیرجان نمودم که سیورسات و مایحتاج خریده[۳۵] موجود نمایند، و خود با عیال روانهٔ رُومنی شده. و بعد از چهار روز چاپاری از جانب محمّد باقر خان وارد و مذکور ساخت که فضلعلیخان با پنج فوج سرباز و سوار و پنج عرّادهٔ توپ دور ما را محاصره دارد و اگر بزودی خود را بما نرسانید ما را دستگیر خواهند نمود.

پس من حکم دادم تا جمیع سوار سوار شوند و تفنگچی و شمخالچیان نیز جمّاز سوار شده حاضر و عیال و بنه و صندوقخانه را گفتم بمانند تا حکم ثانی از من برسد، و سُبای بطریق ایلغار چهار ساعت بغروب آفتاب مانده بشتاب روانه شدیم چون مسافت پانزده فرسنگ بود اوّل طلوع فجر مقابل قلعهٔ زیدآباد سیرجان رسیدیم. همان ساعت از طرف خصم افواج

---

۳۵ ب ۲۹.

سوار و سرباز و توپخانه مستعدّ بمقابله آماده و جنگ شروع شد. و سواران ما سوار و سرباز آنها را شکست دادند و محمّد باقر خان فرصت یافته از قلعه بیرون آمده خود را بما رسانید و من بجهة استخلاص سائرین سپر حفظ الهٰی را بر سر کشیده یورش بقلعه بردم. چون بعد از بیرون آمدن محمّد باقر خان سرباز آنها سبقت کرده داخل قلعه شده بودند چندان شلیک توپ و تفنگ بطرف ما نمودند که اگر محافظت خداوندی نبود یک نفر از ما سالم نمانده بود مع هذا برادرزادهٔ من محمّد جعفر خان و چند نفر دیگر[۳۶] از غلامان زخم دار شدند.

چون سوار و اسبهای ما پانزده فرسنگ بتاخت آمده بودند و نیز قورخانه هم نرسیده بود و چهار ساعت جنگ سخت اتّفاق افتاده بود لهذا توقّف را مجال ندیدم و مستأصلاً روانه شدم. و آنها نیز بقدر چهار فرسنگ دور دور ما را تعاقب نمودند. چون کاری نمی‌توانستند بکنند مراجعت کردند، بلی:

گر شود ذرّات عالم پیچ پیچ
با قضای ایزدی هیچ اند هیچ
چون قضا بیرون کند از چرخ سر
عاقلان گردند جمله کور و کر

---

۳۶ ب ۳۰.

ماهیان افتند از دریا برون
دام گیرد مرغ پرّان را زبون
این قضا بادیست سخت و تندخو
خلق چون خس عاجز اندر پیش او.

ما هم از سبب خستگی خود و اسبها در کنار آبی که محاذی قلعه بود فرود آمدیم و کس بجهة خرید نمودن مایحتاج درب قلعه فرستادیم. اهل قلعه دروازه را بستند. ثانیاً فرستادیم که بهر قیمت که دل شما بخواهد جنس بفروشید و پول بگیرید، قبول نکردند. پس حکم کردم بغلبه قلعه را گرفتند و سیورسات از آنها گرفته. بعد از ادای نماز مغرب و عشا بجهة رفاهیّت زخمی‌ها راه را تغییر داده از طرف سرحد فارس روانه شدیم و حاجی فضل الله کیشکوئی استقبال نموده ما را بقلعهٔ خود برد.[۳۷] و لوازم خدمت‌گذاری را بجا آورد و چند روز در آنجا توقّف نموده زخمی‌ها را روانهٔ بندر عبّاس کردیم. و بجهة آسایش و تدارک مافات قلعهٔ سوغان را تصوّر مأمن نموده از کیشکو روانه شدیم.

و بعد از ورود بمحوّطهٔ سوغان خبر رسید که حیدر خان با تفنگچی بسیار درب قلعه را بسته و راه نمی‌دهند. پس من ناچار حکم دادم بغلبه بگیرند. بعد از تصرّف قلعه بروج را مضبوط و حیدر خان و سایر را بمحبّت آسوده

---

۳۷ ب ۳۱.

کردم و از هر طرف مایحتاج بأحسن وجه از فضل خداوند می‌رسید. اگر چه حکم بجمیع بُلوکات شده بود که ما را در ملک نگذارند و آب و نان بر روی ما به بندند و هیچ چیز بما نفروشند و فضلعلیخان با افواج سوار و پیاده در دو منزلی توقّف داشت ولی حفظ الهٰی در اضطرار شامل حال و قرار ما بود تا این که بدست آوردن غلّه مشکل شد.

در این بین چند سوار از جانب سعید خان بلوچ رودباری بتمنّای حرکت دادن ما بطرف ملک او رسیدند. من هم این مرحله را فرج شمرده روز دیگر از سوغان حرکت کردم و در منازل کهنوپنچرت و بلوک و نوساری سه ماه توقّف نمودم. چون بنه و صندوقخانهٔ ما که با عیال در رومنی بودند، بعد از قضیهٔ زیدآباد فضلعلیخان سوار فرستاده و کلاً را[۳۸] بیغما برده بودند. و عیال من در کوهسارها بسر می‌بردند.

در این چند ماه نوشتم بهر طرف اسباب و ضروریاتی که لازم بود از طرف بنادر و مسقط آوردند، و حکم دادم بردند در باغ نرگس که سرحدّ ملک فارس و متّصل برودبار است خانه‌ها از چوب بجهة هر یک فراخور شأن بنا کنند. و خود بطرف رودان حرکت نمودم. چند ایّامی هم در آنجا بودم و از آنجا نوشتم عیال را بیاورند بباغ نرگس و خود نیز حرکت نموده بخیال آسودگی در باغ نرگس سکونت گرفتم.

---

۳۸ ب ۳۲.

چون این قاعده از قدیم در خانوادهٔ درویشانهٔ ما جاری است که در هر جا ساکن باشیم ارباب حاجت از هر ملک می‌آیند و می‌مانند تا مطلب روا شده روانه شوند لهذا جمعیّت متفرّقهٔ ما زیاد و غلّه کم و از چهار سمت محصور دشمن از این سبب سکونت در آنجا هم مشکل شد. ناچار عیال و اطفال را بطرف کوهساری که ساکن بودند فرستادم و خود در ثانی طرف کهنوپنچرت و بلوک حرکت و دفع خصم را جهة حفظ جان مصمّم شدم و دو عرّادهٔ توپ سرانجام نمودم.

بعد از محرّم ۱۲۵۷ چون اخبار زیادتی لشکر خصم و حرکت علیخان لاری از سمت فارس بمعاونت فضلعلیخان بیگلربیگی کرمان متواتر شد مأیوس شدم و عرصه[۳۹] بغایت تنگ شد. برادر خود میرزا ابوالحسن خان را با صد سوار فرستادم که دشتاب را بغلبه تصرّف نماید. چون علی محمّد خان قبل از جمیع خوانین درکالمند استقبال کرده بود و پیش از همگی سپر بی‌شرمی بر سر گرفته و بمخاصمت برخواسته بود لهذا دشتاب را که ملک و دارالحکومهٔ او بود گرفتند. من نیز بعد از خبر فتح دشتاب از کهنوپنچرت حرکت بطرف اسفندقه که ملک فتحعلی خان مهینی بود نمودم. و مشارالیه فرار کرده بود من یک دو روزی در باغی که قریب بقلعهٔ او بود سکونت ورزیده باستمالت او از هر طرف آدم فرستادم، مگر مفید نیفتاد.

---

[۳۹] ب ۳۳.

و چون خبر رسید که چهار هزار سوار و پیاده بسرداری اسفندیار خان برادر فضلعلیخان بجهة انتزاع دشتاب روانه شده‌اند لهذا جهة دفع او و مدد میرزا ابوالحسن خان حرکت کردم. و یک شب را در درّه کوهی بسر بردم و اوّل طلوع فجر با چهل سوار بتعجیل روانه شدم. و حکم دادم که باقی سوار و پیاده و بنه از تعاقب بیایند.

چهار ساعت از طلوع آفتاب گذشته داخل دربند سیّد علی موسی شدم. و این دربند کوهی است قاف محیط بامامزاده و مرقد در وسط آن واقع است و معبر آن منحصر بدو راه باریک بسیار سخت است. و من[۴۰] بیخبر از این که اسفندیار خان اطراف این کوه را سنگر نموده و خود مستعدّ است که متردّدین را دستگیر نماید. من که از این مقدّمه مطّلع شدم کشته شدن را بدستگیر شدن ترجیح دادم و با همراهان زدیم بکوه.

چون اسفندیار خان و سوارش بالای کوه را که جای اسب تاختن بود داشتند و بالا رفتن ما بسیار سخت بود، از این سبب تا ببالا رسیدن ما بمقابلهٔ پنج دفعه تاخت و شلیک بر سر ما کردند. و نصرالله خان عطاءاللّٰهی و امامقلی خان قاجار و چند سوار بکار از من کشته شدند و به محمّد باقر خان برادرم زخم عظیم رسید تا آن که بالای کوه رسیده مقابل شدیم.

---

۴۰ ب ۳۴.

اگر چه جمعیّت آنها بسیار بود و ما سی و دو نفر، ما دست از جان شسته بجمعیّت آنها تاختیم. و اسفندیار خان سردار آنها را بضرب گلوله از اسب انداختیم. بقیّه اسفندیار خان را بترک گرفته پشت دادند و چند اسب و آدم در تعاقب از آنها زده شد تا خود را بسنگر بزرگ خود که در دامنهٔ کوه واقع بود رسانیدند. من هم بالای سر آنها را گرفته مستعد نشستم تا بمرور سوار و تفنگچی و توپهای من رسیدند. چون جمعیّت آنها چهار هزار بودند لهذا حکم دادم توپها را از بالای کوه مقابل سنگر آنها بستند، و باروت خالی پر کردند و چهار ساعت از مغرب گذشته[۴۱] قریب بتحویل حکم یورش دادم و توپها را سر دادند.

پس چند نفر سواران آنها که مستعد بودند اسفندیار خان را بر داشته فرار کردند، ما بقی خوانین و سر کردگان مثل ولی محمّد خان سرتیپ و محمّد سلیم خان مشیزی و حسین خان قریة العربی و سایر با جمیع سپاه گرفتار و خوانین را بند کرده نزد من آوردند. من حمد الهٰی را بجا آورده و همان ساعت سوار شدم و خوانین را باتّفاق خود گرفته روانهٔ دشتاب شدم. و گفتم باقی نوکرها و سایر گرفتاران را با سامان و اسلحهٔ آنها حمل و نقل نموده بآسودگی روانه شوند.

---

۴۱ ب ۳۵.

روز دیگر جشن عید ترتیب شد. ولی محمّد خان سرتیپ را با سایر خوانین در مجلس طلبیدم و دلجوئی و نوازش بسیار نمودم. پس نوکرهای خود را بفراخور شأن و رتبه بانعام وافی دلخوش کردم و گرفتاران را استمالت و دلجوئی نمودم. آنها هم تعهّد خدمت بصداقت نمودند.

بعد از چند روز که رفع خستگیها شد و خبر قرب علیخان لاری با لشکر فارس متواتر آمد دفع عبدالله خان صمصام الدّوله قراگوزلو سرتیپ را که با تیپ و توپ در بزنجان قرار داشت قبل از ملحق شدن با علیخان مصمّم شدم. و محمّد باقر خان برادرم را بسبب[۴۲] زخمی که داشت با میرزا حسین خان برادرزادهٔ خود، و محمّد سلیم خان مشیزی را با پنجاه نفر تفنگچی و سوار در دشتاب مستحفظ مقرّر کردم، و با این جمعیّت کثیر اسیر نوعهد حرکت بسمت بزنجان نمودم. و بعد از وصول بمحوطهٔ قلعهٔ مذکور خوانین گرفتار را با دسته‌های آنها هر یک را بفاصله در کوهسار جا بجا مقرّر کردم و حکم دادم که هیچ یک از مکان خود حرکت و اقدام بجنگ نکنند تا حکم من نشود، چه:

امید دوستی نو ز دشمنان کهن
چنان بود که طلب کردن گل از گلخن

---

۴۲ ب ۳۶.

و خودم با نوکر خود مقابل قلعه پیاده شدیم و سوار و تفنگچی را سه قسمت نموده از سه سمت قلعه حکم پیش رفتن دادم. از طرف عبدالله خان نیز تیپ سوار و سرباز با توپخانهٔ مستعد مقابل آمد و جنگ شروع شد، جنگی بسیار صعب چون بناحقّ در تلف کردن من میکوشیدند حقّ یاری کرد و من با وجود شلیکهای توپ و تفنگ خودم بطریق یورش حرکت کردم. و بیک دفعه از سه جانب جملهٔ نوکرها یورش آوردند و توپخانه و فوج سوار عبدالله خان پشت دادند چند نفر سرباز گرفتار و باقی در قلعه محصور شدند.

روز دیگر عبدالله خان کاغذی بمن نوشت باینمضمون[۴۳] که من با شما جنگ نمی‌کنم و تعهّد می‌کنم که رفع غائله ما بین بشود. ارکان سلطنت را نوعی بکنم که طرفین مطمئن و آسوده شوید. بالحاصل روز دیگر محمّد علی بیک فارغانی از طرف علیخان لاری وارد و کلام الله شریفی را که علیخان در خاتمه‌اش بدستخط خود باینمضمون نوشته و مهر کرده بود که:

«چون در زمانی که پدرم از ملک و خانه فراری و با عیال و عشایر متواری شد و پناه باین خاندان آوردند، و پنج سال خرج و برج و مجموع را با عزّت و احترام تمام متکفّل شدند، و برادرم نصیر خان و من در خانهٔ شما

---

۴۳ ب ۳۷.

پا بعرصه وجود گذارديم، و خانه‌زاد و نمک‌پروردهٔ شما هستيم، و هميشه مترصّد بوديم که اسبابی مسبّب الاسباب فراهم بياورد که بازای آن همه احسانها خدمتی از ما بشود و حال وقت فرصت است و من از شما توقّع می‌کنم که برويد در مشيز آسوده شويد تا من در تدارک رفع غائله بر آمده دفع تهمت از شما بکنم، و فرمان تفويض حکومت کرمانرا کما فی السّابق بفاصلهٔ دو ماه بشما برسانم و شاهد و حاکم مابين من و شما خداوند تعالی است و کلام او والسّلام.»

و نويدهای زبانی از قول محمّدعلی بيک چندان تکرار رفت که من صدق قول او را يقين نمودم. پس روز ديگر جواب عليخان را حواله بميرزا احمد نمودم و باتّفاق محمّد علی بيک[۴۴] روانهٔ دشتاب کردم که ميرزا حسين خان برادرزاده‌ام را برداشته بردند نزد عليخان. و سبب وقوع اين حوادث را کما هو حقّه باو حالی نموده و استمزاجی از خيالات افعالی آنها حاصل نمايند و مراجعت کند. و خود با عبدالله خان بند و بست نموده با جمعيّت بطرف مشيز حرکت کرديم.

امّا بعد از وصول سيّد حسين خان و ميرزا احمد بادروی عليخان و طیّ گفتگو و بند و بست‌های در خلوت با او، علی الصّباح در اردوی او شيپور کوچ ميزنند. ميرزا احمد از عليخان جويا می‌شود که: شيپور بی وقت بچه

---

۴۴ ب ۳۸.

جهة کشیدند؟ جواب گفته بود: جهة کوچ کردن. پرسیده بود: بکدام سمت؟ گفته بود: بدشتاب. میرزا احمد گفته بود: در دشتاب محمّد باقر خان و جمعیّتی مضبوط هستند و با استعدادند، و شما که بروید بدون جنگ تا جان دارند بشما راه نخواهند داد، و تا جمعی کثیر از طرفین کشته نشوند آن وقت هم تا فتح و شکست نصیب کدام باشد کاری نخواهد شد. پس از قول و قرارداد شما و اطمینان آقاخان چه باقی می‌ماند؟ جواب گفته بود: در این باب[۴۵] من چاره ندارم. احمد بیک یوزباشی مختار است. میرزا احمد از اطوار و گفتگوی علیخان استنباط غدر کرده بود. چون جمعیّت علیخان شش هزار پیاده و سوار و شش عرّادهٔ توپ و جمعیّت احمد بیک نیز از پیاده و سوار چریک شش هزار بودند لهذا میرزا احمد علیخان را خاطر جمع نموده، رخصت مراجعت می‌گیرند. و علیخان محمّد علی بیک فارغانی را با هزار تفنگچی همراه می‌کند که بیایند دشتاب را خالی نموده همگی بیایند در مشیز ساکن شوند. و بعد از ورود بدشتاب چون زخم محمّد باقر خان او را از پا انداخته بود، لهذا دشتاب را تخلیه نموده و روانه می‌شوند. و اردوی آنها بلافاصله وارد دشتاب گشته و ده روز بعد محمّد باقر خان و سایر در مشیز وارد شدند. من متغیّر شدم که چرا دشتاب را خالی کردید؟ میرزا احمد جواب

---

۴۵ ب ۳۹.

داد که: بسبب این که یقین کردم که علیخان بغدر و فریب شما را مشغول نموده و دشتاب را با آن جمعیّت بغلبه می‌گرفتند، زیرا که دسترس بمدد شما نبود.

من با وجود آن قول و عهد علیخان در خاتمهٔ کلام الله حرف میرزا احمد را حمل بخیالات وهمی کردم.[۴۶] و روز دیگر عصری زلفعلی سلطان که در اوقات محاصرهٔ بم یک پای او را گلولهٔ توپ ناقص کرده بود، در راه دو سوار را گرفته با کاغذهای آنها آورد. و بعد از مطالعه معلوم شد که احمد بیک و علیخان بفضلعلیخان نوشته‌اند که ما آقاخان و کسان او را در نهایت اطمینان در مشیز بخواب کرده‌ایم. و شما و عبدالله خان و سردارهای قندهار از سه طرف بنهایت تعجیل خود را برسانید که ما فردا در دو فرسنگی مشیز اردو خواهیم کرد و یک نفر از اینها را اگر پرنده شوند نمی‌گذاریم از این طرف فرار کنند و جملگی از اقبال پادشاهی دستگیر هستند.

بعد از مطالعه حیرت بر من غلبه کرد از مردی و مردمی و اعتقاد علیخان پس گفتم الحکم لله. پس چاپارها را اطلاق نمودم و شب بعد از صرف غذا حکم کوچ دادم و بعزم مقابله و شبیخون زدن باردوی علیخان سوار شدم. مگر برادران و میرزا هادی خان صلاح ندادند و گفتند حال که قضیّه

---

۴۶ ب ۴۰.

برعکس شد باید رفت و بم را گرفت و نشست تا ببینیم خدا چه مقدر می‌کند. پس فسخ آن عزیمت را نموده بطرف قریة العرب روانه شدیم.

روز دیگر بوقت ظهر وارد[۴۷] قریة العرب شدیم که بیست و چهار فرسنگ بود. و یک روز در آنجا توقّف نموده از آنجا منزل بمنزل بطرف بم حرکت کردیم تا بدو فرسنگی بم. و از آنجا میرزا ابوالحسن خان را با پنجاه سوار فرستادم قلعهٔ بم را گرفت. و روز دیگر سوار شده وارد بم شدیم و ارگ بم با توپهای متعدّد بدست تفنگچی عرب و عجم مضبوط بود. بیست و دو روز در بم ماندیم و چند دفعه یورش بارگ بردیم کاری از پیش نرفت، تا این که خبر محقّق رسید که چهار اردو با هم ملحق و بیست و چهار هزار کس می‌باشند. و امروز بدو فرسنگی منزل خواهند نمود.

چون مصلحت بمقابله شدن ندیدم از آنجا بطرف نرماشیر حرکت کردم و قلعهٔ ریگان را که معظم قلاع نرماشیر است منظور نمودم. پس از ورود چون قلعه مملو از تفنگچیان کار بود راه بما ندادند. پس در خارج قلعه پیاده شدم و وسط ظهر حکم دادم قلعه را بیورش گرفتند و شش نفر از آدمهای من کشته و زخمی شدند و بعد از فتح روانهٔ قلعه شدیم. و از

---

۴۷ ب ۴۱.

آنجا برادرم محمّد باقر خان را فرستادم نزد آزاد خان بلوچ که او را با تفنگچی او بجهة حفظ جان بمدد بیاورد.

چهارده روز فاصله لشکر خصم وارد شد.[۴۸] علی الصّباح حکم دادم بنه و بار روانه شود و خود با سوار بعزم مقابله با خصم حرکت کردیم. چون جنگل بود و میدان جنگ نبود خوانین گفتند که باید عقب بنه بآرامی رفت. اینها هم می‌آیند هر جا که میدان تاخت و تاز بنظر آمد بر می‌گردیم و جنگ می‌کنیم. من هم بقول آنها عمل نموده بقدر نیم فرسنگ از قلعه دور شدیم. از حرکت ما خصم جری شده سرعت در تعاقب نموده بقدر تیررس نزدیک شدند. من برگشتم و تفنگی بطرف آنها انداختم و حکم دادم که بر گردید و بزنید. که بیکدفعه سوار ما و میرزا ابوالحسن خان دست از جلو بر داشتند و فرار کردند. اسبهای یدک مرا هم بردند. از قضا اسب سواری من هم گلوله خورد و با من زیاده از هفت کس باقی نماند: محمّد جعفر خان برادرزاده و میرزا هادی خان خراسانی و محمّد رحیم مهردار و میرزا احمد و حسین پیشخدمت و نجفعلی بیک و ملک محمّد بیک. پیدا است که هفت تن با بیست و چهار هزار پیاده و سوار چه می‌کند، مگر حفظ الهٰی. و حال این که گلولهٔ توپ و تفنگ مثل باران می‌بارید و از چپ و راست چهار علم سپاه خصم در جلو ما بودند.

---

[۴۸] ب ۴۲.

باری[۴۹] بطریق جنگ و گریز حرکت مذبوحی کردیم تا عصر به تل بلندی رسیدیم که در آنجا میرزا ابوالحسن خان و سایر سواران قرار گرفته بودند. و از آنجا اسب خود را عوض نمودم و روانه شدیم. و از نوادر اتّفاقات در بین جنگ و گریز دو الاغ که دستهای آنها را بطناب بهم بسته بودند مقابل آمدند و دستهای اسب محمّد رحیم بطناب بند شد. و نجفقلی بیک تاخته پیاده شد و طناب را بریده و سوار شد که در این بین گلولهٔ به دبّهٔ باروت کیسه کمر او خورد و رختهای او آتش گرفت و بدنش سوخت. و مجموع بدن آن بیچاره مجروح شد و از اسب نیفتاد و سالم ماند.

بالجمله بوقت غروب بدهنهٔ تنگی رسیدیم و لشکر خصم نتوانست تعاقب کند. بفاصلهٔ یک فرسنگ ماندند ما هم در آنجا پیاده شده نماز خواندیم و غذا صرف شد و اسبها جو خوردند و سوار شدیم. چون شب بود و ابر و بارش و درّه‌های سخت در راه بود از این سبب جمیعّت ما از یک دیگر جدا ماندند و نصف از راهی و تتمّه از راهی روانه شدند. و روز دیگر بوقت نهار در دامنهٔ قلّهٔ بلندی بهم ملحق شدیم. و منزل بمنزل ما در جلو و آنها[۵۰] از تعاقب می‌آمدند. من با خود تصور کردم مآل حال را، دیدم باینطریقها عمر ضایع کردن حاصلی ندارد. بر فرض این که ده سال

۴۹ ب ۴۳.

۵۰ ب ۴۴.

باینطورها زد و خورد بکنم. پس عزم خود را جزم کردم که از تنگ شمیل روانهٔ بندر عبّاس شوم از آنجا بجهاز سوار شده روانهٔ هندوستان یا عربستان بشوم.

پس باین عزیمت روز دیگر داخل تنگ شمیل شدیم و لشکر خصم این طرف تنگ ماند و فاصلهٔ تنگ البتّه شش فرسنگ بود غرض آمدیم تا قریب بانتهای تنگ سوارهائی که در جلو بودند بر گشته گفتند تفنگچی بسیار دهنهٔ تنگ را از دو طرف بسته‌اند و عبور نمی‌دهند. خود تاختم جلو معلوم شد که چند مدّت است این تفنگچی‌ها با تدارک تمام در اینجا ساخلو[۵۱] هستند بجهة محافظت ملک میناب و بندر عبّاس پس بدلالت و نوید انعام هر چه سعی کردیم راه ندادند. ناچار برگشتیم و در وسط تنگ کنار آبی پیاده شدیم. سیورسات هم اصلاً نداشتیم و در آن کوهسار هم بجز کوه در کوه دیگر آبادی متصوّر نبود. گفتم الحکم لله الواحد القهّار.

نیم ساعت هم بغروب باقی بود در این بین از تفضّلات الهٰی شخصی درویش نوری نام پیدا شد و گفت هر چه ضرورت است مشخص کنید تا من بیاورم. پس میرزا احمد سیاههٔ سیورسات را باو داد و رفت و بفاصلهٔ دو ساعت مراجعت نمود و بقدر ضرورت بار کرده با چند سر گوسفند

---

۵۱ ت: ثاخلو.

آورد. و چند روزی که آبشخور در آن تنگنا بود بر سبیل استمرار درویش مذکور سیورسات را می‌رسانید.

روز سیّم بعد از ظهر برادرهای من و دو نفر از نوکرهای معتبر آمدند من پرسیدم مطلبی دارید؟ میرزا ابوالحسن خان پیشتر آمده گفت: مقصود ما همگی این است که یا حکم بدهید تنگ را بشکنیم و بیرون برویم، یا مرخّص کن باین کوهسار متفرّق شده هر کس بطرفی برود. من جواب گفتم که: اگر بگویم تنگ را بشکنید جمعی کشته خواهند شد، و اگر بگویم در کوهسار متفرّق شوند همه هلاک خواهند شد. صبر کنید از جانب خدا فرج خواهد شد.

ابوالحسن خان گفت: دیگر فرج بجهة ما از این تنگنا محال است و هرگز نخواهد شد. من بشوخی گفتم: اگر فرجی بشود، چه خواهی داد؟ گفت: صد هزار تومان می‌دهم. گفتم: غلط گفتی. از کجا می‌دهی؟ گفت: مقابل روی تو بلشکری که پنجاه هزار باشد خود را می‌زنم. گفتم: این هم غلط است. کشته خواهی شد. گفت: اقرار می‌کنم که پیغمبری!. گفتم: این هم غلط است. پیغمبر جدّ ما بود لکن من دیشب در خواب دیدم که پس فردا یک ساعت و نیم بغروب مانده دو سوار از این طرف خواهند آمد با نوشتجات چند و همان ساعت که آنها رسیدند ما سوار خواهیم شد.

پس آنها رفتند بمکان خود. و دو روز بعد سر ساعت میرزا ابوالحسن خان مکمّل و جلو اسب بدستش آمد نزد من گفتم ابوالحسن خان گویا سر وعده آمده‌ای. پس بعلی بیک تفنگدار گفتم برو از این تل بالا ببین کسی می‌آید. رفت قدری بالاتر و گفت دو سوار بنظر می‌آید. پس چند دقیقه فاصله رسیدند و نوشتجات را دادند و من حکم کردم بنه بار و اسبها را حاضر کردند و سوار شدیم.

اگرچه خوانین کرمان و سایر بالاتّفاق نوشته بودند که ما همگی یکدل کمر بخدمت بسته‌ایم و هرچه زودتر البتّه مراجعت کنید که ما خود اردوی فضلعلیخان و علی خان را بهم می‌زنیم، مگر من اعتماد نکردم و در دل خود قصد رفتن خراسان را مصمّم شده باحدی ظاهر نکردم.

و از تنگ شمیل که سوار شدیم هفت روزه بزرند رسیدیم. و در آنجا چند روزی توقّف نموده رفع خستگی اسبها شده بطرف راور حرکت کردیم. و چند سوار بجهة اطّلاع علیرضا خان راوری فرستادم که وحشت نکنند. مشارالیه ملّا حسین نام وکیل خود را مصحوب آدمهای من فرستاده در خواست کرده بود که در کوبنان منزل بکنم. من حسب التّمنای او بکوبنان نزول نمودم.

چون امیر توپخانه[۵۲] باستعداد تمام از دارالخلافه جهة مدد فضلعلیخان حرکت و بیزد رسیده، و علیرضا خان هم مثل سایر خوانین متوحش بود لهذا سه هزار تفنگچی که جهة محافظت راور معیّن کرده بود فرستاد بکوبنان و بنوکرهای من ملحق شدند. و نوشت بمن که تا ده روز دیگر ده هزار تفنگچی موجود و چنین و چنان خدمت می‌کنم. و بر سبیل استمرار همه روزه چهار صد و پانصد تفنگچی او بکوبنان و بنوکرهای من ملحق می‌شدند.

میرزا ابوالحسن خان و بعضی از نوکرهای معتبر من بخیالات واهی متوهّم شده[۵۳] مکرّر وانمود نمودند که علیرضا خان با خدعه و غدر می‌خواست دست انداز بشما بکند و در نزد امنای دولت وسیلهٔ آسایش و اعتبار او بشود. و چندان از این مقوله اظهار کردند که من ناچار حکم بکوچیدن دادم و تفنگچیان علیرضا خان را بحال خود گذاشته روانه شدیم.

و روز دیگر عصر دامنهٔ گداری که متّصل به خاک یزد بود رسیدیم که ناگاه به تاخت و فریاد کنان ملّا حسین وکیل علیرضا خان رسید و گریبان خود را درید و گفت: به چه سبب حرکت کردید؟ من پیش نفس خود شرمنده شدم و به برادرها و جمیع نوکرها گفتم اگر بلای گرفتاری یا کشته شدن

---

۵۲ ت: بخانه

۵۳ ب از این‌جا به بعد آغاز می‌شود.

نازل باشد، جهة من است. و من لامحاله مراجعت می‌کنم هر یک میل دارید با من بیائید و هر کس مایل نباشد و از جان خود بترسد بهر کجا می‌خواهد برود. پس من مراجعت نمودم و همگی با من موافقت کردند. مگر برادرم میرزا ابوالحسن خان و چند نفری که اعتماد بآنها داشتم رفتند. گفتم بخدا سپرده باشند. و بنوکرها گفتم اینها ده روز دیگر بعضی زخمی و گرفتار و بعضی با ابوالحسن خان خجل و شرمسار مراجعت[۵۴] خواهند کرد.

بعد از ورود بکوبنان یک شب توقّف و روز دیگر بخواهش علیرضا خان حرکت و در باغ محدثی میرزا شفیع خان والد مشارالیه که قریب بقلعهٔ راور است نزول نمودیم و چند روزی در آنجا متوقّف و بکمال فراغت آسودیم و علیرضا خان از لوازم خدمتگذاری دقیقه نامرعی نگذاشت و از امورات اتّفاقیّه، روز دهم میرزا ابوالحسن خان با چهار نفر از همراهان وارد شدند و مابقی زخمی و گرفتار سپاه پادشاهی شده بودند.

بالجمله چون عزیمت خراسان در ممکن خاطر متمکّن بود در چند ایّامی که در راور ماندم علیرضاخان را بنصایح دلپذیر آسوده خاطر نمودم. و نوکرها را از قصد خود مخبر و در همراهی با من و مراجعت باوطان مختار کردم.

---

۵۴ ب ۴۵.

و روز دیگر از آنجا حرکت نموده قریب بلوت منزل ساخته. شب اکثر از همراهان بیخبر برگشتند و صبح بامید الهٰی سوار شده بلوت زدیم. و اسمعیل خان طبسی با چند سوار بلد جلو و بجهة بی‌آبی لوت بتعجیل روان شدیم. مع هذا چندان صدمهٔ تشنگی باسب و آدم وارد آمد که بعضی حیوانات از تاتو و باز و تولهٔ شکاری سقط شدند. تا عصر که از لوت گذشتیم و راویه‌های[۵۵] آب که از نای بندان جلو ما فرستاده بودند رسید. اشهد بالله آب حیات بود که موجب حیات مردمان و دوابّ شد و الحمد خداوند را که آدم اذیّت ندید، چه نادر شاه را خوانین طبس ازین راه بردند و دو ثلث لشکری او چه غرق شدند و چه از تشنگی هلاک شدند. و الحمدالله سالم رفتیم و مغرب وارد نای بندان شدیم.

چون آب و هوای بسیار خوب داشت دو سه روزی توقّف نمودیم. و از آنجا حرکت بطرف قاین را مصمّم شده میرزا هادی خان را فرستادیم نزد امیر اسدالله خان بجهة اطلاع او، و خود منزل بمنزل بفراغت می‌رفتم، تا یک منزلی قاین میرزا هادی خان مراجعت و عذر امیر را باینطریق خواست که می‌گوید آصف الدوله با من دشمن و سرخرابی مرا دارد چنانچه جماعت نخعی را بمخالفت من محرّک شده و الآن مابین ما کار

---

۵۵ ب ۴۶.

بمجادله کشیده است. و اگر شما بیائید در قاین بهمین بهانه مرا پیش پادشاه بدنام و تمام می‌کند.

من ناچار عذر او را پسندیدم و راه را گردانیدم و بطرف سربیشه حرکت کردم. و در آنجا عمّهٔ امیر اسدالله خان خواه مخواه ما را یازده روز نگاه داشت[۵۶] و از لوازم ضیافت و حرمت بهیچوجه فرو نگذاشت. من هم چنانچه بایست توقیر او و پسر او را منظور و از آنجا حرکت سمت قندهار را که از هر طرف مریدهای هر مملکت بمن نزدیکتر باشند مصمّم و روانه شدم.

منزل بمنزل در کمال آسودگی رفتم تا به لاش و جوین که اوّل خاک افغانستان است نزدیک و از دو منزلی سواری جهة اطّلاع نزد شاه پسند خان که مالک ملک بود فرستادم. و در یک منزلی جواب از طرف او رسید و تأکید زیاد در قبول خواهش او که توقّف کنم در چهار فرسنگی تا در آنجا ملاقات بشود و روانه شویم. اگرچه از این کیفیّت اکثر از همراهان بخیالهای دور و دراز افتادند. و در حقیقت جا هم داشت چه بسی احتمالها در نتیجهٔ آن متصوّر می‌شد و لکن من مستظهر بتوکّل و وکیل خود بودم و بی دغدغه در تسلیم بحکم قضا و قدر می‌آسودم فکفی بالله وکیلاً و کفی بالله شهیداً.

---

۵۶ ب ۴۷.

علی الصبّاح که از یک منزلی سوار شدیم میل بمیل و فرسنگ بفرسنگ با بار میوه‌جات و مأکولات متعارفانه چنانکه زیبای میزبانی او بود می‌رسید، تا به چهار فرسنگی در آنجا مکانی بحدّ خود[۵۷] عالی و خروارها میوه‌جات از قبیل خربزه و خیار و هندوانه و غیره انبار. پس پیاده شدیم و من در آن روز در کمال سادگی جبّهٔ پشمینهٔ خودرنگ در بر و نیم‌تاج درویشی با رشته بر سر در مکان معین قرار گرفتم و نوکرها در اطراف مکان نموده آسودند.

یکساعت فاصله شاه پسند خان با اولاد و احفاد و اجانب و اقارب با تجمّلی که ممکن او بود وارد و بآدابهای گزیده و احترامهای پسندیده ملاقات، و بعد از صرف شیرینی و میوه و چای سوار و تفرّج کنان تا دامنهٔ حصار استوار خدا آفرین لاش رسیدیم. خواستیم پیاده شویم مانع آمد و تکلیف رفتن بالای قلعه و منزل کردن بخانهٔ خود را نمود. پس جمیعاً رفتیم بالای ارگ پیاده شدیم. و ظهور این حکایت موجب بروز کمال محبّت و مودّت او شد. چه کامران شاه را که ولی‌نعمت او بود با چهار نفر آدم راه نداد، و فرزند خود را بدستور. پس این مرحله تقلیب مقلّب القلوب است.

بعد از دوازده روز که بعنف ما را نگاه داشت و از وظایف ضیافت دقیقهٔ نامرعی نگذاشت رضا بحرکت ما داد و خود تا جوین مشایعت نموده

[۵۷] ب ۴۸.

آنچه[۵۸] شایستهٔ او و شایان من بود از تعارفات رسمی بعمل آمد. و عبدالقادر خان منسوب خود را با چند سوار همراه نموده ما روانه و او مراجعت کرد.

پس منزل بمنزل آمدیم تا به گرشک. و از آنجا سواری جهة اطّلاع شاهزاده محمّد تیمور حاکم، و میجر رالنسن صاحب کلکتر قندهار فرستادیم. و در چهار فرسنگی قندهار از خوانین و اکابر جمعی کثیر استقبال نمودند، و بعزّت در روز هفدهم شهر ذی قعدة الحرام ۱۲۵۷ وارد قندهار و بخانه‌ای که جهة نزول ما معیّن شده بود پیاده و کلانتر را مهماندار ما کردند.

و بعد از سه روز خرج مهمانی ما را خشکه از قرار روزی صد روپیه مقرّر کردند. و پس از دید و بازدیدها شرح احوال ما را شاهزاده و رالنسن صاحب خود نوشته و بمن هم القاء کردند، نوشتم بلارد مکلاتن صاحب و شاه شجاع و جواب در کمال مهربانی رسید. و مقرّر شد که بمعاونت آنها هرات را گرفته، ساکن شوم. مگر تقدیر مخالف تدبیر آمد و حکایت بلوای کابل متواتر شد و خلل فاحش در احوال صاحبان انگریز ظاهر شد. و رفته رفته قضیّهٔ بلوا در قندهار نشر و خوانین و سردارهای[۵۹] قندهار یاغی شدند. و ملک برهم خورد و افاغنهٔ شهری بی اعتبار و اکثری را اخراج بلد

---

۵۸ ب ۴۹.

۵۹ ب ۵۰.

نمودند. و دروازها خاکریز شد و راهها از تردّد متردّدین مسدود ماند. و مکرّر جنگها واقع شد و من در همهٔ جنگها بودم و بقدر امکان معاونت خلق الله را مواظبت می‌نمودم. چون تفصیلش در دفاتر انگریزیّه ثبت است همین قدر اجمالاً اکتفا رفت.

ولی از فضل الهٰی مریدهای ما از طرف پیشاور و کابل و بلخ و بخارا و بدخشان و سند با وجود سدّ طرق سالم بقندهار رسیدند. چون مدّت محاصره ممتد شد روزی شاهزاده صفدرجنگ و محمّد عمر خان سردار با سایر سرداران و خوانین یاغی کاغذی ممهور بمن نوشتند بایمان مؤکّد که اگر بیرون آمدی و بما ملحق شدی فبها المطلوب و الّا هر وقت دست بیابیم اوّل تو و کسان تو را قتل می‌کنیم، بعد، انگریزان را.

بالجمله بعد که خبر کشته شدن شاه شجاع رسید و صاحبان انگریز مصمّم تخلیه نمودن قندهار شدند، و قورخانهٔ زیادی خود را آتش دادند و شاهزاده صفدرجنگ را طلبیده بحکومت نشاندند و از شهر بیرون آمدند. من هم باتّفاق[۶۰] صاحبان کوچ کردم. و چند روز بجهة بند و بست کار صفدرجنگ در بیرون شهر ماندند، تا روزی کریم خان پیشخدمت شاهزاده آمده مذکور ساخت که: «سردارها افسوس می‌خورند که آقاخان رفت اگر مانده بود سزای او را می‌دادیم». این کیفیّت موجب فسخ عزیمت من

---

۶۰ ب ۵۱.

شد و بجنرل نات صاحب و میجر رالنسن گفتم من بقندهار مراجعت می‌کنم. هر چند مبالغه کردند قبول نکردم.

پس روز دیگر آنها بطرف کابل حرکت و من بقندهار مراجعت نمودم، و در خانهٔ مهردل خان که در وسط خانهٔ افغانها است منزل کردم. و الحمد حافظ حقیقی را که چندان محبّت مرا در دل شاهزاده و سردارها جا داد که شب و روز ساعتی آرامم نمی‌دادند. چون اوضاع آنها را ورای وضع ملک‌داری دیدم مصلحت در سکونت خود ندیدم و چون شاهزاده و سایر از روی محبّت مانع از حرکتم بودند، لهذا سردار ابوالحسن برادر خود را در قندهار گذاشتم. و بملاحظهٔ پاس رعایای فقیر کاغذی بکهن دل خان نوشتم که بزودی روانهٔ قندهار شود تا رعیّت آسوده گردد و خود حرکت نمودم صفدرجنگ[۶۱] اظهار کرد که صالو خان اچک‌زائی یاغی است و سر راه را دارد دو روز تأمّل کن تا تدارک سوار نموده بمدد همراه نمایم. قبول نکردم و روانه شدم.

اگرچه مشارالیه با سه هزار کس سر راه و گدارها[۶۲] را بسته بود، لکن بی دغدغه رفتم و بمجرّد ملاقات لوازم آدمیّت را بجا آورد، و ما را بخانهٔ خود برد و دو روز ضیافت نمود. و روز سیم روانه شدم تا وارد شالکوت که

---

۶۱ ب ۵۲.

۶۲ ب: کدارها.

ملک نصیرخان کلاتی است گشته، و از آنجا سواری بجهة اطّلاع نزد نصیرخان فرستادم او هم نایب محمّد حسن و اکابر ملک خود را باستقبال فرستاد و ما را با احترام تمام وارد کردند و رسم ضیافت را کماکان بجا آوردند. و از آنجا از راه بیلو روانهٔ سند شدیم. و مرحوم میر نصیر خان لوازم اعزاز و اکرام را بجا آورد و در جنب قلعهٔ خود خانهای چند که کفایت من و نوکرهای مرا بکند منزل داد. و بعد از ضیافتها روزی صد روپیه جهة مخارج آدمهای من مقرّر کرد.

و در آن اوقات جنرال سر چارلیس نپیر صاحب و اطرام صاحب در سند بودند، و مقصودشان این بود که میر نصیر خان کراچی را واگذارد بآنها و میر صاحب موصوف[۶۳] تمکین نمی‌کرد. و میر علی مراد خان خیرپوری با جنرال موصوف موافقت نموده و رفته رفته غایله طولانی شد. من از رهگذر خیرخواهی اصرار بسیار بمیرها نمودم که مصلحت شما این است که کراچی را واگذارید و آسوده شوید که علاوه از آنچه مداخل سالیانهٔ کراچی است از دولت انگریز بشما عاید خواهد شد. مگر قبول نکردند تا آنکه لشکر خود را جمع نموده و سراپرده‌ای خارج حیدرآباد زدند من هم سوار شده رفتم در اردوی میر موصوف و اوّلاً آنچه لوازم نصیحت و خیرخواهی بود در ممانعت از جنگ و واگذاردن کراچی بجا آوردم مفید نیفتاد.

---

۶۳ ب ۵۳.

آخرالدّواء جواب داد که فردا شمشیر تالپور را خواهی دید گفتم پس حال که چنین است موافق قانون اسلام نیست که من و نوکرهای من مدد نکنیم لکن چون لباس نوکرها ملبوس ایرانی است شاید بلوچهای لشکر شما نشناسند و خللی واقع شود. پس چند دست لباس سندی بدهید که نوکرهای من بپوشند و با شما بجنگ بیایند قبول نکرد و گفت شما مهمان من هستید هرگز چنین تکلیفی را رضا نمی‌دهم پس من برخاسته[۶۴] مراجعت کردم.[۶۵] و چون قرار داده بودند که شبانه بیخبر در چهاونی شبیخون بزنند، و اطرام صاحب و کسانی که در چهاونی بودند قتل کنند، من محض رضای الهٰی شبانه فرستادم و او را اطّلاع دادم. و شب چهاونی را تخلیه نموده بجهازات سوار شدند و سلامت ماندند.

پس روز دیگر که اردوی آنها بجهة مقابله با افواج انگریزی حرکت کردند من هم از حیدرآباد روانهٔ جرگه شدم بعد از شکست و گرفتاری میرهای سند و تصرّف نمودن حیدرآباد و شورش خوانین بلوچیّه و فساد میر شیر محمّد خان چون صاحبان انگریز مرا خیرخواه خلق الله میدانستند و بمناسبت مسلمانی از من خواهش کردند که چند نفر آدمان بدلالت میر شیر محمّد خان و سایر خوانین بلوچیّه بفرستم که بی غایله اطمینان حاصل نمایند. من هم بخواهش ایشان عمل نمودم. مگر نصایحم ببعضی

---

۶۴ در متن: برخواسته.

۶۵ ب ۵۴.

اثر کرد و باکثری مفید نیفتاد، بلکه میر شیر محمّد خان فرستادهٔ مرا کشت، و با تیپ و توپ بعزم مقابله با لشکر انگریز حرکت، و جنرال صاحب نیز مصمّم شد محمّد باقر خان برادر مرا نیز با خود برد.

و چون بخواهش صاحب موصوف[۶۶] حفاظت از جرگه تا کراچی بدل آسائی و آرامش رعیّت و سکنه و امنیّت طرق مُحوّل بنوکرهای من بود، و من آنها را در لنگر تهته و کراچی و مابین مقرّر کرده بودم، لهذا خود با بیست سوار در جرگه منزل داشتم و قرب هزار نفر مرد و زن از جماعت مریدان هر ملک در جرگه بودند و من مشغول کار آنها بودم. و در جرگه میر شیر محمّد خان جمیع بلوچان سندهه و توابع بمدد و متابعت او حرکت کردند بعضی باو ملحق شدند و بعضی نرسیدند.

بالجمله شیر محمّد خان نوملی با چهار هزار کس و محمّد خان خشک با دو هزار کس در یک شب شیر محمّد خان بجرگه بر سر ما شبیخون آورد و محمّد خان در لنگر تهته بر سر آدمهای من ریخته[۶۷] و در آنجا ده نفر آدمهای من کشته گشتند، و در جرگه هفت نفر از آدمهای من و هفتاد نفر از مریدهای من کشته و زخمی شدند. و من با چند سوار یکتای ارخالق سوار شده، چندان که بهوش بودم در جنگ کوشش کردم، تا اسب

---

۶۶ ب ۵۵.

۶۷ «ریخته» بعداً روی خط اضافه شده است.

من در تاخت یورش بسر افتاد و به پشت بر روی من غلطید. و چهار دندان من شکست و من مدهوش بودم. بقیّة السّیف مرا برداشته از آن[۶۸] مهلکه بیرون برده بودند.

در آن غارت مطابق بیست و سه لک از صندوقخانهٔ من و از آدمهای من بیغما رفت و همین قدرها از مریدان هر ملک و سکنهٔ جرگه غارت نمودند. و چون میر شیر محمّد خان شکست خورده فرار کرده بود شیر محمّد خان هم جرگه را بمستحفظین و تفنگچیان معتمد خود سپرده و خود با اسباب و اموال منهوبه رفته بود من هم شب آن روز را وارد چهاونی شدم. و چند روز تدارک ترتیب سامان دادم تا جنرال صاحب مراجعت نمود. و من برادرزادهٔ خود محمّد جعفر خان را با میرزا احمد و چند نفر نوکر فرستادم بجرگه تا بقیّهٔ جماعت و زخمی‌ها را بیاورند و آنها رفتند و جرگه را از تصرّف بلوچان انتزاع نموده، جماعت و زخمی‌ها را آوردند بچهاونی حیدرآباد، و بمعالجه مشغول شدند.

و جنرل صاحب سیاههٔ اموال غارت شدهٔ مرا خواستند که از بلوچان مطالبه نمایند. مگر مصلحت چنان دیدند که آنچه از ما غارت شده به بلوچان ببخشند تا آنها رام و ملک آرام شود. و در عوض از سرکار کمپنی بما بدهند

---

۶۸ ب ۵۶.

و بعد از چندی که بلوچان اطمینان یافته[69] بالتّمام بسلام شتافتند، بما جواب گفتند که سرکار قبول نکرد که عوض مال منهوبهٔ شما را بدهد. و گفته است که چرا خودشان محافظت نکردند. من گفتم که برادر من سردار محمّد باقر خان را با کلیّهٔ سوار من بخواهش شما همراه شما بجنگ شیر محمّد خان آمده بود، و بعضی از نوکرهای من بحکم شما در لنگر تهته بحفظ طرق مشغول بودند، و من خود با بیست نفر پیشخدمت و عملهٔ خلوت در جرگه بودیم که بیخبر این مقدّمه اتّفاق افتاد. من چگونه جواب چهار هزار کس را می‌دادم؟ جوابی که مقرون بقانون باشد ندادند. من هم ناچار سکوت نمودم و در ثانی در تدارک فراهم آوردن اوضاع خود و نوکر خود بودم.

در این بین فقیر محمّد نام بمفهلی نایب محمّد علی خان بلوچ وارد و نوشته‌جات چند جهة سر چارلیس نپیر صاحب گورنر و من از طرف محمّد علی خان آورد. مضمون این که ملک سندهه و بلوچستان بتصرّف سرکار انگریز بهادر است. من هم خود را و ملک خود را از سرکار و وابسته به سرکار می‌دانم. مگر ازین سبب دین محمّد خان و میر احمد خان و سالار ملوک و سایر خوانین بلوچیّه اکثری در نفاق با من[70] اتّفاق کرده مخالفت

---

۶۹ ب ۵۷.

۷۰ ب ۵۸.

میکنند هرگاه یکی از برادرهای شما بیاید من قلعهٔ بمفهل را باو می‌سپارم و خود کمر بسته خدمت می‌کنم.

من هم تصوّر کردم که بمفهل اگرچه در حقیقت سرحدّ ایران است لکن همیشه تصرّف محراب خان بلوچ پدر محمّد علی خان بوده، و بعد از او تعلّق بپسرش گرفته است و او هم گاهی خدمت بایرانی نمی‌کند. اگر چه در زمانی که من در کرمان بودم سردار ابوالحسن خان برادر خود را بجهة تسخیر آن ملک مأمور کرده بودم، مگر چنانچه ایمائی رفته اُمنای دولت مجال ندادند. و او را قبل از احاطه و تسخیر طلبیدم. حال با وجود تمنّای محمّد علی خان و اطلاع گورنر صاحب اگر بفرستم و ملک را بگیرم ضرری ندارد بلکه یحتمل اسباب التیام مابین بشود.

پس در ماه ربیع الاوّل سنهٔ ۱۲۶۰ سردار محمّد باقر خان برادر خود را با تدارک تمام روانه نمودم. و بعد از ورود محمّد باقر خان به محوّطهٔ بمفهل و ملاقات با محمّد علی خان و ظاهر شدن مخالفت مشارالیه باظهار تمنّای این که اوّل خوانین مخالفین مرا با قلعه‌جات آنها گرفته بسپارند، بعد من قلعهٔ[۷۱] بمفهل را بشما تسلیم می‌نمایم.

ازین سبب از بمفهل مراجعت و سالار ملوک و میر احمد خان متابعت اختیار کرده، میر احمد خان قلعهٔ پیپ را که مسکن او بود تخلیه و تسلیم

---

۷۱ ب ۵۹.

کرده و کمر خدمت بسته بودند. و تفصیل احوال را بمن نوشتند و من بجهة خوانین خدمتگذار خلعت و انعام و مواجب مقرّر کردم و بقدر لازم وقت باستعداد برادر معزّی الیه افزودم. و دو گماشته از کار کنان مریدان معیّن نمودم؛ یکی در بندر کراچی و یک نفر نزد سردار محمّد باقر خان. و حکم دادم که اگر ده لک هم خرج بشود مضایقه نکنند و حتماً بمفهل را تسخیر نمایند.

و در روز پنجشنبه بیست و ششم شهر رمضان المبارک سنهٔ ۱۲۶۰ از کراچی براه دریا جهة سرکشی جماعت مریدین متوطّنین ملک کهچ و بهوج حرکت کردم. اگرچه اوّل سواری من بدریا بود و طوفانی نیز عارض شد ولی بسلامت وارد مدّائی شدیم. سرکار مهاراج راو دیسل جی، مالک مملکت، که الحقّ در عین جوانی از کمال عقل و فتوّت و مردمیّت که مفطور داشت در بندر مدائی آمده ملاقات را اتّفاق دادند. و ضمناً تکلیف[۷۲] رفتن مرا در بهوج که دارالملک ایشان است نموند. من هم اجابت دعوت نموده بعد از پرسش و دیدن جماعت بلوکات بین راه بطرف بهوج عنان‌تاب، و از طرف مهاراج نیز لوازم اعزاز و احترام را در رسومات استقبال نمودن و تعیّن مکان لایق و مقرّر کردن مهماندار و غیره از هر باب بعمل آمد.

---

۷۲ ب ۶۰.

پس از یک ماه توقّف و انجام دادن امور جماعت سکنهٔ بهوج تعارفات رسمی موافق شأن ملوکانهٔ ایشان و درویشی من بعمل آمده، بطرف انجار حرکت نمودم. و بعد از اتمام کار جماعت آن ساحت بسمت هالار و کاتیاوار حرکت نمودم.

و محرّم سنهٔ ۱۲۶۱ را در جام‌نگر برسوم تعزیه‌داری جناب ابا عبدالله (ص) پرداخته و مطابق یک سال در ملک کاتیاوار و هالار و اضلاع آن مختصراً بسرکشی از جماعت آن صفحات نموده و از بندر سورت بطرف دمن روانه، و محرّم سنهٔ ۱۲۶۲ بعد از اتمام لوازم تعزیه داری در اواخر شهر صفر سال مذکور بعزیمت بمبئی حرکت، و بعد از ورود به بندر معمورهٔ مذکور حمد خدای متعال و نعت اجداد بزرگوار از آدم الی خاتم انبیاء و آل او از ماضی[۷۳] تا حال را بجا آوردم.

و الحمد الله تعالی حمداً دائماً ازلیّاً ابدیّاً که این درویش امکان نژاد منسوب متّصل ثمرهٔ شجرهٔ طیّبهٔ مشهورهٔ مشهوده و بقیّهٔ مستورهٔ ظاهره را درین دیر خراب‌آباد از خلوتخانهٔ عدم بتجلیّات وقایع مضمنهٔ طیّ ازمنهٔ ماضیهٔ مرقومة الصّدر نورانیاً و ظلمانیّة، در شدّتها و فرجها در حالاتی که نه مجبور بودم و نه مختار و نه هست و نه نیست، بامر واحد و عین واحده تشریف جلوهٔ ظهور عنایت فرمود. ثم الحمد له علی کلّ حال.

---

۷۳ ب ۶۱.

گهی با خاک همخانه گهی با باد هم‌پیشه
گهی با چرخ همراه و گهی با باد هم بردن
گردد چه خراب تن چه غم جان باشد
ویران چه شود حباب عمّان باشد
داد و ستد عشق زیانش سود است
گر جان برود چه باک جانان باشد

و از عطایای موروثی آباء و اجداد کأنّه أقرب إلیّ من حبل الورید و نحن أقرب إلیه منکم، معلومات درویشانه را بخطاب یا ایّتها النّفس المطمئنّة آسایش اعلائی بخشید. لااله الّا الله فرد و منزّه است خالقی که افراد ممکنات را که در اثبات متّصف بوجود و عدم و در نفی نه موجود و نه معدومند بین الطّریقین خالق متضادّ[۷۴] و حاکم طرفین است. لا حول و لا قوّة الّا بالله العلیّ العظیم. موجود را اتّصاف بمعدوم چه مجال که عدم را اتّصاف بوجود محال است.

خوش گفت در بیابان مرد دهل دریده
عارف خدا ندارد او را نیافریده
در دهر بمستعار آلوده مگرد
هر گز بدی و بهار آلوده مگرد

---

[۷۴] ب ۶۲.

تن در ره تو مشت غباریست رفیق
زنهار باین غبار آلوده مگرد

و ظاهر است که حقّ نور محض و ظلمت محضه است. اگرچه نور منقلب بظلمت و ظلمت منقلب بنور ابداً نمی‌شود، و خلق مابین نور و ظلمت برزخی است که بذاته نه متّصف بظلمت و نه نور است و **الله نور السّموات و الارض** جلّ الخالق که حافظ محفوظ است و ممکنات **بل هم فی لبس من خلق جدید**.

ما فات مضی و ما سیأتیک فأین
قم فأغتنم الفرصة بین العدمین
بی ره نروم تام نگویند بره آی
از ره بروم تام نگویند ز ره برد

کان الله و ما کان معه شیئ.

خدا گواه است که هر جا که هست با اویم.

نی نی غلط این نغمه بموقع نسرودم

و هو معنا اینما کنّا

یار آئینه حسن دلارای خود است
یکدیدهٔ محو در تماشای خود است

این حسن غیور بر نمی‌تابد عشق[۷۵]
موسی و عصا و طور و سینای خود است

سبحان الله،

نمیدانم بیداری است یا که خواب
یا با کیم این سؤالها هست و جواب

همانا این یاوه‌سرائیها و هرزه‌درآئیها نتیجهٔ جنون یا نتایج فنون ذوفنون است. چه گوشم عطا فرمود تا بشنوم و چشمم بخشید تا ببینم. هیهات هیهات **لیس کمثله شیئ و هو السّمیع البصیر**. صامت محض را بنطق چه نسبت.

دلی پر گوهر اسرار دارم
و لیکن بر زبان مسمار دارم
با آن همه نزدیکی و این جملهٔ دوری
من کجا و هوس لاله بدستار زدن

نمیدانم مطلب چه بود و کجا ماند و چرا ماند.

ای دوست چراغ چشم بیدار توئی

۷۵ ب ۶۳.

معشوق توئی عاشق دیدار توئی

آشوب جهان فتنهٔ بازار توئی

خود یوسف مصری و خریدار توئی

بالجمله چون از عهدهٔ وصف حقّ برون ناید کس، رجوع بمطلب مقصود نمودن اولیٰ است. چه بعد از روانگی سردار محمّد باقر خان بتمنّا و تکلیف محمّد علی خان بطرف بمفهل و مخالفت و عذر او نسبت ببرادر معزّی الیه، و حکم من که اگر ده لک خرج شود مضایقه نیست تا بمفهل مفتوح شود، و بعد از مدّتی بجهة تقویت و تأکید[۷۶] در تسخیر ملک مذکور برادر دیگرم سردار ابوالحسن خان را نیز با تدارک تمام مأمور کردم که بعد از تلاقی، بالاتّفاق در فتح بمفهل لوازم جدّ و جهد را مبذول دارند و بعد از ملحق شدن برادران چنانچه رسم اجانب اهل زمانست، جمعی نوکرها خود را ببرادر بزرگ ابوالحسن خان بستند و بعضی به محمّد باقر خان پیوستند. و بمرور اتّفاق برادرها را بنفاق مبدّل ساختند.

و پس از ورود من به بندر بمبئی این خبر متواتر شد. و من برادر خود محمّد باقر خان را طلبیده ابوالحسن خان را سردار مستقل مقرّر کردم. و بمرور بمفهل و سایر قلعه‌جات بلوچستان مفتوح شد و تصوّر آسایش بخاطر غلبه کرد.

---

۷۶ ب ۶۴.

ناگاه پادشاه مرحوم بواسطهٔ وزرای دول خارجهٔ طرفین، ماندن مرا در بمبئی مصلحت دولت خود ندیده و بافساد و اغوای ارباب غرض خواهشمند شدند که مرا بملک بنگاله در بندر کلکتّه منزل بدهند. و نیز لشکری بسرداری فضلعلیخان بطرف بلوچستان بمقابله با ابوالحسن خان فرستادند. و با این که فتح بمفهل بغلبه و یورش تیپ و توپ محال است، مگر بفقدان غلّه و آذوقه. و در قلعهٔ بمفهل[۷۷] یکساله آذوقه از هر چیز موجود و زیست لشکر ایرانی بمحاصرهٔ بمفهل بیش از یک ماه ممکن نبود و نیست. لیکن از سبب نفاق نوکرهای نمک بحرام در شبی که اردوی فضلعلیخان از فتح مأیوس و مصمّم کوچ مراجعت بود، عبدالرّحیم خان و محمّد قاسم خان و فتح الله خان که از نوکرهای معتبر بودند با چند سوار بکار دیگر بهمراهی میرزا ابوالحسن خان بعزم یورش و شبیخون بردن باردوی خصم از طرفی، و سالار ملوک و جمعی از تفنگچیان از سمت دیگر از قلعه بر آمده بودند. و نوکرهای غدّار سردار خود را از بی‌راهه تا قریب طلوع فجر گردش می‌دهند و خارج از اردوی مذکور بقدر هفت هشت فرسنگ به بمفهل فاصله صبح روشن شده بود. پس سردار را مستأصلانه برده بودند. روز دیگر وقت عصر در حالی که اسب سردار از پا افتاده بود و سایر نوکرها در عقب مانده بودند عبدالرّحیم خان نمک

---

۷۷ ب ۶۵.

بحرام او را گذاشته و سواره گریخته بود. پس سردار و قلعهٔ بمفهل بیکروز دستگیر و مفتوح[۷۸] گشت. فاعتبروا یا اولوا الابصار و الملک الله الواحد القهّار.

اوضاع زمانه لایق دیدن نیست
وضعی خوشتر ز چشم پوشیدن نیست
دانی ز چه پا کشیده‌ام در دامن
دنیا تنگ است و جای جنبیدن نیست

بالجمله فرستادن محمّد باقر خان را بطرف بمفهل باستعداد، محض استدعا و تمنّای محمّد خان بلوچ بود. بعد از نقض قول و بروز غدر او که مستحقّ مؤاخذه آمد، بدو ملاحظه حکم دادم بغلبه ملک را از تصرّف او انتزاع نمایند: یکی تنبیه محمّد علی خان و یکی رفاهیّت برادران و نوکرهای خود. چه بلوچستان ملکی بود که متعلّق بهیچیک از سلاطین مقتدر نبود، الا بلوچهای قطّاع الطّریق که همیشه مال و جان اکثری از متردّدین در عرصهٔ نهب و تلف بود. و مطابق پنج لک خرج شد تا ملک گرفته شد و محمّد علی خان متواری، و فراراً پناه بأُمنای دولت ایران برده. بعد از دو سال فضلعلیخان با لشکری شایان بتفصیلی که گذشت ملک را متصرّف شد. مع هذا پس معلوم است سببی نداشت مگر تغیر دادن احکام مقرّرهٔ من و

---

۷۸ ب ۶۶.

نفاق خوانین[۷۹] بلوچیّه و نوکرها بعد از اقتدار، و تحریک نمودن بعضی از سالارهای سرحد را بچاپیدن اطراف بم و نرماشیر، بمخالفت مدد خان سرحد که در خدمت برادر معزّی الیه صداقت و موافقت داشت، و نتیجه ناسپاسی و کفران نعمت: هر کسی آن درود عاقبت کار که گشت.

یارب چه شود گر کرمت یار افتد
لطفت بشکستگان پرستار افتد
غمخوارگی اهل جهان را دیدم
مگذار که با غیر توام کار افتد

پس بتاریخ شهر جمادی الاوّل سنهٔ ۱۲۶۳ از بمبئی بطرف بنگاله حرکت و از راه خشک بخواهش دولتین علیّتین روانه شدیم. اگر چه بین راه در هر شهر و پرگنه‌جات لوازم عزّت و احترام را حکّام انگریزیّه و راجگان فراخور شأن و استعدادشان معمول می‌داشتند، مگر از شدّت گرما و سمیّت حرارت باد سام زحمت بسیار رسید و چند نفر از آدمهای من هلاک شدند تا وارد اکبرآباد شدیم و از آنجا بجهازات آتشی و بادی از شطّ گنگاب و جمناب روانهٔ کلکتّه، و بفاصلهٔ[۸۰] بیست روز وارد کلکتّه گشته به دمدمه که جهة نزول ما نوّاب فرمانفرما معیّن کرده بود ساکن گردیدیم. الحقّ با

۷۹ ب ۶۷.

۸۰ ب ۶۸.

وجود وسعت ملک چندان آبادان بود که مافوق آن متصوّر نیست. مجملاً از اکبرآباد تا کلکتّه دو طرف شطّ مذکور تا بحدّی که نظر کار می‌کرد آبادی متّصل یکدیگر بود.

بالجمله مدّت یک سال هشت ماه بدمدمه ساکن و بامیران سندهه قرب جوار و مؤالفت و مأنوسیّت ما بین پدیدار آمده، رفته رفته رسومات تشیّع را مرتسم و در تعزیه داری ایّام عاشورا لوازم اهتمام را از هر باب مواظب بودند. اگرچه مرحوم میر نصیر خان در عنفوان جوانی و ابتدای جلوس و حکمرانی ره‌سپر مذهب جعفری و مرحله‌پیمای طریق اثناعشری بوده، بخلاف اخوان و ابناء اعمام مگر شعلهٔ شمع ولای اهل بیت پرتو افکن شبستان قلوب اکثر از ایشان، بلکه جملگیشان گشت.

و عالیجاه کپتان کوینه صاحب که الحقّ مردی بود شایسته و لایق مصاحبت بمهمانداری معیّن، و جناب مدک صاحب که نایب نوّاب[۸۱] فرمانفرما بود در لوازم محبّت و مهمان نوازی دقیقهٔ فرو گذاشت نکرد. اگرچه در آن اوقات از سبب شورش و طغیان حکّام و امرای طوایف سینگ و افغان از حدود پیشاور و مُلتان و لاهور و پنجاب، بتصوّر قضایای واقعه در افغانستان بلکه تحریک و مدد محمّد اکبر خان، با جمعیّت و احتشام تمام بلکه ازدحام عام فراغتی جهة صاحبان عظام بهیچ وجه حاصل نبود.

---

[۸۱] ب ۶۹.

چه بعد از قضیّهٔ افغانستان و تدارک جبران شکسته بستگی‌ها وقایع مضمنهٔ چند اتّفاق افتاد که آسایش جهة ایشان دست نداد. بعلاوهٔ این قضیّهٔ بزرگ که اگر جلادت و بهادری شامل نبود هر آینه مقاومت و مقابلت با افواج سواره و نظام و توپخانهٔ سینگ که بشجاعت و دلاوری و بهادری و جنگجوئی ضرب‌المثل جنگ‌آوران عالم اند محال می‌نمود. و اگرچه زحمت بسیار کشیدند و سختی بیشمار دیدند و سردار و صاحب منصبهای بزرگ بقتل رسیدند، لکن مردانه چندان کوشش کردند که خصمان بکلّی مغلوب و ملک و دولت و خزانه و مکنت و اثاثهٔ سلطنت از نقیر تا قطمیر را متصرّف، و برنا و پیر را دستگیر[۸۲] آوردند.

بالحاصل بعد از مدّت بیست ماه توقف در دمدمه، طبیعت از سکونت آن مکان متنفّر و در شوّال سنهٔ ۱۲۶۴ از دمدمه بقصبهٔ چیچره نقل مکان نمودم. و قصبهٔ مذکوره در کنار شطّ گنگاب و جمناب واقع، و هوایش بغایت معتدل و سکنه‌اش از عجم و هندوستانی و سایر بصحبت اهل دل مایل. و حاجی علی نام لواسانی که الحقّ در فضیلت و کمال و اصالت و نجابت بین الامثال امتیازی داشت با برادرش آقا کمال در هر حال طریق مصاحبت را می‌پیمودند، و اکثر اوقات جلیس و انیس بودند و نیز جناب میر کرامت علی که متولی امام بارهٔ هوگلی بود و بواسطهٔ قرب جوار اکثر

---

۸۲ ب ۷۰.

اوقات در مصاحبتش روزگار میگذشت. و آن جناب سرآمد فضلای زمان و در علم ریاضی گوی سبقت از علما و حکمای ماضی ربوده، یگانهٔ دوران بود. همواره همدم و خاطر از درک مجالستش پیوسته خُرّم می‌نمود.

تا در اواخر ذی‌حجّه سال مذکور خبر وحشت‌افزای قضیّهٔ ناگزیر پادشاه خلد مصیر محمّد شاه طاب ثراه رسید، و فی‌الحقیقه موجب زیادتی تألّم و پریشانی خاطر گردید. و چون[۸۳] دست از چاره کوتاه و حاصلی در سوگواری و زاری و آه ندید، برسوم تعزیت چنانچه رسم است پرداخته و فاتحهٔ آن مغفور را بمصیبت جدّ بزرگوار جناب سیّد الشّهدا علیه آلاف التّحیة و الثّناء متّصل ساخته. بعد از انقضای ایّام عاشورای سنهٔ ۱۲۶۵ تهنیت جلوس میمنت مأنوس انوشه ناصر الدّین شاه خلد الله ملکه را وجهه همّت نموده، بتاریخ دوازدهم محرّم بجهاز آتشی سوار و بنهایت استظهار بطرف بمبئی حرکت، و بعد از ورود بمبئی چون اخبار اغتشاش خراسان و مازندران و طغیان فساد سالار و بابی‌ها متواتر و منتشر بود، با خود اندیشیدم که اگر بدون اذن و طلب کردن اولیای دولت بهیّه، بی تمهید مقدّمه بطرف ایران حرکت نمایم، یحتمل از نو سر رشته بدست ارباب غرض بیفتد و باز ماجرای کهنه را مجملی قرار دهند که امر آسان مشکل شود. بهتر این است که چهار صباحی پا بدامن استقامت کشیده، اقامت

---

۸۳ ب ۷۱.

ورزم تا اطراف ملک از خار ادبار مفسدین معاند پیراسته و چمن دولت بآبیاری عنایت حضرت باری عزّ اسمه آراسته گردد و ضمناً عریضهٔ[۸۴] نیازمند با اذن و طلب انباز و پیوند گیرد آن وقت مُحرِم طوف کعبه حضور شوم. و درین ضمن شرحی مخلصانه بمرحوم میرزا تقی خان اتابیک اعظم نوشتم چون عنوانش مخدوم مکرّم بود ظاهراً پسند خاطرشان نیفتاده بود.

و درین بینها، فرزندی میرزا حسین خان، ولد مرحوم میرزا نبی خان بکونسلی بمبئی مقرّر و وارد شد و در ورودش آنچه لازمهٔ عزّت و احترام که شایان و زیبای شأن امنای دولت سلطانی است دربارهٔ ایشان ظاهر ساختم. و «اوّل آن کس که خریدار شدش من بودم». و نخستین شخصی که در دیباچه کتابچهٔ امر خداوندی را خواند و خطّ بندگی سپرد اقدام من بود. پس متعلّقان و نوکرهای من و بعد سایر تجّار و کسبه و سکنهٔ مغلیّه، یعنی سایر ایرانی‌ها بالجمله روز بروز بمتابعت دولت و موافقت با فرزند مقام معزّی الیه می‌افزودم. و از رعایت اولیای دولت بغایت امیدوار بودم که باقصی‌الغایة بعزّتم خواهند افزود و در حقّم عطوفتها خواهند فرمود. و بعد از آنهمه خرابیها که در دولت[۸۵] شاه مرحوم دیده و کشیدم، حال بآبادیم خواهند پرداخت و با جمعی عیال و اطفال سادات متواری فراری،

---

۸۴ ب ۷۲.

۸۵ ب ۷۳.

بالطاف شهریاری بموطن و مسقط‌الرّاس مستقرّ و مستقلّم خواهند ساخت. که ناگاه نائی کون نوائی دیگر نواخت، و صبّاغ کارگاه صنع رنگی دیگر ریخت و معمار کارخانهٔ قضا طرحی دیگر انگیخت، و معنی عرفت الله بفسخ العزایم صورت بست. و موجب سودن دست بدست گشت، و پروانگی بشارت مشتمل بر اشارت اعلیحضرت شهریاری نوک ریز قلم نادره رقم حضرت اتابیکی رسید، و در طلبم مبادرتها در نوید عنایتها ورزیده بودند، مشروط باینکه مرحلهٔ عبور از بندر ابوشهر باشد. با خود گفتم سبحان الله! با این همه اعتبار جای بندگی اختیار کردن است؟ و عقلا در عین اطلاق، خود را مقیّد وثاق ارباب نفاق نمی‌کنند و تقدیر الهٰی اگرچه گاهی با تدبیر بندگان صادق موافق افتد، ولی با تزویر ابداً تصویرپذیر نخواهد شد.

باز[۸۶] نفس‌الامر را سنجیدم و باطن اعلیحضرت شاهنشاهی را نسبت بخود در نهایت صفا و لطافت دیدم. پس فهمیدم که این هم از نتایج فطری وزرای خودبین و خودرای است. و حکم مابین را حواله بانصاف حاکم علی الاطلاق نمودم. بلی:

ابنای زمان دُرد صفا را ندهند
هرگز پرکاه کهربا را ندهند

---

۸۶ ب ۷۴.

این قوم، ولی‌نعمتِ امثال خودند
تا سگ بود استخوان هما را ندهند

بالجمله باخلاص و محبّت باطنی خود نسبت بشاهنشاه جمجاه افزودم، و دعای دوام عمر و دولت دوران عدّت را ورد شبانروزی خود نموده ذخیرهٔ خیری بهتر از این ندیدم، و الحمد لله علی کلّ حال.

دل بندهٔ عشق است و کفیلی دارد
جان و تن سر گشته دلیلی دارد

پس بجهة حمل و نقل نعش مرحومهٔ والدهٔ ماجدهٔ سرکار طاب ثراها، و تبدیل آب و هوا و اجابت استدعای جماعت مریدین هر جا از بمبئی حرکت و قریب یک سال طول مدّت مسافرت شده پس از ورود خبر عزل میرزا تقی خان و اتابیک و نصیب[۸۷] میرزا آقاخان نوری بوزارت متواتر شد. چون با مشارالیه رابطهٔ الفت و ضابطهٔ محبّت از عهد خاقان مغفور فراخور شأن و رتبهٔ ایشان مربوط و مضبوط بود کمال خوشوقتی حاصل شد. و ضمناً مختصر پیشکشی از قبیل پیل و زرّافه جهة خدیو دادگستر و تعارفات دیگر جهة میرزا آقاخان و نظام الملک[۸۸] ولد ایشان با عریضهٔ نیازمندانه ارسال دارالخلافه نمودم. و از کمال رأفت و عطوفت خدیوانه

---

۸۷ ب ۷۵؛ کذا. این کلمه باید «نصب» باشد.

۸۸ نسخهٔ ب فاقد «الملک» است.

مقبول خاطر انور گردیده، بعضی از املاک محدثی مرا بر سبیل انعام واگذار و تحویل کسان من نمودند. و من بغایت خوشوقت و امیدوار و در تدارک روانه ساختن بعضی از متعلّقان و سادات بآن دیار شدم. از قضایای دور فلکی میرزا آقاخان نیز آنچه در طبیعت مفطور داشت بمرور جلوهٔ ظهور داد، بمرتبهٔ که ورد زبانها «رحمة الله علی النبّاش الاوّل» گشت. بالجمله در عهد وزارت آن جناب این قطعه مکرّر ورد زبان بود که:

روزگاریست که از غایت بیداد در او[۸۹]
نیست ممکن که کسی را سر و سامان باشد
چشم نیکی ز که داریم بعهدی که در او
گر کسی بد نکند غایت احسان باشد

بالاخره املاک عطیّهٔ پادشاهی را برگردانید چنانچه پیشینیان کردند. اگرچه مرا بهیچوجه تصوّر منفعتی از آن املاک نبود، مگر جمعی سادات لقمهٔ نانی بخورند و دعا بدوام عمر و دولت شهریاری بکنند.

حال بر صاحبان انصاف بخوبی روشن است که بدطینتی این معتمد دولت پادشاهی تا چه حدّ بود، و تدیّن او در امورات دولت[۹۰] و مملکت و رعیّت

---

۸۹ ب ۷۶.

۹۰ عبارت «پادشاهی تا چه حدّ بود و تدیّن او در امورات دولت» در نسخهٔ ت مفقود است.

تا چه مرتبه. پس گنجایش دارد اگر در مقابل «رحم الله معشر الماضی» حایل آید. هیهات! «گاه حرص و وقت شهوت مرد کو».

پروردگان دایهٔ دولت و تربیت یافتگان دستگاه سلطنت را چنانچه در دولت شاه مرحوم و این دولت روزافزون تا کنون که سال هزار دو صد و هفتاد و هشت است آنچه دیده و سنجیده شد، اشهد بالله بجز پستی فطرت و بدی نیّت و خیانت با ولی‌نعمت و خراب نمودن ملک و رعیّت اصلاً خاصیتی از وجود و بودشان دیده و[۹۱] شنیده نشد، الا اندوختن مال و منال بطریق جبر و رشوت که نزد ایشان از شیر مادر حلالتر است و بس. مگر اکنون که آنچه شنیده و فهمیده شده تربیت‌یافتگان حال و امنا و وزرای نیک‌مآل که اکنون در خدمات دولت و پرستاری سپاه و رعیّت مشغولند، در نظرها مقبولند انشاءالله، عواقب امور جملگی بخیر و در سایهٔ عنایت و تربیت شهریاری مسالک عمر طبیعی را در دولتخواهی سیر نمایند که گفته‌اند:

هر کسی آن درود عاقبت کار که گشت

و مرا اگرچه:

یک چند دل از پی تمنّا گردید

---

[۹۱] ب ۷۷.

جانم هدف طعنهٔ اعدا گردید
گردید ز هر طرف چو راهم بستند
راه سر کوی دوست پیدا گردید
ای درد دوای دل افگار توئی
عاشق توئی و عشق تو و یار توئی
پرگار توئی نقطه توئی دایره تو
یعنی که ز هر پرده پدیدار توئی

عاقبت چشم از هوا و هوسها پوشیدم، و سروری که در دل از رهگذر شوری که بر سر بود بعد از صدمهٔ[۹۲] که بپایم رسید از دست دادم و با خود گفتم:

سر تا سر آفاق همه گردیدی
و ز دیدهٔ دید دیدنیها دیدی[۹۳]
اکنون دامان رنگ و بو را بگذار
تا چند اسیر بیمی و امیدی

---

۹۲ درنسخه‌ها به صورت «سدمه» ضبط شده است.
۹۳ ب ۷۸.

و اینک چند سال است که مدار را بشرط بازی و اسب تازی قرار داده‌ام. گاهی میل شکار و زمانی با مردم زمانه هم‌گفتار و ایّامی با از پا افتادگان هم‌دست و اوقاتی با بینوایان هم‌نشست و بتماشای اهل عالم مشغولم:

در کوی خرابات بسی مردانند
کز لوح وجود سرّها می‌خوانند
بیرون ز شتر گربهٔ احوال فلک
دانند شگفتها و خر می‌رانند

و مقصود من از ایراد این رویدادات این است که بر جمیع نظارگیان اوضاع جهان و جهانیان که در این زمان از کثرت تقلّب تقلیب‌پذیر گشته، سررشتهٔ باشد تا در هر احوال بتصوّرات گذشته و آینده، حال را از دست نگذارند، و خالق ذوالجلال را که مبدع و مخترع و صانع ممکنات است و احد بی مثل و شریک و ضدّ و ندّ، و وجود مقدّسش را نه مرکّب بلکه بسیط و بر جمیع اشیاء محیط دانند.

نه او جسم است و نه جسمانی و نه او را جهتی است و نه مکانی، دیدنش جز بچشم روان روا نی؛ و رؤیتش را غیر از دیدهٔ نفس ناطقه که از آلایش جسمیّت[۹۴] پاک است سزا نه. ذات اقدسش را با حدوث و محلّ حوادث

۹۴ ب ۷۹.

بودن کار نیست و عدم و فنا را بساحت عظمتش بار نیست. روان‌بخش و جان‌ستان و روزی‌ده و قسمت‌رسان کاینات اوست، و معبودیّت شایان رتبه و جلالت و کبریائی شأن اوست.

نخلد بی ارادتش خاری
نگسلد بی مشیّتش تاری[۹۵]

تمام شد کتاب مستطاب عبرت افزا، حسب الفرمایش سرکار شوکت و جلالت و ابهت توأمان عظمت و حشمت، هم‌عنان سیادت و سخاوت و شجاعت، بنیان ممهّد بساط امن و امان، قامع بنیان ظلم و طغیان، راتبه‌افزای وظیفه‌خواران، نقاوهٔ دودمان مصطفوی، شکوفهٔ چمن مرتضوی، نهال بستانسرای سادات الحسینی، بحر عطا و سخای جاودانی، التیام‌دهندهٔ دلهای شکسته از فقر و بینوائی، محمّد حسن الحسینی مشهور به آقاخان ادام الله اجلاله و حشمته. بخطّ اقلّ حاج و عباد الله محمّد ابراهیم الشهیر بآقا المتخلّص به صفا، خلف مرحمت و غفران پناه

[۹۵] متن عبرت‌افزا این‌جا تمام می‌شود. کتیبهٔ نسخهٔ خطی که در زیر آمده است در نسخهٔ ب یافت می‌شود. عبارات کتیبهٔ نسخهٔ بهرام و بهروز در نسخهٔ ت به شکل زیر است: کتاب مستطاب بهرام و بهروز من نتایج الکلام معجز نظام وحید الاعصار افصح المتکلّمین میرزا وقار ابن وصال شیراز حسب الفرمایش سرکار شوکت و جلالت و ابهت توأمان عظمت و حشمت همعنان سیادت و سخاوت و شجاعت بنیان ممهّد بساط امن و امان قامع بنیان ظلم و طغیان راتبه‌افزای وظیفه‌خواران نقاوهٔ دودمان مصطفوی شکوفهٔ چمن مرتضوی نهال بستانسرای سادات الحسینی بحر عطا و سخای جاودانی التیام دهندهٔ دلهای شکسته از فقر و بینوائی محمّد حسن الحسینی مشهور به آقاخان ادام الله اجلاله و شوکته و حشمته بخطّ اقلّ حاجّ و عباد الله محمّد ابراهیم الشهیر بآقا المتخلّص به صفا خلف مرحمت و غفران پناه جنت و رضوان آرامگاه المستغرق فی بحار رحمت الله الملک المنّان محمّد حسین خان اولیا سمیع شیرازی و در کارخانهٔ استاد المطبعّین دادو میان بن محمّد عبدالله دهایلی سمت انطباع پذیرفت فی شهر شعبان المکرم ۱۲۷۸.

المستغرق فی بحار رحمت الله الملک المنّان محمّد حسین خان اولیا سمیع شیرازی و در بندر بمبئی در کارخانهٔ داود میان سمت انطباع پذیرفت فی شهر رمضان المبارک ۱۲۷۸.

نمایه

آ، ا
آزاد خان بلوچ، ۴۳
آصف الدوله، ۵۰
آقا کمال (برادر علی لواسانی)، ۷۲
آقا محمّد باقر اناری، ۳۰
آقا محمّد خان، ۴، ۵، ۸
آقاسی، حاجی میرزا، ۱۱، ۱۲، ۱۲، ۱۳، ۱۴، ۲۴
آقاخان،۱۲، ۱۴، ۲۴، ۴۰، ۴۱، ۵۴، ۸۱
آقاخان نوری، میرزا، ۷۶
ابراهیم خان قاجار، ۲۱
ابوالحسن خان، سردار (برادر آقاخان)، ۸، ۱۵، ۲۰، ۲۱، ۲۸، ۳۴، ۳۵، ۴۲، ۴۳، ۴۴، ۴۶، ۴۷، ۴۸، ۴۹، ۶۱، ۶۷، ۶۸
ابوشهر، ۷۵
اثنی‌عشری، ۷۱، ۱۹
احمد بیک یوزباشی، ۴۰
ارگ بم، ۷، ۴۲
اسفندقه، ۳۴
اسفندیار خان، ۳۵، ۳۶
اسمعیل خان طبسی، ۵۰
اطرام، ۵۶، ۵۷
افغان، ۷، ۹، ۱۷، ۷۱
افغانستان، ۱۷، ۵۱، ۷۱
اکبرآباد، ۷۰
امامقلی خان قاجار، ۳۵
امیر اسدالله خان، ۵۰، ۵۱
انار، ۲۹
انگریز، ۵۳، ۵۴، ۵۶، ۵۷، ۶۰
ایران، ۱۰، ۱۸، ۲۱، ۶۱، ۶۹، ۷۳
ایمانی خان فراهانی، ۴

ب
باغ نرگس، ۳۳
باقر ملک الکتّاب، ۱۳
بخارا، ۵۴
بدخشان، ۲۳، ۵۴
بلخ، ۵۴
بلوچ، ۷، ۹، ۱۵، ۱۷، ۳۳، ۴۳، ۶۰، ۶۱، ۶۹
بلوچستان، ۱۵، ۱۶، ۲۰، ۶۰، ۶۷، ۶۸، ۶۹
بم، ۷، ۸، ۱۴، ۱۵، ۱۷، ۲۱، ۲۲، ۴۱، ۴۲، ۷۰
بمبئی، ۶۳، ۶۷، ۶۸، ۷۰، ۷۳، ۷۴، ۷۶، ۸۲
بمفهل، ۱۵، ۶۱، ۶۷، ۶۸، ۶۹
بندر عبّاس، ۳۲، ۴۵
بنگاله، ۶۸، ۷۰
بهادر، ۶۰
بهرام و بهروز، ۸۱
بهمن میرزا، نوّاب، ۲۶
بهوج، ۶۲، ۶۳
بیلو، ۵۶

پ
پنجاب، ۷۱
پیپ، ۶۱
پیشاور، ۵۴، ۷۱

ت
تالپور، ۵۷
ترکستان، ۲۳
تقی خان امیر کبیر، ۷۴، ۷۵، ۷۶
تنگ شمیل، ۴۵، ۴۷
تهته، ۵۸، ۶۰
توران، ۱۸

ج
جرجان، ۱۲، ۱۴
جرگه، ۵۷، ۵۸، ۵۹، ۶۰
جمناب، ۷۰، ۷۲
جُوین، ۵۱، ۵۲

چ
چهاونی، ۵۷، ۵۹
چیچره، ۷۲

ح
حسین پیشخدمت، ۴۳
حسین خان قریة العربی، ۳۶
حسین خان، میرزا، ۳۷، ۳۹، ۷۴
حسین وزیر، میرزا، ۲۸
حیدر خان، ۳۲
حیدرآباد، ۵۶، ۵۷، ۵۹

خ
خاتم النّبیین، سیّد المرسلین، ۱۹
خاقان مغفور (فتحعلی شاه)، ۵، ۹، ۱۱، ۱۲، ۲۱، ۷۶
خان بابا خان، ۳۰
خدارحم خان، ۲۹
خراسان، ۱۱، ۲۳، ۲۵، ۴۷، ۴۹، ۷۳
خراسانی (ایل)، ۹، ۴۳

د
دارالخلافه، ۵، ۷، ۱۰، ۲۴، ۲۵، ۴۸، ۷۶
دربند سیّد علی موسی، ۳۵
درویش نوری، ۴۵
دشتاب، ۲۸، ۳۴، ۳۶، ۳۷، ۳۹، ۴۰
دلیجان، ۲۵
دمدمه، ۷۰، ۷۲
دمن، ۶۳
دولت آباد، ۱۲

ر
رالنسن، میجر، ۵۳، ۵۵
راور، ۲۰، ۴۷، ۴۸، ۴۹
رومنی، ۳۰، ۳۳
ریگان، ۴۲
ریوگان، ۴

ز
زلفعلی سلطان، ۴۱
زیدآباد، ۳۰، ۳۳

س
سالار، ۷۳
سالار ملوک، ۶۰، ۶۱، ۶۸، ۷۳
سرکار کمپنی، ۵۹
سعید خان بلوچ، ۳۳
سند، ۵۴، ۵۶، ۵۷
سندهه، ۵۸، ۶۰، ۷۱

سهراب خان، ۱۵، ۲۰
سوغان، ۳۲، ۳۳
سیّد الشّهدا، ۷۳
سیّد حسین خان، ۳۹
سیرجان، ۳۰
سیستان، ۱۶
سینگ، ۷۱

ش
شالکوت، ۵۵
شاه پسند خان، ۵۱، ۵۲
شاه خلیل‌الله، ۳
شاه شجاع، ۵۳، ۵۴
شاهرخ خان، ۱۲، ۲۱
شاهزاده محمّد تیمور، ۵۳
شجاع السّلطنه، ۷، ۸، ۱۷
شهر بابک، ۲۹
شیر محمّد خان نوملی، ۵۸
شیروانی، حاجی زین‌العابدین، ۱۱، ۱۲، ۲۳

ص
صالو خان اچکزائی، ۵۵
صفا (تخلص محمّد ابراهیم الشهیر بآقا)، ۵، ۷۵، ۸۱
صفدرجنگ، ۵۴، ۵۵
صوفیّه، ۳

ض
ضیاء السّلطنه، ۱۳

ط
طبس، ۵۰
طهران، ۵، ۷، ۲۳، ۲۹

ظ
ظلّ السّلطان، مسعود میرزا، ۵، ۶

ع
عبّاسقلیخان، ۳۰
عباسقلی خان لاریجانی، ۲۱
عبدالرّحیم خان، ۶۸
عبدالقادر خان، ۵۳
عبدالله خان، ۳۸، ۳۹
عبد المحمّد، حاجی، ۲۴
عتبات، ۲۵
عجم، ۴۲، ۷۲
عراق، ۷، ۱۲، ۲۵
عربستان، ۴۵
عطاءاللّهی (ایل)، ۹
علی رضا مستوفی، میرزا، ۱۰، ۱۵
علی لواسانی، ۷۲
علی محمّد خان، ۲۸، ۳۴
علیخان لاری، ۳۴، ۳۷، ۳۸
علیرضا خان راوری، ۴۷

غ
غلام حسین خان سپهدار، ۷

ف
فارس، ۱۲، ۲۱، ۳۲، ۳۳، ۳۴، ۳۷
فتح الله خان، ۶۸
فتحعلی خان مهینی، ۳۴
فراهان، ۴

فضل الله کیشکوئی، ۳۲
فضلعلیخان، ۳۰، ۳۳، ۳۴، ۴۷، ۴۸، ۶۸، ۶۹
فقیر محمّد (بمفهلی)، ۶۰

ق
قاین، ۵۰
قریة العرب، ۳۶، ۴۲
قم، ۴، ۲۴، ۶۵
قندهار، ۲۹، ۴۱، ۵۱، ۵۳، ۵۴، ۵۵

ک
کابل، ۵۳، ۵۴، ۵۵
کاتیاوار، ۶۳
کالمند، ۲۷
کامران شاه، ۵۲
کپتان کوینه، ۷۱
کراچی، ۵۶، ۵۸، ۶۲
کرمان، ۴، ۵، ۷، ۸، ۹، ۱۱، ۱۲، ۱۴، ۱۵، ۱۷، ۱۸، ۲۱، ۲۲، ۲۳، ۳۴، ۴۷، ۶۱
کلکتّه، ۶۸، ۷۰
کهچ، ۶۲
کهن دل خان، ۲۹
کهنوپنچرت، ۳۳، ۳۴
کوبنان، ۴۷
کیشکو، ۳۲

گ
گلستان سعدی، ۳
گنگاب، ۷۰، ۷۲

ل
لاش، ۵۱، ۵۲
لاهور، ۷۱
لطفعلی خان زند، ۸
لوت، ۵۰

م
مازندران، ۷۳
محراب خان بلوچ، ۶۱
محلّات، ۴، ۸، ۲۴، ۲۵، ۲۶
محمّد ابراهیم، ۸۱
محمّد باقر خان، سردار (برادر آقاخان)، ۲۰، ۶۰، ۶۱، ۶۲، ۶۷
محمّد جعفر خان، ۲۱، ۳۱، ۴۳، ۵۹
محمّد حسن الحسینی، ۳، ۸۱
محمّد حسین خان اولیا سمیع شیرازی، ۸۲
محمّد خان خشک، ۵۸
محمّد خان سرتیپ، ۳۶، ۳۷
محمّد رحیم مهردار، ۴۳
محمّد سلیم خان مشیزی، ۳۶، ۳۷
محمّد شاه قاجار، ۷، ۷۳
محمّد صادق خان، سرکار، ۲۱
محمّد علی (کدخدای ریوگان)، ۴
محمّد علی بیک فارغانی، ۳۸، ۳۹، ۴۰
محمّد علی خان بلوچ، ۶۰
محمّد عمر خان، ۲۹، ۵۴
محمّد عمر خان، ۵۴
محمّد قاسم خان، ۶۸
مدّائی، ۶۲
مذهب جعفری، ۱۹، ۷۱

مسقط، ۳۳
مشک آباد، ۴
مصر، ۱۹
مکلاتن، ۵۳
مکّه، ۲۵، ۲۶
مُلتان، ۷۱
ملک محمّد بیک، ۴۳
ملک نصیرخان کلاتی، ۵۶
مهاراج راو دیسل جی، ۶۲
مهردل خان، ۲۹، ۵۵
مهریز، ۲۶، ۲۷
میبُد، ۲۶
میر احمد خان، ۶۰، ۶۱
میر شیر محمّد خان، ۵۷، ۵۸، ۵۹
میر علی مراد خان خیرپوری، ۵۶
میر کرامت علی، ۷۲
میر نصیر خان، ۵۶، ۷۱
میرزا ابوالقاسم قائم مقام فراهانی، ۸
میرزا احمد، ۳۹، ۴۱، ۴۳، ۴۵، ۵۹
میرزا اسحق، ۳۰
میرزا عبدالغنی، ۲۸

ن

نادر شاه، ۵۰
ناصر الدّین شاه قاجار، ۷۳
نای بندان، ۵۰
نایب محمّد حسن، ۵۶
نبی خان، میرزا، ۷۴
نپیر، جنرال سر چارلیس ، ۵۶
نجفعلی بیک، ۴۳
نرماشیر، ۸، ۱۴، ۱۷، ۴۲، ۷۰
نصرالله خان عطاءاللٰهی، ۲۸، ۳۵
نصرالله صدر الممالک، ۱۳
نصیر خان، ۳۸، ۵۶، ۷۱
نظام الملک (پسر میرزا آقاخان نوری)، ۷۶
نعمت‌اللٰهی، ۱۱، ۱۲
نوّاب شاهزادهٔ آزاده (همسر آقاخان، سروجهان خانم)، ۲۵
نوّاب محمّد رضا میرزا، ۲۳
نوساری، ۳۳

ه

هادی خان، ۴۱، ۴۳، ۵۰
هادی خان خراسانی، ۴۳
هالار، ۶۳
هرات، ۱۴، ۱۷، ۲۳، ۵۳
هندوستان، ۲۳، ۴۵
هوگلی، ۷۲

و

وشناوه، ۲۴
وقار شیرازی، ۸۱

ی

یزد، ۴، ۲۶، ۴۸